Social Class in Contemporary Japan

Post-war Japan was often held up as the model example of the first mature industrial society outside the Western economy, and the first examples of "middle-mass" society. Today, and since the bursting of the economic bubble in the 1990s, the promises of Japan, Inc., seem far away.

Social Class in Contemporary Japan is the first single volume that traces the dynamics of social structure, institutional socialization and class culture through this turbulent period, all the way into the contemporary neoliberal moment. In an innovative multi-disciplinary approach that includes top scholars working on quantitative class structure, policy development, and ethnographic analysis, this volume highlights the centrality of class formation to our understanding of the many levels of Japanese society. The chapters each address a different aspect of class formation and transformation which stand on their own. Taken together, they document the advantages of putting Japan in the broad comparative framework of class analysis and the enduring importance of social class to the analysis of industrial and post-industrial societies.

Written by a team of contributors from Japan, the US and Europe this book will be invaluable to students and scholars of Japanese society and culture, as well as those interested in cultural anthropology and social class alike.

Hiroshi Ishida is Professor of Sociology at the Institute of Social Sciences, University of Tokyo, Japan.

David H. Slater is Associate Professor of Cultural Anthropology and Japanese Studies at the Faculty of Liberal Arts and the Graduate School of Global Studies, Sophia University, Japan.

The Nissan Institute/Routledge Japanese Studies Series

Editorial Board

The Japanese Numbers Game
The use and understanding of numbers in modern Japan
Thomas Crump

Ideology and Practice in Modern Japan
*Edited by Roger Goodman
and Kirsten Refsing*

Technology and Industrial Development in Pre-war Japan
Mitsubishi Nagasaki Shipyard, 1884–1934
Yukiko Fukasaku

Japan's Early Parliaments, 1890–1905
Structure, issues and trends
*Andrew Fraser, R.H.P. Mason
and Philip Mitchell*

Japan's Foreign Aid Challenge
Policy reform and aid leadership
Alan Rix

Emperor Hirohito and Shôwa Japan
A political biography
Stephen S. Large

Japan
Beyond the end of history
David Williams

Ceremony and Ritual in Japan
Religious practices in an industrialized society
*Edited by Jan van Bremen
and D.P. Martinez*

The Fantastic in Modern Japanese Literature
The subversion of modernity
Susan J. Napier

Militarization and Demilitarization in Contemporary Japan
Glenn D. Hook

Growing a Japanese Science City
Communication in scientific research
James W. Dearing

Architecture and Authority in Japan
William H. Coaldrake

Women's Gidayū and the Japanese Theatre Tradition
A. Kimi Coaldrake

Democracy in Post-war Japan
Maruyama Masao and the search for autonomy
Rikki Kersten

Treacherous Women of Imperial Japan
Patriarchal fictions, patricidal fantasies
Hélène Bowen Raddeker

Japanese–German Business Relations
Competition and rivalry in the inter-war period
Akira Kudô

Japan, Race and Equality
The racial equality proposal of 1919
Naoko Shimazu

Japan, Internationalism and the UN
Ronald Dore

Life in a Japanese Women's College
Learning to be ladylike
Brian J. McVeigh

On The Margins of Japanese Society
Volunteers and the welfare of the urban underclass
Carolyn S. Stevens

The Dynamics of Japan's Relations with Africa
South Africa, Tanzania and Nigeria
Kweku Ampiah

The Right to Life in Japan
Noel Williams

The Nature of the Japanese State
Rationality and rituality
Brian J. McVeigh

Society and the State in Inter-war Japan
Edited by Elise K. Tipton

Japanese–Soviet/Russian Relations
since 1945
A difficult peace
Kimie Hara

Interpreting History in Sino–Japanese
Relations
A case study in political decision making
Caroline Rose

Endō Shūsaku
A literature of reconciliation
Mark B. Williams

Green Politics in Japan
Lam Peng-Er

The Japanese High School
Silence and resistance
Shoko Yoneyama

Engineers in Japan and Britain
Education, training and employment
Kevin McCormick

The Politics of Agriculture in Japan
Aurelia George Mulgan

Opposition Politics in Japan
Strategies under a one-party dominant
Regime
Stephen Johnson

The Changing Face of Japanese Retail
Working in a chain store
Louella Matsunaga

Japan and East Asian Regionalism
Edited by S Javed Maswood

Globalizing Japan
Ethnography of the Japanese presence
in America, Asia and Europe
Edited by Harumi Befu and
Sylvie Guichard-Anguis

Japan at Play
The ludic and logic of power
Edited by Joy Hendry and Massimo Raveri

The Making of Urban Japan
Cities and planning from Edo to the
twenty-first century
André Sorensen

Public Policy and Economic
Competition in Japan
Change and continuity in antimonopoly
policy, 1973–95
Michael L. Beeman

Modern Japan
A social and political history
Elise K Tipton

Men and Masculinities in
Contemporary Japan
Dislocating the salaryman doxa
Edited by James E. Roberson and
Nobue Suzuki

The Voluntary and Non-Profit Sector
in Japan
The challenge of change
Edited by Stephen P. Osborne

Japan's Security Relations with China
From balancing to bandwagoning
Reinhard Drifte

Understanding Japanese Society,
Third Edition
Joy Hendry

Japanese Electoral Politics
Creating a new party system
Edited by Steven R. Reed

Social Class in Contemporary Japan

Structures, sorting and strategies

**Edited by Hiroshi Ishida
and David H. Slater**

LONDON AND NEW YORK

First published 2010
by Routledge
2 Park Square, Milton Park, Abingdon, Oxon, OX14 4RN

Simultaneously published in the USA and Canada
by Routledge
711 Third Avenue, New York, NY 10017

Routledge is an imprint of the Taylor & Francis Group, an informa business

First issued in paperback 2011

Typeset in Times by
HWA Text and Data Management, London

British Library Cataloguing in Publication Data
A catalogue record for this book is available from the British Library

Library of Congress Cataloging in Publication Data
Social class in contemporary Japan / edited by Hiroshi Ishida and David H. Slater.
    – p. cm. – (The Nissan Institute/Routledge Japanese studies series)
    1. Social classes – Japan. 2. Social structure – Japan. 3. Social mobility –
Japan. 4. Japan – Social conditions – 1945– I. Ishida, Hiroshi, 1954–
II. Slater, David H., 1960–
HN730.Z9S6756 2009
305.50952–dc22   2009014380

ISBN10: 0–415–47475–2 (hbk)
ISBN10: 0–415–66719–4 (pbk)
ISBN10: 0–203–86915–X (ebk)

ISBN13: 978–0–415–47475–7 (hbk)
ISBN13: 978–0–415–66719–7 (pbk)
ISBN13: 978–0–203–86911–6 (ebk)

Contents

Figures

Tables

Contributors

Amy Borovoy is an associate professor of east Asian studies at Princeton University. Her research concerns the anthropology of Japan's postwar social democracy, focusing on issues of gender, medicine and ethics. She is the author of *The Too-Good Wife: Alcohol, Codependence, and the Politics of Nurturance in Postwar Japan* (University of California Press) and, recently, "Japan's hidden youths: mainstreaming, sheltering, and rehabilitating the emotionally distressed in Japan," in *Culture, Medicine, and Psychiatry*. Her current project explores the role of Japan studies in American social thought as a laboratory for imagining alternatives to liberalism and individualism.

Mary C. Brinton is Reischauer Institute Professor of Sociology at Harvard University. Her research interests include the labor market, gender, social inequality, education, and comparative institutional analysis. She is the author of *Women and the Economic Miracle: Gender and Work in Postwar Japan* (University of California Press), *Women's Working Lives in East Asia* (Stanford University Press), and most recently, *Searching for the Lost Place: The Sociology of the 'Lost Generation'* (in Japanese, NTT Shuppansha).

Aya Ezawa is university lecturer in the sociology of modern Japan in the Department of Japanese and Korean Studies at Leiden University. Her research focuses on the gender and class dimensions of social policy, both in Japan and in a comparative perspective, as well as their implications for the living conditions of single mothers. Her research has been published in the *Journal of Sociology and Social Welfare*, *Japanstudien*, and *Kikan Shakai Hosho Kenkyu* (*Quarterly of Social Security Research*). Currently, she is in the course of completing a book on the regulation of family life in contemporary Japan.

Hiroshi Ishida is a professor of sociology at the Institute of Social Sciences, University of Tokyo. His research interests include comparative social stratification and mobility and school-to-work transition. He is the editor of *Social Science Japan Journal* published by Oxford University Press and co-directs the Japanese Life Course Panel Survey. He is the author of *Social Mobility in Contemporary Japan* (Macmillan Press and Stanford University

Press) and the co-author of *Schools, Public Employment Offices, and the Labor Market in Postwar Japan* (in Japanese, University of Tokyo Press).

Takehiko Kariya is professor in the sociology of Japanese society in the Department of Sociology and Nissan Institute of Japanese Studies at Oxford University, and professor at the Graduate School of Education at the University of Tokyo. His main areas of research are in sociology of education, social stratification, school-to-work transition, educational and social policies, and social changes in postwar Japan. He has published many books in Japanese, including, *Kaisouka Nihon to Kyouiku Kiki* (*Education in Crisis and Stratified Japan*), *Kyouiku Kaikaku no Gensou* (*Illusion of Education Reform*) and, *Kyouiku no Seiki* (*The Century of Education*). His recent article in English is "Japan at the meritocracy frontier: from here, where?" co-authored with Ronald Dore, in *The Rise and Rise of Meritocracy*, edited by Geoff Dench (Blackwell Publishing).

Sawako Shirahase is an associate professor in the Department of Sociology, the University of Tokyo. Her main research interests are on socioeconomic inequality and demographic change in a comparative perspective. She is the principal investigator of the research project examining the structure of social stratification in the ageing society from a gender and generation perspective. She is the author of two books in Japanese, *Unseen Gaps in an Ageing Society: Locating Gender, Generation and Class in Japan* (University of Tokyo Press) and *Thinking about Inequalities in Japan: A Comparative Study of Ageing Societies* (University of Tokyo Press).

David H. Slater is an associate professor of cultural anthropology in the Faculty of Liberal Arts and the Graduate Program in Japanese Studies at Sophia University, Tokyo. His research focuses on youth culture, capitalism, urban space and place, and digitality. Most recently, he has co-authored, "Dysfunctional hegemonic masculinities in neoliberal Japan" in *Mediated Boyhoods* (Peter Lang Publishers). Currently, he is working on a manuscript on neoliberal subjectivities in education and youth labor in Heisei Tokyo.

Ayumi Takenaka is an associate professor of sociology at Bryn Mawr College and at the Center for the Study of Social Stratification and Inequality at Tohoku University. She is the co-editor of *The Changing Japanese Family* (Routledge) and has published various articles on immigration and ethnicity. They include "How diasporic ties emerge: Pan-American Nikkei communities and the Japanese state" (*Ethnic and Racial Studies*).

Series editors' preface

Few modern economies have been through such turbulent times as Japan during the past two decades. After the bubble economy – which had led to many believing that Japan was to become the Number One economy in the world by the end of the century – had burst at the end of the 1980s, the country went into a prolonged recession throughout the 1990s from which it emerged with a sustained period of economic recovery before being flattened, almost more than any other major economy, by the "credit crunch" depression that hit the global markets in 2008. What has this all meant for those who live and work in Japan?

The Nissan Institute/Routledge Japanese Studies Series (the largest series of books in English on contemporary Japanese society) seeks to foster an informed and balanced, but not uncritical, understanding of all elements of contemporary Japan. Few topics are as important yet as little studied for the understanding of Japanese society as class despite the manifest and increasing diversification which has occurred as a result of economic boom being followed by economic recession. Even the Japanese government (well-known for its love of collecting and collating statistics) has been loath to measure the change in class structure in recent years; the team which carried out the most recent *OECD Review of Tertiary Education* in Japan expressed considerable surprise that the Japanese Ministry of Education was unable to provide comparative data on the rates of entry into higher education among young people from families in the lowest and highest quartiles of family income, the most basic data necessary for monitoring rates of educational access and class mobility (Newby *et al.*, 2009: 56–7). The current volume goes a long way towards filling this gap. It explores Japanese perceptions of class and class consciousness as well as the underlying empirical realities of sociological class and social mobility within the society. It looks at the relationship between class and ethnicity and class and gender and it examines in great detail the role of education and marriage in class formation.

The authors of the volume include most of the leading experts on Japanese class currently writing in English and their status in the field allows them to draw on the most up-to-date survey data; as Mary Brinton (2003) has pointed out elsewhere, primary quantitative data in Japan, even if it has been collected using government funding, tends to be much less publicly accessible than it is in other countries. What gives this volume a particularly interesting angle is the way that it combines the use of quantitative data (which has been the bedrock of most class analysis) with qualitative data reflecting the fact that one of the editors, Hiroshi Ishida, is a quantitative sociologist and the other, David Slater, is an anthropologist whose data come from detailed and long-term ethnographic fieldwork. It is this combination of approaches which allows us to understand both how class works and how class is perceived in contemporary recessionary Japan.

Roger Goodman
J.A.A. Stockwin

Sources

Brinton, M, (2003) "Fact-rich, data-poor: Japan as sociologists Heaven and Hell", in *Doing Fieldwork in Japan*, edited by Patricia Steinhoff, Theodore Bestor, and Victoria Lyon Bestor. Honolulu, HI: University of Hawaii Press.

Newby, H, Weko, T, Breneman, D, Johanneson, T and Maassen, P, (2009) *OECD Reviews of Tertiary Education: Japan*. Paris: OECD.

Acknowledgments

This volume has been a long time in preparation. The chapters have been solicited, presented and refined over three years, during which time we held two meetings in Ann Arbor, Michigan, and a meeting in Tokyo. Along the way, we have collected numerous debts. We would like to thank the Center for Japanese Studies at the University of Michigan for funding our conference and workshop in March 2004 and again in October 2005, both in Ann Arbor. In particular, we would like to thank the then director, Mark West, and the staff of the Center for Japanese Studies – Jane Ozanich, Yuri Fukazawa and Sandra Morawski – for their help in organizing these events. We also received financial assistance from the Department of Sociology at the University of Michigan for the October 2005 conference, and would like to thank the chair, Howard Kimeldorf, and business manager, Patricia Preston, for their support. For organizing the Tokyo meeting in January 2005, we are indebted to the 2005 Social Stratification and Social Mobility (SSM) Project, in particular, the principal investigator, Yoshimichi Sato of Tohoku University. We would also like to acknowledge the support of the Grant-in-Aid for Specially Promoted Research (grant number 16001001) of the Japanese Ministry of Education, Culture, Sports, Science and Technology and the Grant-in-Aid for Scientific Research (S) (grant number 18103003) and (A) (grant number 20243029) of the Japan Society for the Promotion of Science.

At these and other meetings many scholars have generously helped us sharpen our theoretical focus and gave comments to our own introduction and to various other chapters in our volume. Most significantly among these are Nancy Abelmann, the late Gary Allinson, Ted Bestor, John Campbell, Sally Hastings, Ken Ito, Sharon Kinsella, John Lie, Tsutomu Nakano, Yuko Ogasawara, Sonya Ryang, Kaoru Sato, the late Gary Saxonhouse, Hitomi Tonomura, Christina Turner and Louise Young. To them, we offer our thanks.

We would like to thank Stephanie Rogers and Leanne Hinves at Routledge for their strong support in turning these chapters into a volume, and to the two readers from Routledge, who subsequently identified themselves, Peter Cave and Roger Goodman, for their constructive comments.

Last, but not least, we owe thanks to Tomoko Abe and Misuzu Nakajima, who were very instrumental in their checking of references and formatting the final manuscript.

Finally, we are grateful to our colleagues who contributed chapters to this volume. They helped us formulate the conceptual framework and agreed to work within the confines of the project as it developed over time. It was a lot of fun to work together, and we feel fortunate to have had the chance to work with such a highly professional and supportive group of diverse and exciting scholars.

Hiroshi Ishida
David H. Slater

1   Social class in Japan

Hiroshi Ishida and David H. Slater

Researching social class in Japan

Prompted by drastic changes in Japanese society and shifts in the foci and methods of social analysis, the social scientific literature on Japan has taken a distinct turn in the past ten years. Japanese society, once represented as unified and homogeneous, is now recognized as fractured along lines of ethnic, racial and gender difference. It is not diverse just at its margins, but often within its very core, and this diversity is not just a recent phenomenon, but one that is now being traced back hundreds of years to the way its very origins have been represented. The literature has demonstrated an exciting shift away from the study of mainstream populations and the mechanisms that unify the population (political, cultural and social) and toward the issue of internal differentiation, autonomy and contestation (Denoon *et al.* 2001, Sugimoto 2003, Weiner 1997). Not only have the discourses that promoted the image of monolithic Japan come under critical scrutiny from many quarters, but there is a growing body of empirical work that documents emergent and increasingly significant fault lines within Japan. Japan has been resituated within a much broader global and comparative context where issues of change, hybridity, and innovation have replaced national and institutional frames of reference. Perhaps most excitingly, this shift has been visible across a wide range of disciplines – literature as well as sociology; political science as well as anthropology; contemporary popular culture as well as the historical roots from which these new forms have emerged.

And yet, in the rush to "diversify" Japan, one important axis of difference and diversity, and source of structure for that difference, has received relatively less theoretical attention or empirical exploration in the English language tradition: social class. This is paradoxical for a number of reasons. There is hardly a society that has experienced more significant class reorganization than has Japan in the past 100 years. Moreover, for much of the postwar period, the rhetoric of social class has supplied the most important ideological foundation for major political social movements. Within the academic literature, Japanese scholars have produced one of the most sustained bodies of work by Marxist and stratification theorists anywhere in the world, and certainly outside the West. Moreover, while acknowledging that there are many ways to measure social structure, for most of the postwar period, the patterns of social mobility have been in the range of most other democratic capitalist societies (Ishida 1993), and yet, the possibility that these processes will generate distinctive social formations has been largely overlooked. In fact, the focus on the formation of middle-class or middle-mass society has so dominated the research agenda that through the postwar industrialization and the rapid economic rise to prominence, including the bubble economy of the 1980s, social science has too often neglected class dynamics that differentiate and divide Japanese society (Chiavacci 2008). While the examination of Japan as a relatively undifferentiated whole, a unit of analysis in and of itself, has provided valuable contrastive examples to analysis of a modernity that is clearly organized around Western models, today it obscures more than it reveals about Japan. In an unexpected shift, as Japan's recession becomes recognized as one more manifestation of the neo-liberal economy characteristic of many late-capitalist societies, the re-emergence of social class rhetoric as a way to frame social anxiety in the popular press has increased as the salience of class analysis is proving new utility in more academic research in Japan (for example, Hashimoto 2003, Sato 2000, Yamada 2004).

Through a re-examination of recent postwar society and this volume demonstrates that the analysis of class formation is a necessary corrective to stratification research and ethnographic work on institutions – family, school and work – and more recently, other sources of collective identity and action, such as gender and ethnicity. Indeed, we argue that without situating our current qualitative and quantitative research within a class context, and without understanding the class dynamics that both generate and cross-cut these other principles of social order, our understanding of Japanese society is fundamentally incomplete and often profoundly misleading. At the same time, understanding how broadly shared patterns of class dynamics have developed in a very different historical and cultural context from the West allows us to gain new purchase and perspective on the parameters and manifestations of class formation.

Before we discuss the needs and requirements of class analysis for contemporary Japan, it is important to see how the issue of social class, both inside and outside the academy, has been developed.

Postwar use of "social class" as a research paradigm in and out of Japan

Both the qualitative and quantitative work on Japanese social structure acknowledges the patterns of social stratification and the keen attention paid to relative status differences within Japanese society. The primary question that has concerned researchers is if these patterns of stratification are sociologically significant and enduring, and if we can identify these patterns as class. And if so, on what basis can we identify the coherence of class groups? More generally, we must ask, what do we gain from such class analysis that we might otherwise lack? We outline the quantitative literature on stratification and the qualitative work from ethnography in an attempt to capture the foci, range and blind spots of these two dominant approaches (which, we might add, show little evidence of referencing each other, even today). We hope that through the reformulation of social class, we are able to be bring to quantitative and qualitative work together in some principled way.

Stratification perspective

Usually based on quantitative survey results, much of the stratification literature addresses a core of issues including the changing patterns of lifestyles in absolute and relative terms; the differences between quantitative indicators of socioeconomic position and the patterns of self-identification; the consistency of openness and closure in the structure of opportunity over time.

The analysis of social divisions within Japanese society became the object of sustained interest in the mainstream sociological and popular press during the 1970s. The intellectual exchanges among three prominent social scientists in *The Asahi Shinbun* newspaper in 1977 were good examples of how the discourse on class took shape during this period. Yasusuke Murakami (1977; 1984) sparked off the debate with his article, "The Reality of the New Middle Class." He claimed that because of the continued increase in living standards in the postwar period, class boundaries were blurred and a huge intermediate group with homogeneous lifestyles had emerged. Shigenobu Kishimoto (1977; 1978), a Marxist economist, critically responded to Murakami's claim. According to Kishimoto, people who identified themselves as middle class in the opinion survey did not possess sufficient personal assets to protect themselves in the face of economic downturn and therefore these people did not in fact occupy the middle class. Japanese society, he argued, continued to be polarized between the capitalists and the workers. Ken'ichi Tominaga (1977), a quantitative sociologist, entered the debate by reporting the empirical findings from the Social Stratification and Mobility (SSM) survey conducted in 1975. Tominaga (1977; 1979; Imada and Hara 1979), insisted that because rewards and resources were distributed by pluralistic criteria in Japan, people scored high on some resources and rewards but low on others. The majority of people did not occupy consistently high or low places on all the dimensions of status scores and thus there was a tendency toward what was called "status inconsistency." Tominaga rejected the idea of homogeneity of lifestyles and claimed that the lack of a clearly identifiable upper or lower class, and the tendency of inconsistent distribution of status characteristics, created a diverse middle class in Japan. At least some of the differences among the three positions reflect different ways of conceptualizing social divisions, including positions within the social relations of production, socioeconomic indicators, lifestyles, and subjective perception of status. However, all of them were confronted with the question of how to understand the profound effects of rapid economic growth on social divisions in the society.

To be sure, Japan has experienced tremendous societal transformations in the postwar period which come into sharp focus when understood as changes in the class structure of society. At the end of the Second World War, almost half of the labor force was engaged in primary production, while this figure decreased rapidly during the period of high-speed economic growth. By the mid-1960s, the proportion of primary production reached around 20 percent, and both the blue-collar sector and white-collar sector were expanding. The educational system, an important mechanism for the social reordering and legitimation of that new order, also experienced rapid expansion through two stages, one from 1960 to 1975 and the other after 1986. The rate of enrollment in university and junior college increased from about 10 percent in 1960 to 38 percent by 1975. The rate was stable until the late 1980s, but it has gone up to more than 45 percent in the recent period. The apparent changes in the landscape of urbanization, upgrading of the educational system, shrinkage of the rural population, and the corresponding expansion of the urban industrial sector all led commentators to predict the emergence of a huge middle group characterized by homogeneous lifestyles, clearly differentiated from both the upper and lower classes in Japan.

However, it is an open question whether these dramatic changes have actually brought about the breakdown of class barriers and the homogenization of lifestyles as predicted by the middle-class thesis. Serious empirical work in Japan suggests otherwise. Despite the transformations as a whole, the relative positions of class status have remained remarkably stable (Hara and Seiyama 1999 in Japanese, 2005 in English). The relative differences in the average level of education and income between class categories did not change much throughout the postwar period. Access to higher education continued to be influenced by family origins in roughly the same pattern. Similarly, the chances of mobility and inheritance according to class origins remained stable as well. Sons of the professional-managerial class were always advantaged in reaching the same positions, compared with the sons of the farmers and the manual working class (Ishida 2000).

At issue here are two distinct, but clearly related issues: first, does the quantitative data suggest a shift in the overall class structure that would support a thesis of either a middle-class or class-less society? In other words, once controlling for overall or absolute change in the affluence and educational upgrading of the whole society during this period of high economic growth, are there greater degrees of openness of opportunity and coalescence of lifestyles? The answer to this question would appear to be "no." The second issue might be phrased as such: given that patterns of reproduction of social inequality over time are roughly equivalent to those of other industrial societies, have there developed sets of cultural forms and social practices that are distinct to the different positions within Japanese society? While we might imagine that the ethnographic literature would address these questions, in fact, it has gone in another direction that has done more to obscure than reveal the patterns of increasing social difference and class formation in Japan.

Ethnographic perspective

During this period, the qualitative or ethnographic literature on Japan documented the transformation of the rural farm economy into the urban industrial and white-collar firm, and the establishment of the latter as the ideological core of Japanese society. The rubric for much of this work was that of modernization theory. Ronald Dore (1967), John Bennett (1967), and others assumed that the modernization of Japan would lead to a functional rationalization of society and a formal convergence of social structure and institutions with more recognizable Western models. There are two clearly identifiable foci within this literature that defined the scope of much subsequent research: first, the assumption of the middle-class as representative, even metonymic, of the whole of Japan, and second, the focus on institutions as the most relevant unit of analysis for ethnographic work.

Ezra Vogel (1963) announced the "new middle class" which signaled the imminent demise of the "traditional working class" based on an agricultural, craft and small factory economy toward newly expanded corporate firms that began to demonstrate increases in scale of operations, productivity, wages, and profitability. Just as importantly, this emphasis signaled the rise of hegemony that led middle-class membership to be considered a component part of Japanese social identity, a part of the social contract, even. Under this model, there was little reason to study social class as a relational ordering of different segments of society because this "residual" segmentation was not central to the development of society, and would likely soon disappear in the transformation into a fully "modern" society. Chie Nakane (1970) challenged the ethnocentrism and teleology of modernization theory in significant ways. She identified the current form of Japanese society not as characteristic of an intermediate step on the path to full modernization, but rather as the embodiment of an "alternative trajectory" of capitalist democracies. In terms of social structure, she argued against the development of any horizontal segmentation of society, such as class, and instead for a society based on the vertical integration of institutional order. Institutional membership, based on workplace participation, would constitute the structure of social identity. Thus, despite the increasingly obvious stratification of the population as a whole, primary subjective identification of individuals with firms would prevent any development of class groups.

The difference between a large and dominant middle class (Vogel) and the lack of any classes at all (Nakane) has often been glossed over in the ethnographic literature. While the theory and politics underneath Nakane's work were distinctly at odds with Vogel's modernization theory, the research agenda that they produced still focused on the large firm as the core of Japanese society, as the shaper of social order and individual social identity. The majority of ethnographic studies of this period fall within some institutional contexts (family, education and work), generating one of the most detailed records in English of human relations of any society. However, the representations of these relations are usually focused on the micro-level and are usually abstracted from any larger sociological context, including social class. Often, the ethnographic sites of research are assumed to somehow represent all of Japan, or else, as falling within the parameters of some un-theorized "middle class," which is itself understood as a default boundary that encompasses more or less the whole society, rather than a specific position in social space generated by a particular set of historical circumstances. During this period, even when there is ethnographic work on clearly non-middle class subjects, they are often represented as "traditional" or transitional populations on their way out of the traditional into the modern (for example, Dore 1958, Smith 1978), as deviant subcultures (Wagatsuma and DeVos 1984) or as firmly entrenched in the institutional context that was thought to form the structural core of Japanese society (Cole 1971; Rohlen 1979). Even more recently, in the best ethnographies we have where social class is an important component to the field site (Bestor 1989, Kondo 1990) the analytical focus is not on the particular and distinctive features of class dynamics as an explanatory mechanism. Interestingly, the ethnographic works on schooling by Rohlen (1983) and Goodman (1990) represent the most systematic attempts to link social class, institutional structure and socialization from this period. While Japanese institutional structure and social identity formation might represent significant counterpoints to a Western-driven social theory of the period, the cost of such relativization has been the lack of any principled analysis of the class diversity within Japanese society and the ways in which such diversity is structured.

It is possible that ethnography was never the best method to document this diversity as the tendency to focus on whole-culture patterns (over internal diversity) has been characteristic of much ethnographic research of Japan and elsewhere. The commitment of ethnographers to the foundational status of the subjective experience of informants makes it quite difficult to capture class dynamics, where these dynamics often function outside or only at the fringes of reflective experience, as in the case of Japan. This is as opposed to, say, the UK, where the idiom of social class is very much part of the popular perspective. Given the sudden and dramatic rise of standards of living during the postwar period and the repeated political projects that emphasized the virtue of social unity and sacrifice at the expense of emerging social differences that have characterized this period (Gordon 1993), it is not hard to understand the marginalization of popular uses of social class, and the failure of ethnographic analysis to capture the workings of class formation.

But this obscuring of social differences, as well as resistance to using the rhetoric of social class to explain them, seems to be breaking down during Japan's period of prolonged recession.

The paradox of social class in recessionary Japan

While the bubble economy for many indicated the realization of the "alternative trajectory" of a non-Western capitalism, free from the divisions and conflicts that so plagued the Anglo-European versions – prominently including divisive formations of social classes – its aftermath has been more difficult to characterize and interpret. What became known as the "bursting of the bubble" seemed at first a catastrophic, but probably temporary, setback to the economic juggernaut that was "Japan, Inc." Today, the effects seem more enduring, and could very well represent a relatively lasting shift in the nature of economic and social activity, and their representation (see Kelly 2002). Japan went into recession as land and stock market prices collapsed by the early 1990s. Banks were overextended and could not collect on outstanding debt, curtailing further loans and slowing any rebound in expansion. Employment opportunities shrank rapidly, bringing a record high unemployment rate, and with it, reduced consumer spending. As absolute growth slowed, the differences in relative class position became more obvious and the promise of middle class membership began to hollow out. Many of the most significant changes are occurring in the labor market: massive restructuring of the economy; increased unemployment rates; shift in the structure of the labor market away from lifetime employment and into part-time and short-term work. Just as important, the confidence that society had in the strength of the economy and in the state to be able to manage prosperity was shaken. Maybe most fundamentally, the stability of the firm as a marker of social identity for individuals has receded as the institutional commitment from the firm has been withdrawn.

While the particular configuration of the recessionary economy is in many ways distinctive to Japan, it is equally part of a much larger economic and social transformation toward a global set of economic shifts that becomes associated with what some call a "neo-liberal economy." While characterizations of this shift vary, most accounts assert that it is less driven by changes in a single sector, instead involving a number of different processes that seem to form a network of loose coupling. These include: a transformation of patterns of work away from production and into a service-oriented economy; the dispersal of the production process out of Japan; a re-definition of value that enables capital creation to proceed independently from labor; a receding of the state's ability to manage the accumulation and distribution of capital (including production) in the national interest; the dispersal of productive relations and class alliances, especially as protected through the state's legal apparatus.

The most common class-related argument at this juncture is that as the dispersal of value-creation and irregularity of work increases, society ceases to be structured on the basis of class segmentation. The once-stable possibility of production as the basis for social status and identity is lost, and thus the likelihood of coherent class-based identity disappears. Instead, the argument goes, consumption and other leisure practices become the primary ways of reflecting and/or expressing social position. Gender, ethnicity and other collectivities of elective affiliation become the poles around which identity is formed (and through which an identity politics replaces labor politics). With this shift, class analysis in the academy loses its explanatory power in the face of fractured social order and multiplex social identities.

While this paradigm shift is already being questioned in many contexts, this shift does not unambiguously represent the Japanese case. While most of the destabilizing dynamics that we have come to associate with this shift in other neo-liberal situations are evident in Japan, the popular response has led to a re-articulation of social structure and individual identity in rhetoric that often resemble social class. The general anxiety in recessionary Japan has led many, from prominent theorists to popular weekly magazines, to invoke the idiom of social differentiation, economic gaps, structured inequality, "winners" (*kachi-*

gumi) and losers" (*make-gumi*) and even social class as the theoretical frame of reference to describe the shifts that are present in the society. Monthly opinion journals, such as *Chūō Kōron, Sekai*, and *Bungei Shunjyū*, have featured special issues on Japan's economic gaps and unequal society (*kakusa shakai*). The prominence of the issue of economic inequality is stimulated by the debate over the impact of economic policies introduced by the Koizumi government. Although the extent of the causal influence of the deregulatory policies of the government on the increased inequality is not clear, there is a tendency among the press to present a fractured vision of society, one broken up into "winners" (*kachi-gumi*) and "losers" (*make-gumi*). The overwhelming majority (75 percent) of the respondents to a national survey in 2007 agreed with the statement that income inequality in Japan is too large (Ishida 2008).

Within the academic community, a resurgence of the discourse on social inequality predates the discourse in the press, as patterns of social divisions became more apparent and anxiety about social position became more widespread in the mid-1990s. Toshiaki Tachibanaki's *Japan's Economic Inequality* (1998) was one of the first publications which identified the heightened economic inequality in Japan. Tachibanaki claimed that the extent of income inequality in Japan increased over the 1980s and into the early 1990s and that the Japanese income distribution is more unequal than the same distributions in other advanced nations. His provocative claim attracted attention from the media and the general public, and his book was heralded as one of the outstanding books in economics published in Japan. However, Tachibanaki's claim was later questioned by other scholars. Fumio Ohtake (2005), based on rigorous empirical investigation of large-scale data, concludes that the main reason for the increased income inequality is the aging of the population. The overall level of income inequality increased because of the increased share of the older population which tends to have a higher extent of inequality, so the drastic increase in the overall level of income inequality in Japan was largely explained by the aging of the population. In another bestseller, *A Nagging Sense of Job Insecurity* (2001 in Japanese, 2005 in English), Yuji Genda has documented an increased uncertainty and (well-founded) fear of risk of economic hardship among the younger generation. The employment opportunities and promotion chances for the younger generation have been seriously undermined at the expense of protecting employment security among the older generations. The spread of unemployment and unstable under-employment in the forms of part-time and temporary work has created divisions and economic gaps among the younger population that has class implications that go beyond generational differences.

In addition to the increased inequality in objective chances, Masahiro Yamada (2004) claims that there is a widening of the gap in people's prospects for future advancement. A clear division exists between those who are confident about individual prosperity and achievement in the future and those who have very little hopes and dreams about their future prospects. According to Yamada, Japan has turned into a "hope-divided society." Toshiki Sato argues in his bestseller, *Japan as an Unequal Society* (2000), that the upper non-manual class, which is composed of managers and professionals, became more closed in the 1990s and there is an increased extent of reproduction of the professional-managerial class. He argues that this has led people to lose faith in their chances and expectations of full membership in the middle class. With the increased reproduction of the intellectual elites (as named by Sato), people have given up the idea of hard work leading to socioeconomic advancement. Remarkable here are not only the findings (increased patterns of inequality and decreased mobility chances), but the class framework in which these findings are expressed and have gained popular salience.

Thus, contrary to what we might have imagined from the purported middle-class thesis or "vertical integration" models, even a preliminary examination of class structure, formation, and more recently the awareness of social instability, have all shown signs of stable or increasingly divergent social trajectories and less than convincing structures of commitment. In contrast to the expectations of the neo-liberal diffusion (post-modern indeterminacy or consumer dispersal – take your pick) there is increased awareness of manifest and enduring social divisions in the society, not their erosion. The demise of the large-scale firm as the ideological structure of society and as the anchor of social identity has not particularly led the Japanese population into the floating signifiers of the consumer market (or at least, not any more than was the case pre-Bubble) or into an exclusionary identity politics. Rather, it has led them back to social class, as one way to understand the increasingly fractured social order and to situate social identity.

What class analysis can do now to explain Japan

In this moment of relatively open questioning of the dominant explanations of Japanese society, it is appropriate to examine the usefulness of class as a tool with which to analyze empirical data on Japanese society. Class analysis today is important in the ways that it has always been important: to the extent to which social class structures, orders and limits the patterns of life course and the opportunities therein. It is important because it allows us to understand how social relations in the key institutions within society function within the larger structure of society, often with very different effects for different segments of the population. Class analysis enables us to see how one dimension of social relations, practice and behavior is organized into collective patterns which cut across the institution, gender and ethnicity. Class analysis allows us to see how individuals form coherent social identity and how those on different life courses develop distinctive goals and strategies for reaching those goals, and how these become disseminated through wide segments of the population. It helps us focus on class consciousness per se, and the generation of political action, as well as helping us understand when and how this does not develop. But we also think that attention to social class can help us rethink the following quite specific dynamics in contemporary Japanese society.

Class diversity of institutions and the role institutions play in class formation

The disorganization of the occupational structure has had effects far beyond the organization of work. At a time when fewer paths lead to stable and desirable jobs, we must reexamine the institutionalized patterns of class diversity that have ordered Japanese social life. It is no longer possible to maintain a principled commitment to the idea of "middle class" membership as the foundation for secure social identity. As a research strategy, to abstract a set of idealized cultural values or social relations and call them "The Japanese Firm" (or for the same reason, "The Japanese Family" or "The Japanese School") might once have served as a useful and illuminating counterpoint to hegemonic images within Anglo-American social theory. But today, the sheer diversity of class forms means that such images are essentializing a certain "Japanese-ness" and distorting the wide range of social forms that are operative. The social relations, practices, goals and strategies are at such wide and increasing variance between, say, high schools preparing elite college students and those that serve as little more than a holding institutions until students can set forth into the low-level service segments of the labor market, that they cannot be understood without a rigorous attempt to link class position of the very different segments of young people who move through these institutions. While there is clear commonality between these schools, they are in effect preparing different groups of people in different ways for different ends.

Perhaps more in Japan than in other countries, the work of class formation is done within an institutional context. Without vibrant and distinct class cultures, it is primarily the role of the institution to carry the burden of sorting, socializing and legitimating the orderly supply of labor for a highly differentiated occupational structure. While this is not a new observation, we are only beginning to understand how it works, and it is impossible to do unless we understand the class dynamics involved.

Class situation and internal diversity among other social "groups"

Class formation is opportunistic, working with other social formations, including gender and ethnicity, in ways that are often divergent and even contradictory. It exploits social attitudes such as chauvinism or racism to fulfill and legitimate its own requirements of a differentiated labor force. The monolithic images of social class analysis of the early modernist period clearly needs to be revised to better describe the complex and often contradictory principles of social structure and sources of social identity to include sources that are decidedly "non-productive" and not generated by or intrinsic to class position. But we also need to understand how class is always already cross-cutting other forms of social order, including especially race and gender. The generally lower wage and reduced responsibilities of women in the labor market are not just the result of male chauvinism, cultural difference or biological timing, but also a function of more flexible capital requirement. On the other hand, the internal diversity of a category referred to as "Japanese women" can no longer be examined without reference to the situation of particular women in particular class positions. Women's work, consumption, marriage and child-rearing practices today do not form a uniform pattern (if they ever did), and the "place" of women solely within the context of the male-dominated family increasingly leaves out important parts of gender and family structure, practice and politics. Unless we understand how gender works with social class in Japan, we run the risk of diminishing the dynamism of both categories.

While seeing that many features of ethnic identity are widely shared, different places within the class position enable individuals to differently deploy, exploit and benefit from the social networks, cultural forms and sub-cultural capital that come with ethnic status. The class complexity of ethnic groups has often been overlooked by theorists of all political orientations in an effort to focus on the set of traits that define a particular minority population relative to the "Japanese" majority, but the results can lead to a lack of appreciation of the dynamism and diversity therein. And, just as class structures ethnic groups' internal diversity it also places parameters on the group as a whole. The streaming of immigrant ethnic groups into the lower reaches of society has as much to do with the shifting needs of capital as it does with racism or claims of "cultural difference." The reproduction of particular class positions within the same ethnic communities is much more likely when both social and economic factors are working in a complementary way. With impending in-migration due to demographic shifts and diminished institutional boundaries (for part-time work is more open to immigrant or ethnic labor) the dispersal of ethnic identities through society is going to be more diffuse, and more influenced by class structuring.

Emergence of class form in the recessionary and post-recessionary economy

Besides the enduring utility of class analysis in helping us understand modern capitalist society, we are faced with new challenges and possibilities of using the tools of class analysis in innovative and revealing ways. Anxiety over the perceptions of increasing patterns of inequality, the lack of coordination between education and the labor market, and inability of many to secure desirable and stable work have led many to question the claims of middle-class membership and entitlements. In the same way, the perceived death of lifetime employment and increased occupational mobility (with a loss of security) has led many to question the feasibility of staking some sort of social identity on institutional affiliation and loyal participation. While for much of the postwar period, the dominant explanatory frameworks described how social order and individual identity worked in Japan, now these same models appear to have been deceptive, incomplete or simply irrelevant.

After the experience of economic recession in Japan, social identity is emerging not as a function of institutional membership, but as a function of the sets of linkages that individuals patch together *among* those institutions. Once middle-class membership cannot be assumed and where individuals grow emotionally, symbolically and economically distant from the once-stable firm, the primary ways in which individuals are locating themselves within society is by virtue of their position on the class map, class-specific goals and strategies, and lifestyles. These destinies are not shared among "all Japanese" or even those in the same company but among those in the same class position, a position that of course cuts across institutional contexts. It is important to add, however, that our approach to highlighting social class does not simply echo the recent popularity of the discourse on economic gaps. The typical representation in the media of Japanese society as one of division into "winners" and "losers" is too simplistic (Miura 2005, Yamada and Ito 2007). The dichotomy is a catchy concept, but often ignores the complexity of social relations involving class. Our aim is to use a class analytic framework in order to go beyond dichotomous understanding and to provide a set of representations of the ever more complex and intricate nature of social inequality in contemporary Japan.

The argument in this volume is not only that social class is always and already an important structuring dynamic when considering these other dynamics. Even a cursory examination of the changes that are occurring within Japanese society seems to confirm this. Nor are we only arguing that class is but one of the many essentially similar sources in some admixture of the composite we call social structure or individual identity. For class analysis to be fully revealing, it must be noted that class does *not* work like gender or race (just as the workings and logic of these two are dissimilar in fundamental ways). We must see that educational credentials or job title is not the same as class position, even if these are both important component parts of the latter. Class formation is a distinct process that has distinct effects that need to be disentangled from other sources of structure and identity to fully understand their relationship. This is especially the case today in Japan, as so many other once-stable sources of order and identity are becoming exhausted.

The first step in this process is to articulate the internal coherence of class formation at the level of structure, and to see the boundaries of and the interrelationships among different class groups. We must specify our use of the term "social class" and what this foundational definition will allow us to do. This is the purpose of the following section.

Theoretical and methodological orientation

Definition of social class

The theoretical construction of social class is complex. To understand social class entails a sorting out of class structure, formation and consciousness, all the while avoiding the reductionist tendency in much of the literature that tends to prioritize one over the other. It is also necessary to avoid the analysis of social class as if it functioned separately from other economic processes, social dynamics and cultural forms that in fact always accompany it. In this section we have two goals: first, to outline the different levels of analysis that often confuse debate so we are able to differentiate and thus link economic, social structural, lifestyle and political manifestations of social class: second, to identify the key class dynamics that we see as most central to our understanding of class formation in contemporary Japan. We start from class structure, reflecting our position that it is necessary to so anchor other levels of analysis.

The most fundamental point in class analysis is the imagery of stratification in society. In the sociological literature, two opposing conceptions of stratification exist: the gradational/quantitative notion and the relational/categorical notion of stratification. Sociologists, and especially stratification theorists of Japan, in Japan and elsewhere, often view social stratification as a hierarchy based on occupational status or income. Individuals are thus ranked from high to low along a uni-dimensional socioeconomic status scale, so the difference between individuals in the stratification system is represented as different relative positions along this single line of hierarchy. Under this model, social mobility is conceptualized as upward or downward movement along the status hierarchy. So, for example, upward social mobility would be expressed by the son who attains ten points more in his occupational status score than his father. This image of stratification thus rests on quantitative differentiation along a gradational hierarchy.

If we are to understand society as organized not by gradient lines but as structured into coherent and recognizable positions in social space, then the image of social stratification as status scale is not sufficient. Social structure is more than a set of weighted socioeconomic indicators, even at the stage of drawing the class map. It is even more obviously insufficient if we are to understand social class to include the relationship between different lifestyles and their quantitative embodiment.

The inadequacy of the gradational/quantitative approach can be illustrated by an examination of one of the most significant transformations in postwar Japanese society: the influx of young people from rural farming to urban industrial sectors. Imagine a father who was an independent farmer and his son who became a bricklayer for a large construction company. The occupational status scores given to these two individuals would be exactly the same (46 points according to the occupational prestige scores based on the 1995 Social Stratification and Social Mobility (SSM) Survey), so from the perspective of the occupational status hierarchy, farmers and bricklayers are ranked at the same position. However, the lives and class implications of independent farmers working in rural communities and those of construction workers hired in large companies in the city are vastly different. Farmers own their land and have autonomy in their work which often requires coordination with other farmers in the community. Bricklayers lack the occupational autonomy and status in the community, and yet, they have better pecuniary returns and higher security in employment with a large company, all the while enjoying urban lifestyles. In order to capture the class implications of these two cases, the point would not be to create a more finely calibrated tool to measure relative occupational prestige scores, but to develop an approach that can represent the fuller set of differences, and in doing so, gain some better understanding of how class works in these two cases.

One way to do this is through the relational/categorical notion of stratification that emphasizes qualitative positions, not quantitative factors, as the defining feature of different groups of people who occupy different locations in the class structure. It is not simply that some people have more or less, but people in different classes occupy qualitatively different positions in the labor market and production relations that cannot be reduced to socioeconomic indicators. Class mobility, under the relational notion of class, is conceptualized as detachment from a certain group (class) and attachment to another group, so that individuals who change class positions may experience fundamental change in their socioeconomic resources, lifestyle, identity and socio-political attitude and behavior. Our approach follows this line of conceptualization. It specifically investigates how individuals and families occupy different class positions and experience mobility within the class structure, how their class positions affect their life-chances, attitudes, and lifestyles, and how their class-related identities and interests are formed.

Membership in and internal coherence of the relational/categorical notion of class structure can be found in either the basis of production or the market. Marxist conceptions of class emphasize social relations of production as the fundamental dimension that defines class, while Weberian formulations put more emphasis on market position. The aim of the volume is not to validate one or another theoretical and political construction of social class but to arrive at a working definition that allows us to use class analysis as a "research program" (Goldthorpe and Marshall 1992). While conceptions of class as a function of productive relations and ownership are not excluded in any way, categories such as "management" and "labor" which are derived more from the abstract motion of capital as understood at the early modern period rather than any particular manifestation of capitalism in a given society, fails to capture the structural complexity, fine gradations of social meaning and global trajectory of new middle-class society (Dahrendorf 1959), let alone late-capitalist society (Giddens 1973). Also, to the extent that we understand social class as something that goes beyond "economic" notions of class to make links with socialization, lifestyles and strategies of different class groups, most of the chapters in this volume attempt to locate their analysis in a more historically- and culturally-specific representations of social class. These dynamics are often better captured in the structural possibilities represented by the specific analysis of the contemporary labor market and particular distributions of capital in Japan.

By the same token, class analysis as a research program does not require – or reject – the understanding of class formation or relations as a necessary function of class exploitation. Observing conflict between classes does not necessarily imply the labor theory of value or any other doctrine regarding exploitation. Further, the adoption of the market as the ordering principle of class does not entail a retreat from critical scholarship, as some scholars have suggested (McNall *et al.* 1991; Wright *et al.* 1992). As our chapters illustrate, the nature and sources of exploitation is an empirical question and can only be addressed through the analysis of different cases. At times, different groups will enter into exploitative relations that are based on class, understood on productive or market basis; at other times, exploitation will revolve around other social dynamics whereby class divisions and/or relations can actually be ameliorating of that exploitation, and conducive to effective mobilization of political movement. The chapters in this volume document how class patterns and class identity are formed by non-productive relations (including market position) and are still quite able to capture the antagonism and exploitation that can be part of the process of class formation.

Methodological challenges and approaches

Even once a foundational definition of social class is established, we have to ask the question, "How is class structure linked to other levels of social, cultural and political phenomena?" While there are many different ways to distinguish and describe different sorts of data, as a heuristic framework for discussion across the disciplines and approaches, we have used the work of a historian, Ira Katznelson:

Levels of Class (adapted from Katznelson 1986: 15–18)

Level 1: capitalist economic development, including ownership of and control of resources and means of production; definition of roles—capitalists, labor, etc., but with no particular phenomenal form; a schematic of the "motion" of capitalism or its universal abstract logic; "experience far" or even "experience absent."

Level 2: the social organization of society lived by actual people in real social formation under capitalism; workplace social relations and labor markets; the extra-work patterns that result from these, including geography of industrialized cities and social networks; "experience close" or at least "experienced" in some way.

Level 3: "lived experience"; shared "dispositions"; cognitive maps and definitions of probable life courses; shared values and an awareness of this sharedness; "class culture"; an interpretation of and responses to the economic patterns in level 2; E.P. Thompson, Geertz.

Level 4: collective action based on shared motivation; collective goals; "class consciousness" proper

Borrowing from Katznelson, we can identify levels of class ranging from the most abstract "motion" of capitalism, and its universal logic (Level 1), to the social workings that these motions generate in any particular society (Level 2), to the lived experience of these social relations (Level 3), to the more discursive representations that emerge with some explicit consciousness of class (Level 4). In our use of this chart, we have followed Katznelson in two principles: "relative autonomy" between levels and "restrictive historicity" among levels. First, each level of class works according to its own distinctive logic that may or may not be shared by other levels. Thus, we would argue that a particular pattern of capitalist accumulation (Level 1) does not determine the patterns of social relations through which that capital is embodied (Level 2), even though these two are directly related with the former being the necessary but not sufficient condition of the latter. In the same way, a particular set of social relations (Level 2) will not determine how individuals will experience and represent these social relations (Level 3). Clearly, each level is related to the next, but we cannot assume that one level will generate any particular form at the next level. Second, to recognize a "restrictive historicity" is to acknowledge that what does emerge from each subsequent level of class formation is dependent upon a range of extra-structural factors that are not restricted or determined by class structure, including global or local social change, political upheaval or cultural transformations.

So, for example, while one's place within the labor market might clearly be a function of the abstract workings of the motion of capitalism, the structure of the labor market and the selection of individuals into its different parts is the result of a long series of circumstances quite specific to Japan's postwar history that cannot be extrapolated from or reduced to the abstract workings of capitalism. Thus, patterns of some distinctive sets of class culture, set off by mechanisms of closure and self-awareness, may or may not emerge. And of course, as noted above, the generation of the political mobilization of certain groups legitimated by appeals to "class interests" may not occur as anything we could recognize as "revolutionary class consciousness," as E.P. Thompson (1966) long ago argued. In the case of postwar Japan, such higher level manifestations of an enduring class structure have only infrequently occurred. In adapting this sorting of data to the main themes in our project, we can thus say that the class structure of Japan does not determine the sorts of selection processes among key institutions, the ways in which each institution structures the socialization process, or how the strategies of different class groups will develop. One important goal of class analysis is to be able to establish these non-deterministic linkages. But the considerations of these higher level dynamics do not suggest that class structure is any less important to our analysis. Quite the opposite. Our attempt is to preserve the influence of class structure by resisting the conflation of structure with other levels of analysis that too-often takes place.

The position we take in this volume is that many of the most intransient controversies and methodological shortcomings within the history of class analysis of Japan stems in large part from a failure to fully articulate the different levels of analysis within a principled framework. Consider the above-mentioned debate on "middle-class." The criteria invoked to define "middle-class" are in fact a mishmash of different examples from different levels of analysis with no particular understanding of their relative position: a Marxist is arguing from the level of structure as defined by productive relations (Level 1), while a stratification theorist is arguing over occupational status position (Level 2), while a sociologist is talking about lifestyles (Level 3), and the survey data depends upon self-reporting via individuals' self-conscious reflection (Level 4). While we applaud the diversity of perspectives, we doubt that productive research can be accomplished until the different types of data and their relationship to each other is first clearly articulated.

The framework proposed here also allows us to re-analyze assumptions within the field that have in fact retarded the investigation of social class. Take, for example, Nakane's claims about the classless society we mentioned above. Recall that she asserts that social organization in Japan is a function of institutional membership (household and later firm). She writes that despite a clearly and enduringly stratified population, horizontal strata or classes in Japan have failed to form due to the exceptionally high levels of vertical integration among and within institutions or groups of institutions. Nakane argues that it is these vertical units that organize social structure and define social identity. She writes "even if social classes [class structure] like those in Europe can be detected in Japan ... the point is that in actual society this stratification is unlikely to function" (1970: 87) so as to allow for the positive identification of individuals with classes as such.

By sorting out the different levels of analysis, it is possible to reformulate her argument as follows: because there is no class consciousness (Level 4), there is no class structure in Japan (Level 2), or at least, it does not "function" in society. By conflating the different levels of analysis, Levels 2 and 4, in Katznelson's chart, Nakane is unable to see the significance of social class except insofar as it rises up to the level of explicit consciousness or leads to political mobilization. Of course, this is putting the cart before the horse. That is, she reads backwards from one of many historically contingent outcomes of class structure (consciousness and political mobilization), and finding nothing, concludes that there is no operative class structure at the more fundamental levels of society. What we miss by Nakane's reading are the many intermediate forms that may never rise to the level of consciousness but nevertheless still structure class-specific practices and correlated subjective (social and individual) aspects of class to a more objective class structure. These include the following: the sorting and selection mechanism that redistributes the population; the differential ways in which different groups are socialized for vastly different futures; the different sorts of social practices and strategies that coalesce around particular positions in social space.

This is not characteristic of Nakane's work alone, and is shared with much of the ethnographic work done on Japan. Ironically, these theorists have no problem teasing out bits of social behavior as illustrations of "Japanese cultural" pattern persistence, and yet seem less willing to accept the same analytical practice in the study of social class. Our framework has helped us uncover the institutional and social aspects of class formation and closure that may never come up to the level of individual conscious reflection, and yet still play a role in the structuring and informing of the inarticulate practices of social classes. Our goal is to be able to differentiate distinct levels of analysis in order to be able to link them back up (where the empirical data would justify such attempts) so we can see the wider range of class formations, even when these are not the primary popular idiom through which social order, identity and difference are articulated.

The diversity of class effects

One of the ways to revitalize class analysis and to demonstrate its utility is to specify and at times limit, the claims made for it. While the term "class analysis" once signaled a mono-causal myopia, in this volume (as indeed in much contemporary research that focuses outside Japan) class relations are recognized as but one of many factors that constitute, bind and divide society. Class membership can be relativized as one of many considerations in the complex process of identity formation, both local and more remotely global. One way to capture this diversity is to understand the diversity of institutional forms and of group memberships, as argued in Section 1 of this Introduction. The question is not if social class (or generation or geography, institutions or gender) is the best or most fundamental way to understand Japan, or any society. Clearly, these are all always and already in the mix together. Rather, the examination of social class should complement and develop, instead of replace or compete with, some of the fascinating research and approaches that are currently being undertaken in many disciplines. But we would stress that class is always there.

Thus, it should also be recognized that just as subcultures are important in the shaping of social groups, most subcultures also exist at particular places in the class structure, have been sorted in different ways, and have developed strategies for expression that are just as significant in shaping their development as the particular cultural content. We would argue that the examination of youth, family and aging – all critical and crisis-level topics within the literature on Japan – must include some awareness that different class trajectories offer very different pictures of what are all too often represented as unitary phenomena. We cannot study consumption (of images or products), without some explicit identification of the many different strategic aspects that organize this centrally important social practice in different ways for different classes. "Women" cannot be considered some undifferentiated political, social or cultural unit of analysis, any more than can "labor" or "race." The differential patterns of sorting and socialization that these different groups go through, collectively or in their diversity, alert us to dynamics that are obscured otherwise. The representations of global flows of money, ideas and individuals into, out of and through Japan is virtually incoherent until we see at what points the money is accumulated and spent, at which level of society particular ideas become operative, and most fundamentally, what positions people are moving to and from within Japanese society. One important way that these positions are defined is by the class map of Japan, and the point of class analysis is to see the ways this structure can be linked more broadly to correlations in sorting, socialization and strategies that can lead to larger social forms and social identities.

We examine the intersection among these different dimensions of institutional forms and functions, of ethnicity and race, of gender and generation, of geography and global flows, arguing that even where the most explicit patterns of representation of social relations revolve around these other sorts of social difference, this does not imply that social class becomes any less present or influential, nor should it be marginalized in analysis. Indeed, it is all the more important to seek out the material conditions that relate to these patterns of social difference when they are otherwise obscured. The goal of this study is to explore the ways in which social relations and identity formation in Japan always exist within particular material conditions in a particular class structure. Our goal of this volume is not to isolate class effects, but to see how class dynamics work within the broader fabric of society.

Four dynamics of understanding social class

One of the characteristics of the literature on social class is its methodological breadth and theoretical diversity. While this is a welcome and invigorating feature in any literature, it has also led to a balkanization of subfields and polarization of specialties around stratification, labor economics, cultural studies and political justice. Most evident is that different approaches take wholly different phenomena as their object of explanation. In our own project, we attempt to bridge the methodological distance between the qualitative and quantitative approaches, between the survey study, discourse analysis and ethnography. Since our understanding of social class is expansive, and includes structural, institutional and cultural manifestations, one of the exciting methodological challenges of putting together this volume has been to bring these different approaches together. We had to ask ethnographers to pay more attention to situating their field sites within a class map; to ask quantitative researchers to draw out the more cultural implications of their surveys; and to have everyone make an attempt to link their own work in ways more broadly understood than is usual within their subfield. Thus, you will find more tension over shared models of analysis in this volume than in others more narrowly constructed by sub-discipline, or where the sorting out of different types of data is less of a priority. The collective understanding of class analysis for us began not so much with a singular definition of social class, but a shared appreciation of the necessity of locating the different definitions of what we all considered relevant "data."

Sorting out the different disciplinary perspectives and levels of analysis is the first step to begin a principled class analysis, but it does not tell us what to look for. "Class analysis as a research program" aims to explore four separate but related dynamics which are essential to the understanding of society from a class perspective: they are *class structure, class-differentiating selection, class-based socialization*, and *class strategies*. These four Ss constitute the thematic structure of our research enterprise. It should be noted that these four *dynamics* are different from the four *levels of analysis* we have just introduced, and that both are necessary in order to have a robust and disciplined research program. Each of these dynamics can occur at different level of analysis, in the sense outlined above, even while there is a rough correspondence. So, while it is more likely that the structuring dynamics of class formation will be understood at Level 1 or 2 of Katznelson, "selection" or class-based sorting occurs also at Level 2 or 3 (and sometimes at Level 4), albeit through different mechanisms. By the same token, the development of class "strategies" is most often thought of as being part of Level 4 (an explicit program of class consciousness and political action) but probably more often, occurs through the inarticulate process of lived culture (Level 3) and sometimes goes as low as Level 2 (as a pattern of social behavior that is often intrinsic to the structure of the workplace relations). While the levels of analysis allow us to order our data, the four class dynamics allow us to focus our substantive inquiry.

The first S stands for *structure* and is concerned with the task of locating individuals and families within the class map. Above, we have argued for the importance of a relational approach to class structure. Indeed, the whole project begins with the question of class structure, and the research that demonstrates the reproduction of class structure over time (Ishida 1993).

Ishida's chapter asks whether socioeconomic resources are mapped along class lines and whether people's mobility chances and perceptions are affected by their location on the class map in contemporary Japan. The analysis of large-scale survey data sets points out that education, occupational status, and income are unequally distributed among different class categories not only in Japan but also in the United States and Germany, and that the patterns of the ranking of class categories are very similar across the three nations. When we move our attention to intergenerational mobility, we find strong propensity towards class inheritance, that is, the tendency for the children to stay in the same class position. Again the Japanese pattern of class immobility is very similar to those found in the United States and Germany. However, because of the late and rapid industrializing path of economic development in Japan, the Japanese manual working class possesses weakly developed demographic identity: the Japanese manual working class is recruited more extensively from other classes and less likely to remain in manual positions than the manual working class in the West. Ishida's chapter also shows that people's subjective perception of social standing is influenced by social class in three nations, and Japan is not different in terms of the importance of class in subjective social status. Social class constitutes a crucial dimension in contemporary Japan, shaping and re-shaping people's life chances and perceptions.

Shirahase examines the linkage between class map and the institution of marriage. She begins by asking who gets married and who remains single. One of the main reasons for the recent decline in fertility rates and the emergence of a low-birth society is the declining marriage rate because there are very few births outside marriage in Japan. Married couples have shown a tendency to have fewer children only very recently, and the main social force driving the low fertility rate is that fewer people are getting married in Japan. The chances of remaining single are related to class origin and education, especially among men. Among those who do get married, there is clear evidence of homogamy by class origin and education. People from the same class background and from the same educational level tend to marry each other. The selection of marriage partners is not done at random. Partners are screened and carefully chosen on the basis of the location on the class map of the family and the ranking in the educational hierarchy. Marriage is another institution where social class has profound influence, and at the same time, exerts impact on class. Through marriage, class structure is reproduced from one generation to the next.

In a fundamental way, the chapters in this volume are a response to the findings on class structure: if we find patterns of intergenerational reproduction of class inequality at rates roughly comparable to other advanced capitalist democracies, then should we not also expect to find concomitant effects of differentiation and structuring in Japanese society as a whole? While being mindful of the fact that the social mechanisms and cultural forms of class in Japan will be different from what we find in other societies, it is necessary to explore the possibility if we are to put Japan into a larger comparative framework.

We assume that the structural locations on the class map that provide the basis of class categories do not determine how these patterns shape people's lives, be it around class or other dynamics. In Giddens' (1973) terms, the question could be stated, "How does economic or objective class structure become manifest as social or subjective orders of social class?" That is, if productive and/or market relations represent the mediate principles of class structure as understood through mobility chances, in order to speak of the *social* existence of a class, we must also consider the more proximate institutional mechanisms and ordered social behavior that structure shared life conditions within class groups. We identify three such dynamic mechanisms that produce boundaries between classes and structure coherence within classes: selection, socialization and strategies.

Selection refers to the processes of sorting and class closure. Within the limited patterns of social mobility in postwar Japan, as outlined above, we would expect to see concomitant patterns of social closure (Parkin 1979). Institutional closures involve limiting access to resources and opportunities to members of a particular class group (Grusky and Sorensen 1998; Weeden and Grusky 2005). In Japan, it is the educational system that is usually considered to be the primary mechanism for the reallocation of individuals through the class structure. But of course, the selection mechanism can be found elsewhere. For example, employers screen candidates based on cognitive skills including educational qualifications, non-cognitive skills and dispositions, reputations, and demographic attributes, and in the end, they tend to select those candidates who match the attributes of the incumbents. In fact, as the school-to-work linkages become disordered and frayed in the neo-liberal economy of recessionary Japan (Honda 2005), we are seeing increased emphasis on the formal filtering criteria, such as licenses and certifications, which are used to sort out levels of professional and non-professional occupations. There is also self-selection on the side of the applicants. This dynamic is notably illustrated by the strident, if in the end, usually self-defeating rhetoric of "freedom" used by the part-time workers known as "freeta" to contextualize their loss of secure and stable employment opportunities (Kosugi 2003). Prospective employees self-select the positions for which they apply based not only on their qualifications and credentials but also on their beliefs about whether it is a good match in terms of dispositions, lifestyles, and demographic attributes (Kariya 1991). The selection mechanism thus generates institutional closure by assuring that members of the same class group share not only cognitive traits that may be directly relevant to productivity but also non-cognitive and demographic attributes. The sorting of individuals in this way ensures class closure while the institutionalization of credentials legitimates this selection process.[1]

In order to understand the structural reproduction of class over time and to make concrete the abstractions of class formation, we require close case studies of the mechanisms that (re)-allocate individuals into society. Note that both of these studies take particular note of the policy and market changes that have both transformed the school and dramatically altered the institutional linking between school and the labor market.

Kariya provides an important example of the sorting mechanism by looking at what is imparted by education. According to Kariya, Japanese people used to subscribe to the idea of "the Japanese mode of educational credential society" (J-mode credential society). It emphasized cognitive achievement as represented by success in test scores and entrance examinations, which in turn, assured job security and advancement in lifelong employment system. Education imparted knowledge (or memorization of knowledge) and test-taking skills. The J-mode credential society, however, has been criticized by academics, policy makers, and the public as the leading cause of the excessive competition known as "exam hell," as well as juvenile delinquency, bullying and school violence. Educational reforms introduced in the 1990s were aimed at addressing the problems of the J-mode credential society, by introducing a new curriculum which emphasized less competition and learner-centered pedagogy. The objectives of education under these reforms highlighted self-learning competence and the ability to discover and solve problems, rather than teacher-centered teaching and memorization. What has replaced the J-mode credential society is what Kariya calls "the learning capitalist society" which emphasizes the significance of learning competency – a combination of eagerness to learn, active learning habits, and skills to know how to learn. However, the unintended consequence of educational reforms, according to Kariya, was that as learning competency became more important in education, social class difference in learning competency emerged. There are clear gaps in learning competency according to students' family background, and there is a division between the "haves" and "have nots." Kariya argues that there is emerging a new form of class society based on learning competency.

Brinton looks at the class sorting effects of the school-to-work transition during the same important period of the recessionary economy for a certain stratum of the youth labor market: high school graduates. In light of Ishida's macro-level findings demonstrating reproduction of class structure over time, Brinton asks if the force of intergenerational reproduction of labor market success has become stronger for the cohort who came of age in Japan at the end of the twentieth century in ways that suggest an increase in class closure and divergence in the economic profiles of different social classes. In this recessionary economy, the desire for a more "flexible" labor force has resulted in decreased full-time hiring of "fresh" graduates just out of school, and thus an overall increased inability of young people to secure stable jobs, a departure from the experiences of other post-Second World War cohorts. While Brinton uses the term "lost generation" to describe the effects upon this young cohort across classes, she also points out that this labor market shift is differentially affecting different classes in different ways. Participation in this recruitment system was one way for all classes, middle and working class, to secure stable employment and earnings, but with its demise, it is those at the bottom who are robbed of the more significant mobility mechanism. Brinton's chapter argues that for students from low-ranked high-schools social class is an increasingly important determinant in their labor market outcomes.

Socialization mechanisms act to establish and solidify class-based skills, attitudes, and interests. Formal education in school and training within the company are the most obvious site of socialization in Japan. High schools of different academic levels socialize and prepare their students to inhabit and accept different class positions in the society. In Japan where the geography (both urban and rural) does not always exhibit clear-cut class-based residential patterns, it is at high school where students are most clearly prepared for their future locations in society, not only through formal teaching but also through informal interactions with teachers who guide them and friends who share their general social background and future life trajectory. It is in high school that their class position is given the tangibility of institutional form through the highly differential structures, practices and symbols characteristic of different schools at different ranks. This socialization process continues into post-secondary education, where in the past ten years we have seen not only a huge increase in numbers of students attending regular four-year colleges, but various two-year training schools that expose students to the more specific skills, pedagogy, and structures of institutional authority that anticipate their selection into more particular places in the occupational structure. Both levels of education demonstrate the importance of the establishment and diffusion of socializing patterns in forming class-based orientations and aspirations.

Slater's chapter is set against the backdrop of "normal" educational practice, normal in the sense of "normative" popular image, but also the overwhelmingly dominant image in the academic literature. The fact is that most Japanese high school students do not go to competitive colleges and so different high schools are preparing them for very different futures. Through the progressive marketization of secondary school students are tracked into high schools that prepare them for, and predispose them to accept as legitimate, very different social destinations. While this process is the same as in any capitalist society (despite the fact that it has yet to be documented in the case of Japan), what is distinctive is the set of cultural forms through which this reallocation, preparation and legitimation is managed. In middle school, where the default social unit is a collective (group living), efficient and effective sorting must break down this collective in order to individuate outcomes as the natural result of achievement. The first part of this chapter documents how students narrate their descent to the bottom of the middle school, how being at the bottom becomes part of their "class resource" and situated worldview. The second part of this chapter outlines the various contradictions of the working-class high school: an exam-oriented curriculum that holds virtually no meaning or utility to students not going to college and yet, an authority structure that teachers deploy just to keep order in a school of compromised moral foundation. The end result is a socialization process that generates not only a social and institutional self, but also one that is distinctively classed, as they enter the lower reaches of the service labor market.

Borovoy examines the ways in which three very different tertiary educational institutions prepare three very different groups of students for three very different positions in the occupational structure. She begins by historicizing the definition of "valued human capital," especially documenting the ways in which this organizing cultural form has structured and legitimated the school-to-work transition in the postwar period. During the recession, a move into increased part-time labor and a neo-liberal ethic of market flexibilization has destabilized the pillars of lifetime employment and seniority wage structure, as well as transformed the ways in which the firms recruit young workers. By analyzing the effects of this larger market transition on three groups of students in their job search, we are able to see how universities are resituating and socializing youth labor and how students are navigating these shifts; we are able to see how class capital is being produced in new ways. Those at the elite universities are struggling to stay atop the wave by accumulating marketable skills and certificates to be more competitive in a market that hires more on skills rather than the traditional criteria of "character" and university prestige. Those at the lower-level universities often lack the social and cultural capital to take advantage of this shift, and find themselves slipping into the strata of the irregular labor market, demoralized by the deterioration of the respectable working-class stability and status they once enjoyed. Those at the bottom, who have always had to navigate the irregularities of a fluid and piecemeal occupational existence, have perhaps most dramatically exploited this discursive shift as record numbers opt for training schools (*senmon gakkō*) that re-represent the skills that they have to offer in a more positive light (even if their actual working conditions appear to have changed very little).

Class *strategies* is the most heterogeneous dynamic. It here refers to the regularization of behavior into patterns that are distinctive to different groups as they negotiate their class position, selection and socialization processes mentioned above. Individuals in different class positions will find themselves presented with particular circumstances which they must adapt to, explain and work through. They generate distinctive goals that seem "reasonable" to someone in their position and develop strategies to meet those goals. These strategies can be seen as orderly and shared responses to the differential predicaments characterizing different positions on the class map. Thus, while linked to this class map, these strategies are not determined by that map, or by the sorting and socialization mechanisms that are distinctive to particular class positions. We might think of the class map presenting a horizon of possibilities. So, for example, someone coming out of a bottom level school will have different networks, resources and goals than someone from a top private school. Indeed, it is through the study of strategies that we can see how class structure is transformed through individual agency, and thus, extend our understanding of how class becomes a feature of lived experience. With the increasingly fractured educational and job market, it might very well be that these shared class strategies are emerging as the most influential mechanism in the process of class formation, both a result of exposure to particular class situations and a generative mechanism for coherent social action in a world where institutional bonds are weakening.

As we have pointed out, these strategies rarely rise to the Level 4 articulated by Katznelson. More often, we see partial awareness, and incomplete or unrealized attempts, somewhat disorganized practices that reflect the objective conditions of lived experience in certain class positions, but are not fully regularized through institutional structure, articulated through shared values, or legitimated by symbols of distinct identity in any way available to conscious reflection. Often, it is the inaccessibility of these strategies as objects of conscious reflection that makes them silently effective in the larger process of class formation.

We have made the point that the dynamics of social class never exist in isolation from other ordering principles (such as ethnicity, gender or generation) that constitute the complex we call social identity. Throughout this volume, our effort is to identify – but never exclude – these other principles in our understanding of social class. But we can push the argument one step further to say that when examining strategic deployment of identity, it is through these other principles of distinction that class distinctions are manifest and sometimes encoded because they, rather than class position, are often more readily available to conscious reflection. Unlike other societies (say, the UK at certain historical periods), social class does not provide the rhetoric of social identity. This is a point made above, but in the context of using class as a research tool, often the discursive elements are provided by other, less self-evidently related parts of a complex social identity. Of course, there are many more socially acceptable ways of talking about social identity than class. By the same token, there are other ways to be talking about what amounts to class distinctions than calling them by name. This pattern requires the invocation of another, more accessible set of distinctions that can be invoked and manipulated so as to provide the tools for strategic aspects of representation and generation of social action. The discourses and dynamics underlying gender and race are just such available sources of order and distinction that are essential to understanding class strategies and class effects.

Aya Ezawa demonstrates a range of strategies required to navigate the intersection of social class and gender ideals in her analysis of how single women with children struggle and strategize in their attempt to be "good mothers" and "professional housewives." While these normative notions are already linked to larger patterns of the middle-class lifestyle of the stay-at-home mother who lives on the salary of her husband, this lifestyle is not available to these women. Just as her own class identity becomes called into question without a husband, so her claims to moral standing become jeopardized by single motherhood. The interesting point is that from different class positions, just what constitutes a "good mother" becomes quite different, and with unequal material resources available to different class positions, these mothers evolved social meanings that are operationalized to different extents and in different directions. Based on a much larger sample, Ezawa offers examples of three different women, all of whom share the stigma of an "irregular" household and limited recourses (as child support is very rarely paid by fathers in Japan and the state's public assistance is quite limited) as they try to balance work and child care. Women of more elite backgrounds can do some part-time jobs because they have more resources to call upon (educational credentials, housing loans and a family network to share child care). This enables them to secure the personal control and family peace that was absent when they were married, even as they struggle with the fact that a divorcee in an elite family can generate pervasive negative social opinion from peers and co-workers and even jeopardize future opportunity. A second woman, middle-class in many ways, thrust into a precarious position by divorce, opts to keep her full-time job, even if it means extended day-care for her child and her own separation from him so as to be sure that she can pay for her son's future education. For her, being a "good mother" is about making the sacrifice to secure her son's financial future. A final woman, from a family on welfare, does not see the securing of future educational or financial opportunity for her young children to be a realistic goal or even a responsible pursuit for a mother. Rather, she opts to stay on welfare so she can devote her full attention to her family, with little of the stigma felt by those women in higher class positions. All of these women are engaged in a moral struggle about what constitutes a "good mother," but the answers and strategies that are engendered are closely linked to class position.

Finally, the chapter by Ayumi Takenaka examines the intersection between ethnicity and class, a relationship that points not only to the global flow of people that has been characteristic of Japan for many years, but also to the inextricable political dimension as the Japanese state attempts to manage its borders, labor markets and national identity – all projects that have distinctive class effects. Takenaka examines a very recent intersection of ethnicity and social class in her study of Peruvian migration into Japan, where once again, the issues of social class are inextricably bound up with political history. Unlike Koreans, Peruvians were brought into Japan under a rhetoric of "ethnic kin," with the immigration policy giving preference to those of Japanese descent. Also brought over were Peruvians of non-Japanese descent, and interestingly, these two groups also represented different social classes as well. At least initially, like many patterns of in-migration cross-nationally, the situation of new migrants at the bottom of the labor market served to structure Japanese representations of Peruvians. The "ethnicization" or typification of certain forms of labor for Peruvians (and many other Latin Americans) as temporary and undesirable "*dekasegi*" jobs is essentially a process where class positions are re-represented through the imputation of ethnic characterization, regardless of education or family status in Peru (much of which was decidedly middle-class). While the chance to exploit "ethnic resources" (cultural identity and network) might have led to the establishment of a more cohesive community, it is primarily class differences that have prevented it. Despite the class and ethnic privilege that most Peruvians of Japanese descent have enjoyed relative to those of non-Japanese descent, they have been unable to transform their cultural capital in any advantageous way in Japan. Moreover, their ethnic identification with the Japanese population in Japan has made it more, not less, difficult to accept compromised social identity and poor working conditions. The result is that Peruvians of non-Japanese descent have proven to be more able to improve their economic status and establish a viable class position (as witnessed by social integration and work promotion).

Taken together, these four class dynamics – class structure, selection, socialization and strategies – allow us to expand the complexity of class analysis beyond just "structural" or "cultural" readings and to see how these work together and sometimes in contradiction. Our focus on these dynamics allows us to situate the institution in the larger social whole, and recognize the complexity of individual and collective practice, all as linked to the class structure of society. The degree to which these patterns are regularized and shared among individuals in the same social class, and are distinct from those in other classes, will determine their utility as dynamics in class analysis.

Notes

1 The extreme stratification within the section of employment positions that are often misleadingly lumped together under the notion of "freeter" obscures the re-sorting process that is the key to the efficient use of youth labor in this changing economy, and hides the class reproduction that is going on as much through the youth labor market as it has been through the education system.

References

Bennett, J. (1967) "Japanese economic growth: background for social change," in R.P. Dore (ed.) *Aspects of Social Change in Modern Japan*, Princeton, NJ: Princeton University Press.

Bestor, T.C. (1989) *Neighborhood Tokyo*, Stanford, CA: Stanford University Press.

Cole, R.E. (1971) *Japanese Blue Collar: the changing tradition*, Berkeley, CA: University of California Press.

Chiavacci, D. (2008) "From class struggle to general middle class society to divided society," *Social Science Japan Journal*, 11 (1): 5–27.

Dahrendorf, R. (1959) *Class and Class Conflict in Industrial Society*, Stanford, CA: Stanford University Press.

Denoon, D., Hudson, M., McCormack, G. and Morris-Suzuki, T. (2001) *Multicultural Japan: palaeolithic to postmodern*, Cambridge: Cambridge University Press.

Dore, R.P. (1958) *City Life in Japan: a study of a Tokyo ward*, Berkeley, CA: University of California Press.

—— (1967) *Aspects of Social Change in Modern Japan*, Princeton, NJ: Princeton University Press.

Genda, Y. (2005) *A Nagging Sense of Job Insecurity: the new reality facing Japanese youth*, trans. Jean Connell Hoff, Tokyo: LTCB International Library Trust, International House of Japan.

Giddens, A. (1973) *The Class Structure of Advanced Societies*, New York: Harper & Row.

Goodman, R. (1990) *Japan's "International Youth": the emergence of a new class of schoolchildren*, Oxford: Oxford University Press.

Goldthorpe, J.H. and Marshall, G. (1992) "The promising future of class analysis," *Sociology,* 26 (Aug): 381–400.

Gordon, A. (1993) "Contests for the workplace," in A. Gordon (ed.) *Postwar Japan as History*, Berkeley, CA: University of California Press.

Grusky, D.B. and Sorensen, J.B. (1998) "Can class analysis be salvaged?," *American Journal of Sociology*, 103: 1187–1234.

Hara, J. and Seiyama, K. (2005) *Inequality amid Affluence: social stratification in Japan*, trans. Brad Williams, Melbourne: Trans Pacific Press.

Hashimoto, K. (2003) *Class Structure in Contemporary Japan*, Melbourne: Trans Pacific Press.

Honda, Y. (2005) *Wakamono to Shigoto: "gakkō keiyu no shūshoku" wo koete* [Young people and employment in Japan: beyond the "school-mediated job search"], Tokyo: Tokyo Daigaku Shuppankai.

Imada, T. and Hara, J. (1979) "Shakaiteki chii no ikkansei to hiikkansei [Consistency and inconsistency of social status]," in K. Tominaga (ed.) *Nihon no Kaisō Kōzō* [The Japanese Stratification Structure], Tokyo: Tokyo Daigaku Shuppankai.

Ishida, H. (1993) *Social Mobility in Contemporary Japan: educational credentials, class and the labour market in cross national perspective*, Stanford, CA: Stanford University Press.

—— (2000) "Industrialization, class structure, and social mobility in postwar Japan," *British Journal of Sociology*, 52 (Dec): 579–604.

—— (2008) *Sedaikan Ido no Heisasei wa Jyōshō Shitanoka* [Did the Barriers to Mobility Increase?], Panel Survey Discussion Paper, No. 17, Tokyo: Institute of Social Science, University of Tokyo.

Kariya, T. (1991) *Kaisōka Nihon to Kyōiku Kiki* [Stratified Japan and Education in Crisis], Tokyo: Yūshindō.

Katznelson, I. (1986) "Working-class formation: constructing cases and comparisons," in I. Katznelson and A. R. Zolberg (eds) *Working-class Formation: nineteenth-century patterns in Western Europe and the United States*, Princeton, NJ: Princeton University Press.

Kelly, W. (2002) "At the limits of new middle class Japan: beyond mainstream consciousness," in O. Zunz, L. Schoppa and N. Hiwatari (eds) *Social Contracts Under Stress: the middle classes of America, Europe and Japan at the turn of the century*, New York: Russell Sage Foundation.

Kishimoto, S. (1977) "Shin chūkan kaisōron wa kanō ka [Can the new middle class theory be sustained?]," *Asahi Shinbun* [Asahi Newspaper], evening edn, 9 June.

—— (1978) *Chūryū no Gensō* [The Illusion of the Middle Class], Tokyo: Kōdansha.

Kondo, D.K. (1990) *Crafting Selves: power, gender, and discourses of identity in a Japanese workplace*, Chicago, IL: University of Chicago Press.

Kosugi, R. (2003) *Furītā Toiu Ikikata* [Freeter as a Way of Life], Tokyo: Keisō Shobō.

McNall, S., Levine, R. and Fantasia, R. (1991) *Bringing Class Back In: contemporary and historical perspectives*, New York, Westview Press.

Miura, A. (2005) *Karyū Shakai* [Lower-class Society], Tokyo: Kōbunsha.

Murakami, Y. (1977) "Shin chūkan kaisō no genjitsusei [The reality of the new middle class]," *Asahi Shinbun* [Asahi Newspaper], evening edn, 20 May.

—— (1984) *Shin Chūkan Taishū no Jidai* [The Age of the New Middle Mass], Tokyo: Chūō Kōronsha.

Nakane, C. (1970) *Japanese Society*, Berkeley, CA: University of California Press.

Ohtake, F. (2005) *Nihon no Fubyōdō* [Japan's Inequality], Tokyo: Nihon Keizai Shinbunsha.

Parkin, F. (1979) *Marxism and Class Theory*, New York: Columbia University Press.

Rohlen, T. (1983) *Japan's High Schools*, Berkeley, CA: University of California Press.

—— (1979) *For Harmony and Strength: Japanese white-collar organization in anthropological perspective*, Berkeley, CA: University of California Press.

Sato, T. (2000) *Fubyōdō Shakai Nippon* [Japan as an Unequal Society], Tokyo: Chūō Kōron Shinsha.

Smith, R J. (1978) *Kurusu: the price of progress in a Japanese village 1951–1975*, Stanford, CA: Stanford University Press.

Sugimoto, Y. (2003) *An Introduction to Japanese Society*, 2nd edn, Cambridge: Cambridge University Press.

Tachibanaki, T. (1998) *Nihon no Keizai Kakusa* [Japan's Economic Inequality], Tokyo: Iwanami Shoten.

Thompson, E.P. (1963) *The Making of the English Working Class*, New York: Vintage Books.

Tominaga, K. (1977) "Shakai kaisō kōzō no genjō [The current state of social stratification]," *Asahi Shinbun* [Asahi Newspaper], evening edn, 27 June.

—— (ed.) (1979) *Nihon no Kaisō Kōzō* [The Japanese Stratification Structure], Tokyo: Tokyo Daigaku Shuppankai.

Vogel, E.F. (1963) *Japan's New Middle Class: the salary man and his family in a Tokyo suburb*, Berkeley, CA: University of California Press.

Wagatsuma, H. and DeVos, G.A. (1984) *Heritage of Endurance: family patterns and delinquency formation in urban Japan*, Berkeley, CA: University of California Press.

Weeden, K.A. and Grusky, D.B. (2005) "The case for a new class map," *American Journal of Sociology*, 111: 141–212.

Weiner, M. (1997) *Japan's Minorities: the illusion of homogeneity*, London: Routledge.

Wright, E.O., Levine, A. and Sober, E. (1992) *Reconstructing Marxism: essays on explanation and the theory of history*, London: Verso.

Yamada, M. (2004) *Kibō Kakusa Shakai* [Hope Divided Society], Tokyo: Chikuma Shobō.

Yamada, M. and Ito, M. (2007) *Kakusa Supairaru* [Economic Divide Spiral], Tokyo: Yamato Shobō.

Part I
Class structure

2 Does class matter in Japan?

Demographics of class structure and class mobility from a comparative perspective

Hiroshi Ishida

Introduction

There has been a resurgence of interest in issues of social inequality in Japan, beginning in the 1990s. Popular books describing the increased level of income inequality and the barriers to mobility have become bestsellers. Toshiaki Tachibanaki, a noted economist, argues in his book, *Japan's Economic Inequality* (1998), that the extent of income inequality in Japan has risen sharply and has even reached a level equivalent to that of the United States. Toshiki Sato, a sociologist, claims in his book, *Japan as an Unequal Society* (2000), that entry into upper white-collar employment has become more closed since the 1990s. The public perception of and concern about inequality has recently showed a dramatic increase. An opinion survey conducted by the *Mainichi* newspaper reports that about two-thirds of the respondents agreed with the statement: "Japan is becoming an unequal society where children's occupational and income attainment is determined by parents' income and family environment."[1] Similarly, the great majority (75 percent) of the respondents to a national survey on life trajectory agreed with the statement that income inequality in Japan is too large.[2] The survey also shows that the responses vary by education and social class. University graduates and the professional-managerial class are the least likely to agree with the statement, and those with a high school education or less and the non-skilled manual working class are the most likely to agree that income inequality is too large in Japan (Ishida 2008).

The renewed interest in social inequality, however, does not necessarily imply a revival of class analysis. Class has not occupied the central position in the sociological discourse on Japanese society. Except for Marxist sociologists who always advocate the primacy of the concept of class in understanding Japan (see, for example, Hashimoto 2003, 2006), sociological discussions of social inequality usually focus on differentiation by occupational status, education, and income. Social inequality is often viewed by sociologists studying Japan as the unequal distribution of various resources, and individuals are located along a hierarchy of occupational status, education, and income. Differences in individual positions in this hierarchy are thus expressed as a quantitative difference in the amount of socioeconomic resources possessed. The notion of social class does not usually enter into sociological investigations of Japanese inequality.

Indeed, authors from many perspectives have displayed deep skepticism regarding class analysis in Japan. One of the most provocative critics has been Chie Nakane, a social anthropologist, whose book *Japanese Society* was widely read by both Japanese and foreign audiences. She claims that the dominant mode of group formation and group inter-relationships is "not that of horizontal stratification by class or caste but of vertical stratification by institution or group of institutions" (Nakane 1970, p. 87). Japanese society is not characterized by the relationship between different social classes but instead by relationships between business enterprises. People who work for a particular firm are therefore organized against those working for another firm. The notions of stratification developed in the West, such as that of class, are too foreign to be applied to the Japanese case. "Even if social classes like those in Europe can be detected in Japan, and even if something vaguely resembling those classes that are illustrated in the textbooks of western sociology can also be found in Japan, the point is that in actual society this stratification is unlikely to function and that it does not really reflect the social structure" (1970, p. 87). Nakane dismisses class analysis because it is too universalistic, ignoring indigenous social relationships.[3]

Ken'ichi Tominaga, a prominent sociologist, casts doubt on class analysis not because it does not take into account Japanese cultural specificity but rather because it ignores the universal process of industrialization. As a strong believer in the industrialism thesis (Kerr *et al.* 1960; Kerr 1983), Tominaga claims that class analysis is outdated and neglects the developmental logic of industrialism which brought "openness" and "fluidity" to postwar Japanese society (Tominaga 1979, p. 83). The postwar transformation of the Japanese stratification system, according to Tominaga, followed closely the course of development predicted by the industrialism thesis. Through rapid industrialization, urbanization and accompanying reforms, the barriers to social and geographical mobility have weakened substantially and a more open form of stratification, not based on class origin or kinship, but on achievement, has emerged in contemporary Japan (Tominaga 1988). In the end, as far as the criticism of class analysis is concerned, Tominaga's argument echoes that of Nakane by concluding that the concept of social class based on the particular historical experience of Western European societies does not accurately map out differentiation in Japanese society. The Western European-type of working class never fully emerged in Japan and the rapid economic growth in postwar Japan undermined the development of working-class consciousness and working-class culture (Tominaga 1988, Chapter 4).

These criticisms are primarily directed against Marxist writings, but the scope of the criticisms clearly goes beyond Marxism and seriously questions the usefulness of any concept of class. Class is not a concept unique to Marxist scholars. Class analysis does not always have to resort to the Marxist conception of class, which assumes antagonism between capitalists and the working class or the historical mission of the working class to transform capitalist society. Class categories can be operationalized by employment relations in the labor market, representing qualitatively different locations in the class structure. The key to class analysis is the recognition of the existence of different social groupings within the labor market. This differentiation corresponds to ownership of the means of production, as Marxists would emphasize, but it may also be manifested in the possession of marketable skills, including educational qualifications, as Weberians would point out.

This chapter presents quantitative analyses of large-scale social surveys conducted in Japan, the United States, and Germany. Its aim is to show the continuing relevance of class analysis in understanding contemporary Japanese society, with comparative findings from American and German society. It is crucial to present cross-national evidence because we would like to examine whether class "works" in a similar fashion in Japanese society, in comparison to other societies. Three sets of empirical analyses are presented. First, this study examines whether socioeconomic resources are unequally distributed along class lines. If class is not a relevant concept in contemporary Japanese society, various resources are less likely to be distributed among different class categories in Japan than in other societies. Second, this study addresses the question of intergenerational class mobility – the movement of people in different generations across the class structure. The detailed pattern of intergenerational mobility is examined in Japan and then compared to those in the United States and Germany. The study will examine whether class origins affect people's mobility chances in a similar way in the three societies. If class does not "function" in Japanese society, we expect that class origins do not shape people's life chances, at least their chances of mobility across generations.

Third, this study takes up the subjective aspect of social stratification. When asked in a public opinion poll, almost invariably over 90 percent of Japanese respondents say that they belong to the middle stratum. During the late 1970s and early 1980s, it was commonly said that all 100 million Japanese were in the middle (*ichioku sōchūrū*), and Murakami invented the term "the emergence of the new middle mass" (Murakami 1984). However, it is not clear whether the Japanese are the only people who choose to identify themselves as "middle" (Hashimoto 2003; Hayashi 1995; Scott and Watanabe 1998; Sugimoto 2003; Chiavacci 2008). This study will examine the responses to survey questions about subjective perception of status when the question is asked cross-nationally in a comparable manner in the three countries. It will then ask whether social class influences how people perceive their position in society. In particular, we will examine whether social class plays a more important role in explaining people's subjective perception of status than education, occupation or income. If class does not matter in Japan, social class should not influence how people place themselves in society.

Data and variables

The data sets used in this study derive from national surveys conducted in the 1980s and 1990s in the three countries. They contain information about the respondents' and their fathers' employment, respondents' education, occupation, and income, as well as respondents' subjective social status. The Japanese data comes from the 1995 Social Stratification and Social Mobility Survey (SSM) and the 2000 and 2001 Japanese General Social Surveys (JGSS).[4] The U.S. data comes from the 1983 to 2000 General Social Survey (GSS). The German data comes from the 1990 to 2000 German General Social Survey (ALLBUS).[5] The analyses are restricted to respondents aged 20 to 69. The age range is determined by the 1995 SSM survey, which had the most restricted age range.

Social class is operationalized using the Erikson-Goldthorpe-Portocarero (EGP) class schema (Erikson *et al.* 1979; Erikson and Goldthorpe 1992; Goldthorpe 2000). Although there has been a continuing debate over the optimal form of social class categories in the sociological literature (see, for example, Goldthorpe and Marshall 1992; Marshall *et al.* 1988; Grusky and Sorensen 1998; Grusky and Weeden 2001; Wright 1985, 1997), the EGP class schema has become one of the most prominent and widely-used classifications, especially in cross-national studies (Erikson and Goldthorpe 1992; Evans 1997; Hout 1989; Ishida *et al.* 1991; Ishida *et al.* 1995). The validity of the EGP class schema has been tested (Evans 1992; Evans and Mills 1998), and its theoretical justification is grounded in the literature of economics and sociology (Goldthorpe 2000; Erikson and Goldthorpe 2002). The analyses are based on the six-category version of the EGP schema: the professional-managerial class or the service class (I+II), the routine non-manual class (III), the petty bourgeoisie (IVab), the farming class (IVc+VIIb), the skilled manual class (V+VI), and the non-skilled manual class (VIIa).[6] The social class variable is constructed using four questionnaire items: employment status (employer, self-employed, employee, or family worker), occupation, managerial status (manager, supervisor, or non-management), and firm size (large or small). Information about the respondents' current employment is used to construct class destination, and information about the fathers' employment is used to construct class origin.[7]

Education is represented by a four-category variable: (1) primary level, (2) high school level, (3) junior college level, and (4) university and graduate school level. For the analyses of the relationship between class and socioeconomic resources, education is operationalized as the proportion of college graduates.[8] Occupation is measured by international standard occupational prestige scores (Treiman 1977). The detailed occupational categories for each nation are converted to the international prestige scores, which represent the ranking in the occupational hierarchy. Income is expressed as the log of annual individual income (after applying the appropriate exchange rate). In some analyses, occupational prestige and income are expressed by four quarterly groups. In the analysis of the determinant of subjective social status, in addition to the father's class, the father's and mother's education level (measured in the same manner as the respondent's education) are included as social background.

Social class and the distribution of resources

The first set of analyses reports the relationship between social class and various socioeconomic resources, including education, occupational status, and income. The main purpose of the analyses is to examine whether social resources are unequally distributed along class lines, and if so, whether class differentiation in socioeconomic resources is less pronounced in Japan than in other societies.

Table 2.1 shows the distribution of education, occupational status, and income by class categories. First, regarding the distribution of education – that is, the proportion of college graduates – the professional-managerial class (I+II) stands out in all three nations. For both men and women in the three countries, the proportion of college graduates among the professional-managerial class is often more than twice as much as those of other classes. In order to enter professional occupations and management ranks, educational credentials are often considered to be a prerequisite, especially among younger cohort members. Indeed, the proportion of college-educated among the professional-managerial class is much higher for the younger cohort than the older cohort (table not shown). In Japan, in addition to the professional-managerial class, a relatively high proportion of men in the routine non-manual class (III) are college graduates, though this is not true of Japanese women in the routine non-manual class. This is because male college graduates are recruited into white-collar occupations (clerical jobs) and continue to occupy non-management positions for several years before they are promoted (Ishida *et al.* 2002; Koike and Inoki 2002). Clerical jobs are used as a training ground for male managerial prospects, but most women in clerical jobs remain in a clerical position for the rest of their career, except for the small minority recruited into the managerial-track (especially after the enactment of the Equal Employment Opportunity Act in 1985). In contrast, in the United States and Germany, college graduates normally occupy managerial positions soon after they join a firm, if not immediately after entry. In Germany, the advantaged position of the professional-managerial class is most conspicuous. College graduates are rarely found in other classes, with the exception of the petty bourgeoisie. Some segments of the petty bourgeoisie have technical skills and are well-educated.

Shifting our attention to the distribution of occupational prestige across different class categories, we find a clear rank hierarchy, with the professional-managerial class at the top and the non-skilled manual working class at the bottom. The hierarchical ranking of prestige scores is similar not only between men and women and but also among the three nations. Regarding the distribution of income (the average log of income), we find a clear income gap between different class categories. The professional-managerial class occupies the highest end of the income distribution, and the non-skilled manual working class or the farming class occupies the lowest end. However, for the rest of the classes, there seem to be some subtle cross-national differences. In Japan and Germany, the urban petty bourgeoisie have attained an average income level equivalent to the professional-managerial class, so the self-employed and small employers in these countries are relatively well-off. It is worth noting, however, that the coefficient of variation, which is the measure of the variation in income within class categories, is high among the petty bourgeoisie and farming class, suggesting that there is wide variation in income among the self-employed both in the farming and the non-farming sectors. In the United States, the income level of the skilled manual class is higher than that of the routine non-manual class, so skilled manual workers

Table 2.1 Distribution of education, occupational prestige, and income by class categories for men and women in Japan, the United States and Germany

	Education				Occupational Prestige				Income			
	Men		Women		Men		Women		Men		Women	
	Mean	C.V.	Mean	C.V.	Mean	C.V.	Mean	C.V.	Mean	C.V.	Mean	C.V.
Japan												
Prof-managerial	0.506	0.990	0.311	1.490	51.160	0.225	54.062	0.138	11.095	0.051303	10.103	0.098
Routine non-man	0.353	1.356	0.108	2.873	39.607	0.169	39.308	0.150	10.472	0.066452	9.679	0.082
Petty bourgeoisie	0.159	2.307	0.073	3.586	40.492	0.220	38.980	0.240	10.833	0.065099	10.040	0.103
Farming	0.031	5.649	0.000	0.000	36.208	0.168	37.723	0.128	10.365	0.104006	9.520	0.103
Skilled manual	0.077	3.471	0.021	6.820	36.700	0.143	34.778	0.133	10.570	0.056528	9.442	0.084
Non-skilled manual	0.083	3.337	0.025	6.286	27.855	0.244	23.935	0.274	10.324	0.068092	9.229	0.083
Total	0.279	1.608	0.112	2.815	41.374	0.291	38.337	0.297	10.737	0.067558	9.655	0.093
USA												
Prof-managerial	0.527	0.948	0.442	1.125	57.315	0.154	56.131	0.128	10.569	0.076822	9.840	0.096
Routine non-man	0.206	1.975	0.076	3.498	33.579	0.228	38.661	0.269	9.837	0.101412	9.302	0.102
Petty bourgeoisie	0.205	1.995	0.067	3.771	35.000	0.251	28.917	0.347	9.896	0.091653	9.102	0.140
Farming	0.030	5.746	0.083	3.466	33.182	0.283	29.154	0.289	9.829	0.099816	8.999	0.152
Skilled manual	0.028	5.924	0.013	8.769	38.866	0.150	37.091	0.155	10.181	0.066788	9.556	0.080
Non-skilled manual	0.046	4.552	0.019	7.119	27.202	0.296	27.162	0.293	9.652	0.11082	9.167	0.115
Total	0.249	1.737	0.198	2.015	42.211	0.356	42.762	0.327	10.151	0.095441	9.505	0.107
Germany												
Prof-managerial	0.482	1.038	0.340	1.394	53.776	0.226	51.048	0.212	10.315	0.039921	9.749	0.052
Routine non-man	0.070	3.670	0.030	5.661	40.479	0.268	38.849	0.191	9.995	0.03755	9.388	0.053
Petty bourgeoisie	0.127	2.633	0.125	2.674	41.930	0.214	43.490	0.205	10.330	0.048633	9.797	0.062
Farming	0.000	0.000	0.087	3.311	39.476	0.277	37.991	0.274	9.742	0.0499	8.799	0.072
Skilled manual	0.008	11.138	0.023	6.552	38.394	0.176	37.473	0.260	9.927	0.032358	9.369	0.056
Non-skilled manual	0.014	8.390	0.008	10.952	31.032	0.232	28.053	0.326	9.858	0.02671	9.205	0.047
Total	0.208	1.955	0.170	2.212	44.217	0.285	42.947	0.291	10.101	0.042374	9.530	0.058

Note: C.V. = the coefficient of variation.

are highly paid in this country despite their relatively low educational level. In Germany, the income gap between the skilled and non-skilled manual workers is very small. In fact, the income distribution (as expressed by the coefficient of variation for the total sample) seems to be most equal in Germany, followed by Japan and then by the United States.

We next examine the strength of the relationship between social class and socioeconomic resources using a simple statistical measure, the correlation coefficient.[9] This measure expresses the degree or strength of association between the two variables and ranges from –1.0 to +1.0. When the coefficient is either plus or minus 1.0, it implies that there is a perfect correspondence. A coefficient of zero implies that the two variables are not related at all. Table 2.2 reports the correlations among the four variables – education, occupational prestige, income, and class. The coefficients above the main diagonal are for men, and the coefficients below the main diagonal are for women. The main findings can be summarized as follows. First, for both men and women, correlations involving class are strong in all three nations. In particular, the correlations between class and occupation are higher than 0.7. Occupational prestige also has strong correlations with education and income in all three nations. Second, for both men and women, the pattern of correlations is similar across the three societies. Correlations involving class are relatively strong, and correlations involving income are relatively weak in all three nations. The only cross-national difference that emerges from the analyses is that in Germany the correlations are generally stronger than in Japan and the United States. Third, there is no clear difference in the pattern of the correlation matrix between men and women. Although the pattern is similar between genders,

Table 2.2 Correlations among class, education, occupational prestige, and income by gender and by nation

	Education	*Occupation*	*Income*	*Class*
Japan				
Education	–	0.412	0.216	0.448
Occupation	0.356	–	0.361	0.723
Income	0.151	0.325	–	0.488
Class	0.330	0.826	0.357	–
USA				
Education	–	0.485	0.284	0.537
Occupation	0.414	–	0.441	0.866
Income	0.185	0.307	–	0.420
Class	0.482	0.818	0.296	–
Germany				
Education	–	0.634	0.356	0.620
Occupation	0.540	–	0.423	0.737
Income	0.338	0.444	–	0.531
Class	0.507	0.728	0.447	–

Note: Figures above the main diagonals are men and below are women.

most correlations are stronger for men than for women. This result suggests that the crystallization or the consistency of the indicators of social status is higher among men than women.

In summary, socioeconomic resources are distributed unequally by social class in all three nations. The professional-managerial class is the most advantaged and the non-skilled manual class is located toward the bottom of the socioeconomic hierarchy. The pattern of the ranking of class categories is very similar across the three nations. There is no evidence to suggest that class lines are less determining of the distribution of socioeconomic resources in Japan than in the other nations. The correlations between social class and other resources indicate that class is strongly related to education, occupational prestige, and income in the three nations. The findings do not lead us to the conclusion drawn by previous research on status inconsistency in Japan, namely that various status indicators are more inconsistent in Japan. A direct comparison of these findings with the existing literature, however, is not warranted because our method of using correlations is different from the clustering methodology used by previous studies, which report that the majority of the respondents belong to the status-inconsistent clusters (Imada and Hara 1979; Tominaga 1988).

Intergenerational class mobility

We move to the topic of intergenerational movement of people within the class structure. Our analyses are based on class mobility tables, which are the cross-classification of class origin (father's class) by class destination (respondent's current class); these are separate for men and women in the three nations.[10] In order to examine the pattern of class mobility, we use three indicators of mobility. First, we compute the total mobility rate: the proportion of people who changed class position between the two generations. The total mobility rate indicates the gross total amount of mobility that is observed in a particular table. Second, the patterns of outflow and inflow rates are examined. Outflow rates show where the members of a particular class origin are found in the next generation, whereas inflow rates show where the current members of a particular class destination originated. Third, the chances of mobility and inheritance from members of different class origins are compared. These relative inheritance and mobility chances show how class origins affect the chances of mobility and immobility. In other words, these relative rates suggest the extent to which class origins make a difference in life chances. The stronger the effect of class origin, the larger the difference in life chances between class categories.

We first examine men's total mobility rates, which imply mobility between fathers and sons. The proportion of men who attained class positions different from those of their fathers is 0.693 in Japan, 0.660 in the United States, and 0.581 in Germany. Japan shows the highest rate. About two-thirds of male respondents experienced mobility between generations in Japan and the United States. The main factor increasing the total mobility rate derives from the changes in class structure between the father's and the son's generation. Table 2.3 reports the distribution of class origin and class destination by gender and nation.[11] Among men in Japan, the father's generation is dominated by the petty bourgeoisie and the farming class, which together constitute the majority of the class origin distribution. In contrast, in the son's generation, the professional-managerial class and the routine non-manual class, the two white-collar segments, constitute the majority. In order to understand the magnitude of the changes in class structure between generations, we compute the index of dissimilarity between class origin and class destination distribution. The index ranges from 0 to 100 and indicates the percentage of cases that must be re-classified in order to make the two distributions identical. In Japan, the index of dissimilarity is 31, whereas the same index is 15 in the United States and 16 in Germany. In other words, the scope of the changes in class structure in postwar Japan is much larger than in the United States and Germany, and the high total mobility rate in Japan must have been affected by these large structural transformations. In the United States, however, the relatively high total mobility rate is more likely to be affected by the fluidity in the society than by changes in class structure between the two generations because the index of dissimilarity is much lower than that in Japan.

Total mobility rates among women are 0.793 in Japan, 0.741 in the United States, and 0.712 in Germany. Japanese women experienced the highest mobility, followed by American and then by German women. It should be noted that women's total mobility rates are substantially higher than men's rates in all three nations. This finding derives from the fact that the difference in class origin and class destination distributions involves not only the difference in generations but also the difference in gender. In other words, the kinds of positions that can be attained by men and women differ in the labor market, and gender segregation in the labor market induces mobility among women. When we compute the index of

Table 2.3 Distribution of class origin and class destination by nation

	Class origin			Class destination		
	Japan	USA	Germany	Japan	USA	Germany
Male						
Professional-managerial	21.1	30.9	21.4	34.8	40.1	35.9
Routine non-manual	6.0	6.3	3.6	12.0	9.3	5.0
Self-employed	25.8	9.0	10.8	17.1	4.3	8.2
Farm	27.3	12.6	12.9	5.3	3.2	4.0
Skilled manual	11.2	19.3	38.7	17.5	18.6	37.3
Unskilled manual	8.7	22.0	12.6	13.2	24.4	9.6
Female						
Professional-managerial	21.5	28.5	25.3	17.2	42.8	44.2
Routine non-manual	7.9	6.6	3.8	37.8	30.8	25.9
Self-employed	24.1	9.7	10.6	7.0	4.4	6.2
Farm	26.4	12.2	13.0	6.2	0.7	2.5
Skilled manual	11.4	18.6	36.1	14.5	5.5	9.3
Unskilled manual	8.6	24.4	11.1	17.3	15.8	12.0

dissimilarity between class origin and class destination distributions, the index is about the same in the three countries: Germany (42 percent), Japan (42 percent), and the United States (39 percent).

We next examine the pattern of outflow rates. Table 2.4 (first three columns) shows the rate of intergenerational stability for class origin categories – that is, the proportion of those who remained in the same class as their fathers. For example, the rate for Japanese men of professional-managerial class origin is 57.9. This implies that 57.9 percent of Japanese men with professional-managerial class origin remained in the professional-managerial class. We begin with the rates for male respondents. Although the rate of intergenerational stability is similar for the professional-managerial class in the three nations, the other rates show some cross-national differences. The stability of the routine non-manual class (24.0) and the petty bourgeoisie (28.4) is higher in Japan than in the United States and Germany. In contrast, if we group the skilled and non-skilled manual working classes together and compute the rate of intergenerational stability (not shown in Table 2.4), the Japanese rate (43.8) is lower than those found in the United States (54.6) and Germany (62.9), suggesting that the Japanese manual working class possesses relatively weak intergenerational stability. These distinctive features are related directly to the cross-national difference in class destination distribution. Japanese class destination is characterized by the relatively large routine non-manual class and petty bourgeoisie, and by the relatively small skilled and non-skilled manual working classes. Therefore, the intergenerational stability of the routine non-manual and the petty bourgeoisie tends to be high, while that of the two manual working classes is generally low.

Table 2.4 Outflow rates and inflow rates by nation

	Outflow (intergenerational stability)			Inflow (self-recruitment)		
	Japan	*USA*	*Germany*	*Japan*	*USA*	*Germany*
Male						
Professional-mangerial	57.9	57.8	63.4	35.1	44.5	37.7
Routine non-manual	24.0	17.6	11.7	11.9	11.9	8.5
Self-employed	28.4	8.2	24.3	42.6	17.1	31.8
Farm	17.4	15.9	25.0	89.2	61.7	81.6
Skilled manual	29.1	24.6	50.5	18.7	25.5	52.4
Unskilled manual	19.2	34.4	20.2	12.6	31.0	26.5
Female						
Professional-mangerial	28.0	57.1	65.2	35.1	38.0	37.3
Routine non-manual	42.0	32.4	44.6	8.7	6.9	6.6
Self-employed	11.3	6.3	17.4	39.2	13.9	30.0
Farm	18.6	2.8	13.7	79.7	48.8	72.2
Skilled manual	15.8	6.4	10.8	12.4	21.8	42.2
Unskilled manual	21.8	21.9	28.0	10.8	33.8	25.7

When we shift our attention to women respondents, we find another distinctively Japanese pattern in the very low extent of intergenerational stability in the professional-managerial class. Only 28 percent of women whose fathers belonged to the professional-managerial class reached the same position. In contrast, the same rate for the United States is 57.1 and for Germany is 65.2. In the United States and Germany, the intergenerational stability of the professional-managerial class is about the same for males and females, but in Japan, the rate for women is less than half that of men. This finding derives from the fact that the class positions attained by women are different from those attained by men in Japan. As shown in Table 2.3, 42.8 percent of American women and 44.2 percent of German women reached the professional-managerial class, while only 19 percent of Japanese women did. The gender gap in the attainment of professional-managerial positions clearly reduced the intergenerational stability of the professional-managerial class among Japanese women.

Table 2.4 (last three columns) reports the self-recruitment rate for different class destinations by gender and nation. These rates show what proportion of the members of the current class came from the same class. For example, among Japanese men who occupied the professional-managerial class, 35.1 percent came from the same class origin; that is, their fathers were also in professional-managerial positions. A distinctive Japanese pattern appears to emerge for both men and women. In Japan, the self-recruitment rates of the petty bourgeoisie and the farming class are higher and the rates of the skilled and the non-skilled manual working classes are clearly lower than in the United States and Germany. The Japanese manual working class is much more extensively recruited from the farming and the petty bourgeoisie classes than from the working class in either the United States or Germany. These features are related to the shape of class origin distribution in the three nations. Japan shows a larger share of the farming and petty bourgeoisie classes and a smaller share of the two manual working classes than do the United States and Germany.

When the low self-recruitment and the low intergenerational stability are taken together, the Japanese manual working class can be characterized by weakly developed demographic stability, or "demographic identity" (Goldthorpe 1982, 2000), at least in comparison with the American and German working classes. This distinctive feature of the Japanese working class has been pointed out throughout the postwar period (Ishida *et al.* 1991; Ishida 2001). Moreover, it is possible that because the Japanese manual working class has never developed a stable demographic core in the Japanese postwar class structure, there has been weak working-class consciousness and the corresponding prevalence of middle-class consciousness expressed in opinion surveys.

As we have seen, the rates of intergenerational stability and self-recruitment are heavily influenced by the marginal distributions of class origin and class destination. For example, the farming class, which was a major component of Japanese class origin distribution, was dramatically reduced in size, producing movements out of farming to other sectors. In contrast, due to the rapid expansion of both the blue-collar working classes and the white-collar sectors during Japan's postwar economic development, Japanese class destination distribution contains a large share of the professional-managerial class and the routine non-manual class, thereby producing intergenerational movements into these classes. It is therefore not possible to determine, from the rates of intergenerational stability and self-recruitment, whether the patterns of mobility and immobility are produced by the changes in marginal distribution or the movement of people independent of these changes.

In order to evaluate the chances of mobility and immobility, the net effect of changes in class structure, we compute the relative chances or compare the immobility chances of people from different class origins. Table 2.5 reports the relative chances of class inheritance, expressed by log of odds ratios. For example, the figure (1.233) for Japanese men of the professional-managerial class indicates that these men are 3.43 times ($e^{1.233} = 3.43$ because 1.233 is the log of odds ratio) more likely to occupy the professional-managerial class than men of other class origins. It shows the relative advantage of reaching the professional-managerial class for those who come from the same class origin as opposed to those of other class origins. Three points stand out from Table 2.5. First, all the rates are positive, implying that class inheritance is prevalent in all three societies. Second, the pattern of the inheritance rates is similar across nations and genders. The chances of relative inheritance are highest in the farming class, suggesting that this class has a high barrier to entry. The relative inheritance chances for the professional-managerial class are also high in all three nations. The advantage of the professional-managerial class is passed on from one generation to the next. The tendency for the petty bourgeoisie class to reproduce itself is also apparent in all

Table 2.5 Relative chances of class inheritance by nation

	Japan	USA	Germany
Male			
Professional-managerial	1.233	1.058	1.472
Routine non-manual	0.916	0.805	0.985
Self-employed	0.954	0.775	1.562
Farm	3.279	2.574	3.672
Skilled manual	0.766	0.452	0.917
Unskilled manual	0.494	0.646	1.059
Uniform difference	*1.000*	*0.865*	*1.313*
Female			
Professional-managerial	0.852	0.813	1.159
Routine non-manual	0.189	0.075	0.876
Self-employed	0.768	0.432	1.422
Farm	2.577	1.947	2.991
Skilled manual	0.116	0.212	0.283
Unskilled manual	0.314	0.562	1.246
Uniform difference	*1.000*	*0.845*	*1.247*

three nations, although the German petty bourgeoisie shows a higher inheritance rate than in other nations.

The last row of Table 2.5 shows the cross-national difference in the overall relative chances of mobility. The uniform difference parameters indicate whether the strength of association between class origin and class destination is uniformly stronger or weaker between nations. The Japanese parameter is set at 1.00 as the base nation. The American parameters for both men and women are smaller than 1.00, indicating that the association is weaker in the United States and that American society is relatively more open than Japanese society. In contrast, German society is more closed than Japanese society because the parameters are greater than 1.0 for both men and women. The German class structure may be considered more rigid than the American and Japanese class structures because the German parameters and inheritance rates are always higher than the American and Japanese rates.

In addition to cross-national comparison, it is important to examine the trends in societal openness in Japan because there is a recent resurgence in the interest in inequality in Japan. The notion that Japanese society has become more unequal in recent years has dominated the public discourse. In order to test the long-term trend in intergenerational mobility, we examined six mobility tables generated from the SSM surveys conducted in 1955, 1965, 1975, 1985, 1995, and 2005. The detailed analyses can be found elsewhere (Ishida and Miwa 2008). The results from the analyses indicate that the association between class origin and class destination shows a remarkable stability in postwar Japan. Despite the growing concern with increased inequality, there is no clear tendency towards increased rigidity in recent years.

In summary, the rates of total mobility, intergenerational stability, and self-recruitment are influenced by the changing shape of class structure. Our analyses point to the impact that postwar Japan's rapid industrialization and economic development had on its rates of intergenerational stability and self-recruitment, especially regarding the manual working class. Our analyses also show that the ways in which class origin affects people's life chances (at least intergenerational mobility chances) are similar across the three nations. The pattern of the inheritance rates is similar across nations and genders. Class background is a powerful determinant in shaping people's prospects for mobility not only in Japan but also in the United States and Germany.

Class and subjective social status

This section focuses on the subjective aspect of social inequality. It examines how people perceive their social standing in society and how their perception is influenced by social class and other socioeconomic resources they possess. To begin with, it is not easy to compare people's subjective perception of their status across nations because each nation has its own way of asking the question of subjective status. In Japan, a typical question used in many opinion surveys about subjective social status is the following:

Table 2.6 Distribution of subjective social status with differing questions in three nations

Japan		USA		Germany	
Upper stratum	0.6	Upper class	3.8	Upper class	1.2
Upper-middle stratum	10.3	Middle class	45.2	Upper middle class	10.3
Middle-middle stratum	47.8	Working class	45.4	Middle class	54.8
Lower-middle stratum	33.3	Lower class	5.0	Working class	30.3
Lower stratum	6.4			Lower class	2.1
Don't know, no answer	1.7	Don't know, no answer	0.1	None of these	1.3

If we divide society into the following five strata, which do you think you belong to: the upper, the upper-middle, the middle-middle, the lower-middle, or the lower stratum?[12]

The American GSS asked the following question:

If you were asked to use one of four names for your social class, which would you say you belong to: the lower class, the working class, the middle class, or the upper class?

The question asked to German respondents in the ALLBUS was the following:

There is a lot of talk about social class these days. What class would you describe yourself as belonging to: the upper class, the upper middle class, the middle class, the working class, the lower class, or none of these classes?

The distributions of the responses are shown in Table 2.6. As we already know from the wording of the questions, it is not possible to compare the responses across nations. In Japan, the proportion of respondents who chose one of the three "middle" categories adds up to over 90 percent, whereas the proportion who chose middle class in the United States is 45 percent and the combined proportion of those who chose upper middle class and middle class in Germany is 65 percent. However, we do not know how many of those who chose the category of "working class" in the United States and Germany would respond had they not been given the choice of "working class." Moreover, the term "stratum" rather than "class" was used in the Japanese survey, creating further complication in the cross-national comparisons.

In order to have a better measure of the subjective social status that can be used in a more cross-nationally comparable fashion, the surveys from the three nations used the following question:

In our society there are groups which tend to be towards the top and groups which tend to be towards the bottom. Below is a scale that runs from top to bottom. Where do you put yourself on this scale?

Top
1
2
3
4
5
6
7
8
9
10
Bottom

There are several advantages to using this question. First, the respondents did not find this question difficult. The proportion of those who did not answer (did not know and no answer) is less than 4 percent in the three societies. Second, the question does not use terms like "working class" or "middle class" which might have different connotations in the three societies (Evans *et al.*, 1992; Evans and Kelly 2004). Third, the question does not force the respondents to accept labels, such as "middle class," that are given to the categories. Pre-labeling the categories may affect the respondents' perception of how they place themselves in the status hierarchy (Nakao 2002).

Table 2.7 presents the distributions of responses to the 10-point scale version of the subjective status question in the three nations for the two time periods. In Table 2.7 and the following tables, the scoring of the categories is reversed. The top category is assigned a score of 10 and the bottom category is assigned a score of 1, for ease of presentation. Several important findings can be drawn from this

Table 2.7 Distribution of subjective social status by nation

Year	Japan		USA		Germany	
	2000, 2001	1995	2000	1983, 1987	2000	1990, 1991, 1992
10 (top)	0.7	0.4	3.1	4.6	1.3	0.6
9	1.7	1.0	2.8	3.9	1.4	1.7
8	6.8	5.4	11.0	12.7	6.2	10.1
7	10.2	12.0	15.3	15.2	10.6	19.3
6	41.6	29.8	31.6	30.1	21.8	33.3
5	14.8	22.6	16.3	13.6	34.7	17.8
4	11.5	17.1	10.8	9.6	15.6	9.9
3	7.5	8.2	5.6	5.9	6.5	4.8
2	2.4	2.0	1.7	1.8	1.7	1.7
1 (bottom)	2.8	1.6	1.7	2.6	0.1	0.8
Proportion of 5 and 6	56.4	52.4	47.9	43.7	56.5	51.1

table. First, the distributions of responses are very similar across the three nations and two time periods. In Japan, the proportions of the two lowest categories (1 and 2) are slightly larger than those in the other nations, and in the United States, the proportions of the two highest categories (10 and 9) are slightly larger. However, the differences are minor. Second, since the respondents are asked to pick one number among the ranking of 1 to 10, there are two middle numbers: 5 and 6. The proportion of respondents who selected either 5 or 6 is shown at the bottom of the table. In Japan and Germany, the figures are almost the same: just over 50 percent. In the United States, the figures are slightly lower, at 48 and 44 percent. If we assume that the values 5 and 6 represent the "middle categories" or the "middle status," there is no clear difference in the proportion of respondents who identify themselves as "the middle" in the three societies. In other words, on the basis of these findings, it is hard to confirm that Japan is the only country with a prevalent "middle-class consciousness." The majority of the people perceive themselves as belonging to the middle in all three societies.

We next examine what kinds of factors explain the difference in people's perception of status. Table 2.8 presents the average and the spread (measured

Table 2.8 Subjective social status scores by class, education, occupation and income

	Japan		USA		Germany	
	Average	*C.V.*	*Average*	*C.V.*	*Average*	*C.V.*
Class						
Professional-managerial	5.957	0.254	6.518	0.255	6.426	0.198
Routine non-manual	5.364	0.292	5.890	0.309	5.969	0.224
Self-employed	5.670	0.315	5.657	0.343	6.364	0.224
Farm	5.479	0.305	5.870	0.351	5.500	0.362
Skilled manual	5.218	0.318	5.758	0.312	5.577	0.254
Unskilled manual	4.931	0.336	5.284	0.379	4.985	0.297
Total	5.469	0.302	5.981	0.312	5.969	0.244
Education						
Middle/Primary Secondary	5.054	0.340	5.195	0.423	5.648	0.266
High school/Abitur	5.423	0.301	5.862	0.298	6.063	0.251
Junior college/Politec	5.573	0.284	6.133	0.278	6.401	0.188
University	5.960	0.258	6.802	0.244	6.847	0.178
Occupational prestige						
First quartile (bottom)	5.118	0.336	5.439	0.347	5.462	0.267
Second quartile	5.314	0.305	5.782	0.332	5.932	0.235
Third quartile	5.605	0.280	6.216	0.284	6.087	0.231
Fourth quartile (top)	5.894	0.270	6.540	0.259	6.515	0.194
Income						
First quartile (bottom)	5.263	0.315	5.672	0.346	5.495	0.315
Second quartile	5.126	0.330	5.774	0.304	5.482	0.273
Third quartile	5.368	0.296	6.139	0.254	5.756	0.243
Fourth quartile (top)	6.223	0.236	6.786	0.213	6.492	0.200

Note: C.V. = coefficient of variation

by the coefficient of variation) of the subjective status scores (1 as the lowest and 10 as the highest).[13] The first sub-table (the section labeled "class") shows the difference by social class categories. As can be seen from the difference in the average scores, people occupying different class positions have different perceptions of their location in the status hierarchy. In all three societies, the professional-managerial class has the highest subjective status score, and the non-skilled manual working class has the lowest score. There are, nonetheless, subtle differences across the three nations. In Germany, the petty bourgeoisie show an average score as high as the professional-managerial class. This is probably related to the fact that the German petty bourgeoisie tend to have high average income and academic and vocational credentials, as already shown in Table 2.1. In Japan, the average score for the professional-managerial class appears to be lower than in the United States and Germany. However, this should not be too surprising because the overall average is lower for the Japanese respondents. Indeed, it may be noted that the Japanese respondents are more "modest" in reporting their status scores than those in the United States and Germany, since the overall average score in Japan (5.469) is lower than in the United States (5.981) and Germany (5.969). Nonetheless, it should be emphasized that the pattern of the difference in average scores across class categories is very similar in the three nations.

Table 2.8 also reports the relationship between subjective status and education, occupational prestige, and income. Regarding the difference according to educational level, we find that the higher the educational attainment, the higher the subjective scores. In Japan, the difference between high school graduates and those who completed junior college and technical college is not as large as in the other two nations. In the United States and Germany, there is a clear difference in the average subjective status scores at all four levels of education. Similarly, when the four groups of occupational prestige are examined, there seems to be a linear pattern in all three societies: the higher the occupational prestige, the higher the subjective status. The pattern of income difference in the subjective status scores is similar in Japan and Germany; the average scores for the richest (the top 25 percent of the income group) stand out. In the United States, a large difference in the subjective score is found between the bottom half and the top half, in addition to between the top 25 percent and the top 50 percent. In summary, the subjective status scores differ not only according to social class but also according to education, occupational prestige, and income.

Which of these four factors is the most important determinant of subjective social status? Furthermore, does the relative importance of these factors vary across nations? In order to answer these questions, we conducted a multiple regression analysis of the determinants of subjective status. The results are shown in Table 2.9.[14] Column (1) presents the effect of each factor after we controlled for the age and sex of the respondent, and column (2) presents the effect after we controlled for age, sex, and social background (the father's and the mother's education and the father's class) of the respondent. The figures represent the changes in the coefficient of determination (R-squares) when each factor is added to the regression equation. In other words, these figures measure the effect of each

Table 2.9 Explanatory power of class, education, occupational prestige, and income

	Japan		USA		Germany	
	(1)	*(2)*	*(1)*	*(2)*	*(1)*	*(2)*
Class	0.0727	0.0613	0.0608	0.0398	0.1549	0.0989
Education	0.0466	0.0336	0.0940	0.0577	0.1227	0.0670
Occupational prestige	0.0491	0.0397	0.0255	0.0104	0.1141	0.0676
Income	0.0503	0.0433	0.0570	0.0362	0.0910	0.0592

Note: (1) After controlling for gender and age; (2) After controlling for gender, age, and social background (father's education, mother's education, and father's class)

factor, the net influence of the variables already in the equation. For example, the figure for class in Japan (column [1], 0.0727) shows that when we control for the respondent's age and sex, the class of the respondent explains 7.27 percent of the variance in the subjective status scores.

Rather than examining the details of these figures, we turn to the major findings of the regression analysis. In Japan and Germany, social class explains greater variation in people's perception of status than does either education or occupational prestige or income. This picture does not change when we control for sex and age only, or if we control for social background as well. In other words, class appears to be the most important determinant of subjective social status in Japan and Germany. On the other hand, in the United States, education exerts the strongest influence, and social class is the second most important factor. This pattern holds for different controls (columns [1] and [2]). Because the United States has achieved mass higher education, with the highest proportion among the three nations of people advancing to institutions of higher learning, the social stigma attached to high school dropouts might be particularly strong and have accordingly reduced their subjective status scores. At the same time, the socioeconomic returns of a college and graduate school degree tend to be higher in the United States than in Japan and Germany (Ishida 1999; Ishida and Yoshikawa 2003), so university graduates might have relatively high subjective scores.

When we compare the magnitude of R-squares across nations, the values of R-squares are generally larger in Germany than in Japan and the United States. This finding suggests that subjective perception of status is more likely to be determined by socioeconomic factors, including class, in Germany than in Japan and the United States. In summary, in all three societies, social class plays an important role in explaining how people perceive their social standing. Although people also take into account education, occupation, and income in evaluating their standing in society, social class is one of the most significant factors when people place themselves subjectively in a status hierarchy.

Conclusion

The primary objective of this study has been to examine whether social class is an intellectually useful concept in understanding contemporary Japanese society. In order to achieve this objective, this chapter presented three sets of empirical analyses. First, we examined whether socioeconomic resources are differentially distributed by social class. With respect to all three dimensions of socioeconomic resources – education, occupational prestige, and income – there are clear differences among class categories. The professional-managerial class is the most advantaged, and the non-skilled manual working class is located towards the bottom of the socioeconomic hierarchy. Most crucial in our analyses is that this pattern of the distribution of socioeconomic resources by class is largely similar across the three nations for both men and women. There is no empirical evidence to suggest that the distribution of socioeconomic resources is less related to social class in Japan than in the other nations.

We also examined the extent to which social class is correlated with other socioeconomic resources. The pattern of the correlations among class, education, occupational prestige, and income shows a similarity across the three nations. Social class showed strong correlations with other socioeconomic resources in all three societies. In previous work on status consistency and inconsistency in Japan (Imada and Hara 1979; Tominaga 1988), the majority of the respondents belonged to the status-inconsistent clusters, leading these scholars to conclude that status inconsistency characterizes Japanese society. Our analyses are not consistent with this conclusion. If we assume that the correlations among class, education, occupational prestige, and income are indicators of the degree of status consistency, the Japanese coefficients were by no means lower than the American and German ones. In other words, Japanese society does not exhibit any higher tendency towards status inconsistency than do the United States and Germany.

The second set of empirical analyses focused on the movement of people within the class structure between two generations. Two conclusions may be derived from these analyses of intergenerational mobility. First, with regard to intergenerational stability and self-recruitment, Japan shows some distinctive patterns. In comparison to American and German manual working classes, the Japanese skilled and non-skilled manual working class is characterized by a low level of intergenerational stability and a low level of self-recruitment. In Japan, the children of the manual working class are more likely to be found in other classes, and the manual working class is more extensively recruited, especially from the petty bourgeoisie and the farming class, than are their German and American counterparts. This finding primarily derives from the rapidly changing shape of class structure in postwar Japan. In particular, due to the late and rapid economic growth beginning in the late 1950s, Japanese class structure underwent substantial transformation: the rapid contraction of the farming class occurred almost at the same time as the expansion of the blue-collar working class and the white-collar sector. Consequently, the class structure of the father's generation and of the children's generation differed to a much greater extent than in many other industrial nations, producing distinctive outflow and inflow patterns. In addition, among Japanese women, the professional-managerial class exhibited a distinctively low intergenerational stability, reflecting gender segregation in the Japanese labor market. Because women are much less likely to be found in the professional-managerial class in Japan than in the United States and Germany, a much smaller proportion of the daughters of the professional-managerial class ended up in the professional-managerial class in Japan than in the other nations.

Second, however, when we examine the intergenerational movement of people net of changes in class structure, a different picture emerges. The pattern of class inheritance – that is, the relative chance of inheriting the same class position – is very similar across the three nations for both men and women. If we equate the pattern of relative immobility chances with the indicator of closeness of class structure, the Japanese class structure is neither more nor less closed than the American or German class structures. In other words, class origins affect people's life chances (at least intergenerational mobility chances) in a very similar manner in the three societies.

Our class analysis points out some distinguishing features of Japanese class structure, in particular, with regard to the Japanese manual working class and professional-managerial class. Because we used comparable class schema for the three nations, we were able to identify some crucial cross-national differences. And these differences may be explained in large part by the Japanese path of late but rapid industrialization and the extent of gender segregation in Japanese class structure. At the same time, our class analysis discloses a pattern of class inheritance and reproduction that is common to all three societies. There is a tendency for class positions to be passed on from one generation to the next, and class background continues to shape people's prospects of mobility not only in Japan but also in the United States and Germany.

The third set of empirical analyses took up the issue of people's subjective perception of status. By using a cross-nationally comparable survey question about subjective perception of status, we found that the distribution of subjective status scores is similar across the three nations, with the majority of respondents selecting the middle scores. When we examined the determinants of subjective status, social class, along with education, occupational prestige, and income, are found to affect subjective social status in the three societies. Among these four factors, class is the most important factor in Japan and Germany and the second most important factor following education in the United States. These findings suggest that social class continues to influence how people perceive their position in the rank ordering of society. Social class is related not only to objective allocation of resources but also to subjective evaluation of standing in society.

The linkage between objective position and subjective perception, however, requires a more thorough treatment than the quantitative analyses of the kind presented in this chapter provide. Sociologists who employ a quantitative approach are less equipped than ethnographers to bring subjective reality into the analytic picture. It is not clear from this set of analyses why the respondents placed themselves in a given position in the ten-point scale. For example, some respondents felt exploited and placed themselves at the bottom of the scale, while others simply located themselves at the bottom based on their niche in the labor market. Similarly, it is difficult to infer the subjective feelings of the many respondents who placed themselves at the middle of the scale. Only through careful ethnographic studies are we able to understand the social reality of class differentiation and consciousness.

In summary, these conclusions highlight the usefulness of a class analytic perspective. If class categories of any kind, including those used in this study, are meaningless and do not function in Japanese society, it is hard to explain why there is cross-national similarity in the distribution of socioeconomic resources along class lines, why there is similarity in the effects of class origin on mobility chances, and why social class plays an important role in explaining people's perception of status in all three societies. Class functions in a very similar manner in Japan and the other two nations. Social class continues to shape and re-shape people's life chances and perception in contemporary Japanese society.

Notes

1 The figure comes from the daily edition of the *Mainichi* newspaper (January 6, 2006).
2 The figure is computed from the 2007 Japanese Life-Course Panel Survey (JLPS), a nationally representative survey of men and women aged 20 to 40 residing in Japan in 2007. For details of the JLPS, see Ishida *et al.* (2008).
3 Nakane's view is often associated with the range of literature called *nihonjinron* (theories of Japaneseness), which stipulates the uniqueness of the Japanese (Dale 1986; Sugimoto and Mouer 1995; Yoshino 1992).
4 I am grateful to the 2005 SSM Research Committee for permission to use the SSM Surveys. The Japanese General Social Surveys (JGSS) are designed and carried out at the Institute of Regional Studies at Osaka University of Commerce in collaboration with the Institute of Social Science at the University of Tokyo under the direction of Ichiro Tanioka, Michio Nitta, Hiroki Sato and Noriko Iwai, with Project Manager Minae Osawa. The project is financially assisted by a Gakujutsu Frontier Grant from the Japanese Ministry of Education, Culture, Sports, Science and Technology for the 1999–2003 academic years, and the data sets are compiled and distributed by SSJ Data Archive, the Information Center for Social Science Research on Japan, and the Institute of Social Science, University of Tokyo.
5 I have restricted my analysis to (the former) West Germany, since earlier ALLBUS included only West Germany. The German data sets were obtained from GESIS-ZA. The U.S. data sets were obtained through the ICPSR. Davis, James A., Tom W. Smith, and Peter V. Marsden. GENERAL SOCIAL SURVEYS, 1972–2006 [CUMULATIVE FILE] [Computer file]. ICPSR04697-v2. Chicago, IL: National Opinion Research Center [producer], 2007. Storrs, CT: Roper Center for Public Opinion Research, University of Connecticut/Ann Arbor, MI: Inter-University Consortium for Political and Social Research [distributors], 2007-09-10. doi: 10.3886/ICPSR04697.
6 For justification of collapsing the full ten-category version to the six-category version, see Ganzeboom *et al.* (1989). On the use of more disaggregated tables, see Hout and Hauser (1992).
7 The surveys asked about the father's employment when the respondent was growing up (around the age of 15), except for the 1995 SSM survey, which asked for information about the father's main employment.
8 The German educational system differs from the Japanese and American systems, so it is difficult to construct a comparable measure of education. The four categories in the German survey represent: (1) primary education level, (2) those with *Abitur* or qualifications to enter polytechnics, (3) polytechnics level, and (4) university and graduate school level. In the analyses of the determinants of subjective social status, I have included vocational qualifications in addition to the above four categories, in order to maximize the effect of education.

9   Since social class is a categorical variable with six categories, I compute a multiple correlation coefficient rather than a simple correlation coefficient. Correlation coefficients among education, occupational prestige, and income are expressed by simple correlation coefficients.

10 The analyses of intergenerational mobility tables are based on the surveys conducted in the 1990s and 2000/2001. In Japan, 1995 SSM and 2000/2001 JGSS data sets are combined. In the United States, 1990, 1991, 1993, 1994, 1996, 1998, and 2000 GSS data sets are used. In Germany, 1990, 1991, 1992, 1994, 1996, and 1998 ALLBUS data sets are used.

11 It should be noted that the distribution of class origin does not reflect the distribution of class structure of any particular period. Instead, it represents the class distribution of respondents' fathers.

12 This question is used by the opinion surveys conducted regularly by the Prime Minister's Office. The 2000/2001 JGSS used the same question, and a number of other surveys have a very similar question. The SSM surveys asked a similar question, but the possible response categories were: the upper, the upper-middle, the lower-middle, the upper-lower, and the lower-lower.

13 The analyses of the determinants of subjective status (Tables 2.8 and 2.9) are based on the following data sets: the 2000 and 2001 JGSS for Japan; 1983, 1987, and 2000 GSS for the United States; and 1990, 1991, and 1992 ALLBUS for Germany.

14 The social class variable is entered into the multiple regression equation as a nine-category rather than six-category variable with the following categories: the upper professional-managerial class (I), the lower professional-managerial class (II), the routine non-manual class (III), the petty bourgeoisie with employees (IVa), the petty bourgeoisie without employees (IVb), the farming class (IVc/VIIb), the supervisor of the manual working class (V), the skilled manual working class (VI), and the non-skilled manual working class (VIIa). These categories are entered as dummy variables, with the exception of the reference category. Education is measured as a five-level variable in Japan and the United States: junior high school, senior high school, junior college/technical college, university, and graduate school. In Germany, we entered the five levels of academic qualifications and three levels of vocational qualifications: primary academic, secondary academic, *Abitur* (including qualifications for entry into polytechnic), polytechnic degree, university degree, manual vocational qualifications, commercial vocational qualifications, and *meister* qualification. Occupational prestige is measured by international occupational prestige scores, and income is represented by the log of annual income. Educational levels of the father and mother in Japan and the United States are represented by three levels: junior high school, senior high school, and higher education (including both junior college and university). For Germany, the same categories used for the respondent's education are used for the father's and mother's education. The father's class is measured by a six-category version of the EGP class schema. The reason for using these variables with more detailed categories is to maximize their explanatory power.

References

Chiavacci, D. (2008) "From class struggle to general middle class society to divided society," *Social Science Japan Journal*, 11 (1): 5–27.

Dale, P. (1986) *The Myth of Japanese Uniqueness*, London: Routledge.

Erikson, R. and Goldthorpe, J.H. (1992) *The Constant Flux: a study of social mobility in industrial societies*, Oxford: Oxford University Press.

—— (2002) "Intergenerational inequality: a sociological perspective," *Journal of Economic Perspectives*, 16: 31–44.

Erikson, R., Goldthorpe, J.H. and Portocarero, L. (1979) "Intergenerational class mobility in three Western European societies: England, France, and Sweden," *British Journal of Sociology*, 30: 415–41.

Evans, G. (1992) "Testing the validity of the Goldthorpe class schema," *European Sociological Review*, 8: 211–32.

—— (ed.) (1997) *The End of Class Politics? Class voting in comparative perspective*, Oxford: Oxford University Press.

Evans, G. and Mills C. (1998) "Identifying class structure: a latent class analysis of the criterion-related and construct validity of the Goldthorpe class schema," *European Sociological Review*, 14: 87–106.

Evans, M. D. R. and Kelly, J. (2004) "Subjective social location: data from 21 nations," *International Journal of Public Opinion Research*, 16 (1): 3–38.

Evans, M. D. R., Kelly, J. and Kolosi, T. (1992) "Images of class: public perceptions in Hungary and Australia," *American Sociological Review*, 57: 461–81.

Ganzeboom, H.B.G., Luijkx, R. and Treiman, D.J. (1989) "Intergenerational class mobility in comparative perspective," *Research in Social Stratification and Mobility*, 8: 3–84.

Goldthorpe, J.H. (1982) "On the service class, its formation and future," in A. Giddens and F. Mackenzie (eds) *Social Class and the Division of Labour*, Cambridge: Cambridge University Press.

—— (2000) *On Sociology: numbers, narratives, and the integration of research and theory*, Oxford: Oxford University Press.

Goldthorpe, J.H. and Marshall, G. (1992) "The promising future of class analysis: a response to recent critiques," *Sociology*, 26: 381–400.

Grusky, D.B. and Sorensen, J.B. (1998) "Can class analysis be salvaged?," *American Journal of Sociology*, 103: 1187–1234.

Grusky, D.B. and Weeden, K.A. (2001) "Decomposition without death: a research agenda for a new class analysis," *Acta Sociologica*, 44: 203–18.

Hashimoto, K. (2003) *Class Structure in Contemporary Japan*, Melbourne: Trans Pacific Press.

—— (2006) *Kaikyū Shakai* [Class Society], Tokyo: Kodansha.

Hayashi, C. (1995) *Sūjikara Mita Nihonjin no Kokoro* [Japanese Minds Seen from the Figures], Tokyo: Tokuma Shoten.

Hout, M. (1989) *Following in Father's Footsteps: social mobility in Ireland*, Cambridge, MA: Harvard University Press.

Hout, M. and Hauser, R.M. (1992) "Symmetry and hierarchy in social mobility," *European Sociological Review*, 8: 239–66.

Imada, T. and Hara, J. (1979) "Shakaiteki chii no ikkansei to hiikkansei [Consistency and inconsistency of social status]," in K. Tominaga (ed.) *Nihon no Kaisō Kōzō* [The Japanese Stratification Structure], Tokyo: Tokyo Daigaku Shuppankai.

Ishida, H. (1999) "Gakureki shutoku to gakureki kōyō no kokusai hikaku [International comparison of educational attainment and its returns]," *Japanese Journal of Labour Studies*, 472: 46–58.

—— (2001) "Industrialization, class structure, and social mobility in postwar Japan," *British Journal of Sociology*, 52: 579–604.

—— (2008) *Sedaikan Ido no Heisasei wa Jyōshō Shitanoka* [Did the Barriers to Mobility Increase?], Panel Survey Discussion Paper, No. 17, Tokyo: Institute of Social Science, University of Tokyo.

Ishida, H. and Yoshikawa, H. (2003) "How profitable is Japanese education? An international comparison of the benefits of education," *Social Science Japan*, 23: 3–7.

Ishida, H. and Miwa, S. (2008) "Trends in intergenerational class mobility and education in Japan," in H. Ishida (ed.) *Social Stratification and Social Mobility in Late-Industrializing Countries*, Tokyo: The 2005 SSM Research Committee.

Ishida, H., Goldthorpe, J.H. and Erikson, R. (1991) "Intergenerational class mobility in postwar Japan," *American Journal of Sociology*, 96: 954–92.

Ishida, H., Muller, W. and Ridge, J.M. (1995) "Class origin, class destination, and education: cross-national comparison of ten industrial nations," *American Journal of Sociology*, 101: 145–93.

Ishida, H., Su, K. and Spilerman, S. (2002) "Models of career advancement in organizations," *European Sociological Review*, 18: 179–98.

Ishida, H., Miwa, S. and Ōshima, M. (2008) "Tokyo daigaku shakaikagaku kenkyūsho no paneru chōsa [Panel survey of the Institute of Social Science, University of Tokyo]," *Chūō Chōsahō* [Central Research Services Report], 604: 1–9.

Kerr, C. (1983) *The Future of Industrial Societies*, Cambridge, MA: Harvard University Press.

Kerr, C., Dunlop, J.T., Harbison, F.H. and Myers, C.A. (1960) *Industrialism and Industrial Man*, Cambridge, MA: Harvard University Press.

Koike, K. and Inoki, T. (eds) (2002) *Howaito Karā no Jinzai Keisei: nichi bei ei doku no hikaku* [Skill Formation among White-collar Workers: comparison among Japan, the U.S., Britain and Germany], Tokyo: Tōyō Keizai Shinpōsha.

Marshall, G., Rose, D., Newby, H. and Vogler, C. (1988) *Social Class in Modern Britain*, London: Unwin Hyman.

Murakami, Y. (1984) *Shin Chukan Taishu no Jidai* [The Age of New Middle Mass], Tokyo: Chūōkōronsha.

Nakane, C. (1970) *Japanese Society*, Berkeley, CA: University of California Press.

Nakao, K. (2002) "Kaisō kizoku ishiki to seikatsu ishiki [Subjective strata identification and life consciousness]," *Riron to Hōhō* [Sociological Theory and Methods], 17 (2): 135–49.

Sato, T. (2000) *Fubyōdō Shakai Nihon* [Japan as an Unequal Society], Tokyo: Chūō Kōron Shinsha.

Scott, J. and Watanabe, M. (1998) *Kaikyūron no Genzai: igirisu to nihon* [The Current State of Theories of Class: Britain and Japan], Tokyo: Aoki Shoten.

Sugimoto, Y. (2003) *An Introduction to Japanese Society*, 2nd edn, Cambridge: Cambridge University Press.

Sugimoto, Y. and Mouer, R. (1995) *Nihonjinron no Hōteisiki* [The Japanology Equations], Tokyo: Chikuma Shobō.

Tachibanaki, T. (1998) *Nihon no Keizai Kakusa* [Japan's Economic Inequality], Tokyo: Iwanami Shoten.

Tominaga, K. (1979) "Shakai kaisō to shakai idō no sūsei bunseki [Trend analysis of social stratification and mobility]," in K. Tominaga (ed.) *Nihon no Kaisō Kōzō* [The Japanese Stratification Structure], Tokyo: Tokyo Daigaku Shuppankai.

—— (1988) *Nihon Sangyō Shakai no Tenki* [Change in Japanese Industrial Society], Tokyo: Tokyo Daigaku Shuppankai.

Treiman, D. (1977) *Occupational Prestige in Comparative Perspective*, New York: Academic Press.

Wright, E.O. (1985) *Classes*, London: Verso.

—— (1997) *Class Counts: comparative studies in class analysis*, Cambridge: Cambridge University Press.

Yoshino, K. (1992) *Cultural Nationalism in Contemporary Japan: a sociological enquiry*, London: Routledge.

3 Marriage as an association of social classes in a low fertility rate society

Towards a new theory of social stratification

Sawako Shirahase

Sociological observation of population shifts

Japan's total fertility rate stood at 1.32 in 2005, very far indeed from the 2.08 required to maintain the population at a steady level. In 1989 the fertility rate fell to 1.57, below the figure recorded in 1966, the last "year of the fiery horse."[1] The realization that a fertility rate which looked like a drastic but temporary fall just 20 years ago was now the norm provoked a wave of panic that came to be called the "1.57 shock." That shock prompted the government to start work on policies to combat the falling fertility rate. The 1990s saw a series of government initiatives such as the "angel plan," the "new angel plan," a new system of childcare leave, and the Basic Law for a Gender-equal Society, among other attempts to counteract the falling fertility rate. Even so, the fertility rate has continued below replacement rate for over 30 years now, and in 2006, a year earlier than forecast, the population itself started to decline.

In a country like Japan with only a limited amount of living space, a decline in the overall population is not, in itself, a problem. What *is* problematical, however, is the structure of the population. The active working population is in relative decline, while the retired generation that needs to be supported by that working generation is increasing relative to the whole. The decline of the active working generation is widely seen as liable to sap Japan's economic vitality, or even the vitality of the nation as a whole, and much hope is invested in policies to fight the falling fertility rate. In the background to the high-growth days of the 1960s was a demographic profile that guaranteed a rich supply of young newcomers to the Japanese workforce. Today, however, Japan has become a graying society comparable to those of Europe and America. This monumental demographic shift is now shaking the foundations of many social systems. Already the drastic decline in the fertility rate has made reform of the social welfare system an urgent imperative.

Population problems arise from changes in the distribution of different kinds of people who make up society. Those people are society's natural resources; at the same time they are also recipients of socioeconomic resources. As such, social groupings are formed in response to social rules that govern the distribution of these various resources. In short, the principle of resource distribution determines the people's level of well-being, and irrational elements in the working of that principle lead to social inequalities. Within the framework of sociology, the fairness or otherwise of the distributive principle has been argued mainly in terms of social stratification theory, and many problems in existing distributive processes have been discussed. As shifts occur in the distribution of the elements making up society, a need arises to reconsider the distributive principle and a whole range of social systems. It thus becomes a meaningful enterprise to look at demographic change, as represented by the problem of the falling fertility rate and aging society, from the perspective of social status theory.

Population problems have long been debated by social scientists, originally mainly as an issue of food supply. There is also a long history of theoretical attempts to view population problems in terms of inequality issues. In Europe, the Myrdals' *The Crisis of the Population Problem* was published in 1934, and the Myrdals went on to make a major contribution to the development of the universal welfare state in Sweden (Miyamoto 1999). In Japan, meanwhile, Yasuma Takata published his famous treatise, *Kaikyū oyobi Dai-San Shikan* (Class and the Third View of History), a good ten years before Myrdal's work, in 1925 (Takata 1925). The following year, Takata published a thesis entitled "Give Birth and Proliferate" (Umeyo Ueyo), in which he argued that overpopulation was not necessarily as problematic as others had argued (Takata 2006). This work was roundly condemned by Marxist economist Hajime Kawakami, who accused Takata of advocating overpopulation as a way of lowering wages for workers (Sugita 2006; Nakanishi 2003). Kawakami's critique of Takata reads too much into Takata's text and distorts its meaning in quite a few places. Opinion on Takata's writing about population problems remains divided to this day, but at the very least it deserves attention for identifying population as the quantitative and qualitative structure at the foundation of society.

Demography is not just a matter of counting heads. It deals with the question of how the members of society are distributed, and how they live their daily lives amid the limitations and blessings of the social systems around them. Moreover, the distribution of economic, social and cultural resources is governed by a certain principle, a distributive principle that has not been generated out of the "free competition" that is the cornerstone of modern economics. Rather, the process of resource distribution is frequently subject to restrictions and disruptions from various systems. Moreover, people do not receive their share of the distribution of resources directly: the individual's acquisition of resources is mediated through the household and the family: the locus of the basic unit of consumption. Among those residing within the household are some who are not capable of acquiring income through their own labor and managing their own personal finances. The most typical examples would be small children and the elderly. The household, as the basic unit of consumption, is essentially formed of a couple – usually a married couple. It therefore makes sense to look at the coming together of couples in terms of class origins and the level of achievement, in fields such as education, of each partner.

Now the most striking recent changes in household composition have been an increase in single-person households, and in the proportion of people who go though their lives without ever marrying. Even today, however, the majority of people do get married at some point in their lives, and since a plural-member household based on a married couple remains the dominant style of household, it is still appropriate to study the married couple as the basis of household structure. Changes in population structure play out in concert with changes in household structure, and influence the way people actually live their lives. The main objective of the research presented here is to look at population change, as represented by the falling fertility rate and aging society, in terms of the social class structure underlying the principle governing distribution of socioeconomic resources. In particular I hope to look at patterns of marriage, as a form of class alliance, with a view to seeking out new ways of thinking about social class, appropriate to the coming age.

A constantly declining fertility rate and extreme aging of population

It is customary in Japan today to speak of the declining fertility rate (*shōshika*) and aging society (*kōreika*) as a single unit (*shōshi-kōreika*), but if we examine them separately, we find that the former exerts a particularly large impact in explaining overall demographic change (Atō 2000). The literal meaning of the Japanese term *shōshika* is a situation where the total fertility rate (an estimation of the average number of children which a woman in the reproductive age range of 15 to 49 is supposed to have throughout her life) consistently runs below population replacement level, that is 2.08.

Figure 3.1 shows trends in the total fertility rate (TFR) since 1950. It is clear enough that the TRF has been running below replacement level for over 30 years since 1970. This constant decline in the fertility rate has led to a striking increase in the age of the overall population. It took just 24 years for the proportion of over-65s in the population to double from 7 percent to 14 percent. In France – the industrialized country with the slowest rate of aging – the doubling period was 115 years, over four times as long as for Japan.[2] The aging index used in Figure 3.1 is the ratio between the child population (14 and under) to the old population (65 and over). Those in the former group will eventually enter the workforce and join the ranks of those supporting society. By contrast, members of the elderly population will continue to be on the side requiring support, however long they may live. If the elderly population expands relative to the child population, the imbalance between generations will widen further.

However, an increase in the proportion of old people in the overall population is only one aspect of the aging population problem. Another important index is the increase in life expectancy. Whereas the increase in the elderly proportion of the population is a macro value, increasing life expectancy means that individual members of the elderly population will continue to be in that population for a longer period of time. This naturally gives rise to the issue of how large numbers of very old people are going to be looked after. The long-term care issue is part of the

Fertility rate   Aging index

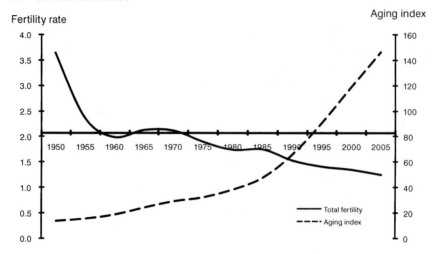

Figure 3.1 Japan's declining fertility rate and aging population

Note: The aging index is calculated by dividing the population of over-65s by the population of under-15s, and multiplying by 100. The bold horizontal line represents a total fertility rate of 2.08 – the level required for population replacement.

Source: Latest Demographic Statistics 2007 (National Institute of Population and Social Security Research 2007)

problem of inter-generational imbalance (since younger generations have to look after older generations), but it is also a micro-level problem, affecting individual lives, since an increase in life expectancy is not necessarily accompanied by an increase in *healthy* life expectancy – the period for which a person can expect to live independent of any nursing assistance.

The declining number of children in the population has two main underlying factors. One is the increasing number of unmarried people (*mikonka*) and the other is a decline in fertility among those who *have* got married. Until the mid-1990s, the declining fertility rate was explained mostly in terms of the former factor. As Yamada (1999) pointed out, one reason why young people tended to avoid or postpone marriage was because they tended to wait longer and longer before leaving the parental household. Since in Japan it is still relatively rare for children to be born out of wedlock, marriage and childbirth are closely related issues, and the decision of each individual on whether to marry or not can have a direct impact on the fertility rate.

Figure 3.2 shows trends since 1950 in the non-marriage rate for each age group. Looking first at the data for men, from the 1970s onwards over half of all men were still unmarried even in their late twenties. By 2005 the non-marriage rate for men in their late twenties had reached 70 percent. Even for men in their late thirties, some 30 percent remained unmarried. As for the women, in recent years the non-marriage rate for those in their early twenties has approached 90 percent, leaving almost everyone in this cohort unmarried. During the 1990s non-marriage rate

Male

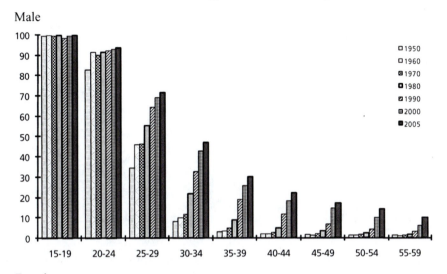

Female

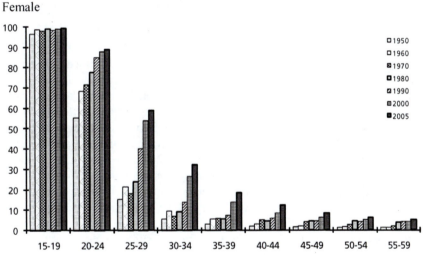

Figure 3.2 Trends in non-marriage rate, by age group

Source: Ministry of Internal Affairs and Communications Statistics Bureau, National Census for each year. Reproduced from National Institute of Population and Social Security Research 2007, Latest Demographic Statistics 2007, Table 6-24.

levels also rose rapidly for women in their thirties, passing 30 percent by 2005. However, these trends must be read with caution. They represent cross-sections of the population at various age levels, and the significance of being unmarried changes with time. Naturally, the older the age cohort, the more likely are its members to remain permanently unmarried; for those still in their late twenties, being unmarried may well mean simply that marriage has been postponed.

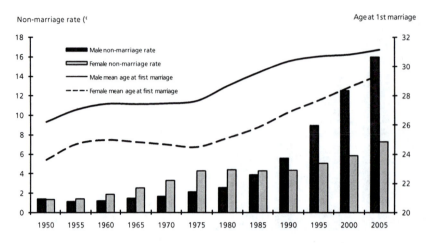

Non-marriage rate ('   Age at 1st marriage

Figure 3.3 Trends in male and female non-marriage rates and mean age at first marriage

Source: *Latest Demographic Statistics 2007* (National Institute of Population and Social Security Research 2007)

Figure 3.3 shows trends in the average age at first marriage for men and women, and changes in the proportion of people who never marry throughout their lives.[3] Both men and women have shown a striking tendency to marry later and later in life. In the 45 years from 1960 to 2005, the average age at first marriage has risen by roughly five years for men and six years for women. More recently we have also seen a narrowing of the age gap between husband and wife, roughly halving from a peak of about 3.7 in 1985 to 1.7 in 2005. The proportion of people spending their whole life unmarried rose sharply in the 1990s, especially among men. Until the 1980s there were more women than men who never married, but that pattern was reversed in the late 1980s and the proportion of men who never marry has continued to climb steeply ever since. Among the overall population of unmarried men, those in their forties and fifties are still a minority, but these are the age groups growing fastest.

At the same time the constant decline in the fertility rate has led to a decline in the size of the younger age groups, meaning that the impact of non-marriage among these groups is having less impact than before on the decline in the fertility rate. That brings us to the other major factor in falling fertility: the decline in the numbers of children being born to couples who *have* tied the knot. Since the start of the 1990s, this trend has had a growing impact on the broader demographic picture (Hiroshima 2000, Iwasawa 2002, Kaneko 2004).

However, this decline in the fertility rate among married couples does not necessarily signify an increase in the number of childless couples. Figure 3.4 shows the mean number of children born to couples who have been married for 16 to 20 years, treating that figure as the complete fertility rate (i.e. the mean number of children born to couples who are supposed to have completed their

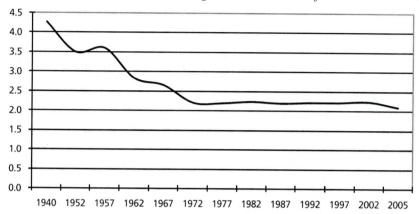

Figure 3.4 Trends in complete fertility rate (married couples only)

Source: *The 13th National Fertility Survey* (National Institute of Population and Social Security Research 2006)

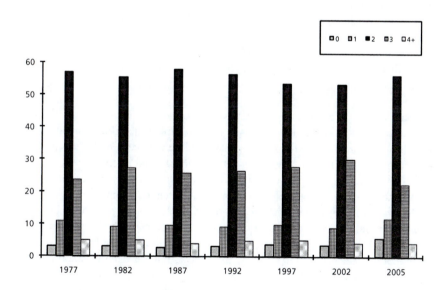

Figure 3.5 Trends in the complete number of children (%)

Source: *The 13th National Fertility Survey* (National Institute of Population and Social Security Research 2006)

reproductive activity).Even in 2005, the complete fertility rate stood at 2.09, and although as I write the latest figure is slightly lower at 2.07, it is still running at or very close to population replacement rate.

Figure 3.5 shows the distribution of numbers of children born to the couples who have been married for 16 to 20 years and who are supposed to "have completed" their fertility behavior. The percentage of couples still childless after 16 to 20 years of marriage stood at 5.6 percent in 2005, and although that was an increase from the 3 percent recorded in 1977, childless couples remained a very small minority. On the other hand, three-child families have shown a sudden decline in very recent years, to only about 20 percent of the whole, and there has been a corresponding increase in families with one or two children. Even so the overall picture is one of relatively little change in the final distribution of children born to married couples over the last thirty years.

From 2005 to 2006, the total fertility rate recovered somewhat, from 1.26 to 1.32, although it was still running far below the population replacement rate of 2.08. Among the factors in this recent modest revival has been a rise in the fertility rate among 30–34 year old women (members of the so-called *dankai* junior generation, or the offspring of the baby boom generation), and a trend toward childbirth later in life among older age-groups. It is possible that this is merely a temporary upturn caused by the occurrence of a large age cohort reaching childbirth age, and it is too early to know whether the recovery may be sustained (Japan Ministry of Health, Labor, and Welfare 2007). Still, it is probably fair to say that recent changes in fertility rate have been increasingly explicable in terms of fertility trends among married couples, as opposed to the decline in marriage. In the background to that is the decline of large households with three or more children.

Very well – let us next ask ourselves *why* couples are having fewer children. One point often raised in debate over policy to combat the falling fertility rate is that the ideal number of children people would like to have is not necessarily that low. It follows that the fertility rate is not declining because people are *refusing* to have children. Many couples would like to have two or three children, but end up having none or one. They want to have more children, but cannot. This is the nub of the problem. This is one of the most important reasons for promoting policy to counter the falling fertility rate, because if the fundamental willingness to have children is there, the chances of increasing the fertility rate through socioeconomic policy tools is far better than if that willingness is not there in the first place. Let us therefore look at the reasons preventing couples from having as many children as they would wish. Table 3.1 tabulates those reasons, as identified in a recent national survey.

By far the most commonly cited reason for having fewer children than would be ideal is the excessively high cost of child-rearing and education, cited by close to two-thirds of the sample surveyed. It simply costs too much money to have children. If that is the case, then a bold program of cash incentives might well be effective. Indeed the scope of the child allowance system has expanded since April 1, 2007. The amount of the monthly payment was increased to 10,000 yen

Table 3.1 Reasons why people expect to have fewer children than they would ideally like to have (%)

Excessive cost of child-rearing and education	65.9
Reluctance to have a baby at the old age	38.0
Unable to cope with any further mental and physical stress of child-rearing	21.6
Social environment not conducive to relaxed childhood	13.6
Health reasons	16.9
Interferes with work/career	17.5
Want children but physically unable to have them	16.3
Not enough space at home	15.0
Lack of cooperation from husband in chores and child-rearing	13.8
Want to concentrate on own and husband's life	8.1
Want last-born child to reach adulthood before husband retires	9.5
Husband does not want more children	8.3
Other	8.5

Source: The 13th National Fertility Survey (National Institute of Population and Social Security Research 2006).
Note: multiple answers

for children under the age of three, and the ceiling of income restrictions was eased (Japan Ministry of Health, Labor, and Welfare 2007). Starting April 2006, the period for which the child allowance is paid was also extended, to cover all children still at elementary school as well as the pre-schoolers originally covered.

Marriage viewed in terms of social class

The high cost of child-rearing is often cited as a background factor in the declining fertility rate. But that does not mean that more children are born when the marital household is in good shape financially. The average number of children has actually declined fastest among high-income families (Shirahase 2008). Individual reproductive behavior is heavily influenced by class factors, and the decline in childbirth has by no means been uniform across the whole of society.

Homogamy and endogamy – the practices of marriage with a partner of similar social background (homogamy), and marriage within one social group (endogamy) – are important topics within the study of social class. Industrialization theory posits a shift in the distributive principle governing society, from attribute to achievement. In the course of industrialization, an individual's social class would come to be decided by what he or she had achieved, rather than by attributed characteristics deriving from the circumstances of birth. It was further argued that this new distributive principle would bring change not only to how one attained social class, but also to marriage patterns, which determine who becomes allied with whom in the class system. In a homogamous/endogamous society, marriage is encouraged between partners from similar class backgrounds, and marriage thus serves to perpetuate and harden the class system. However, as industrialization brings the shift to meritocracy, marriage changes from a balanced deal between two lineages, to something based on the will of two individuals. Industrialization and modernization would change marriage patterns, along with all the other social institutions.

The British sociologist D.V. Glass was one of the first researchers to look at homogamy from a class perspective (Glass 1954). Lipset and Bendix (1959) and Blau and Duncan (1967) also tried to investigate the degree to which society had become liberalized and fluid by starting with marriage patterns. Kalmijn (1991) proposed that prevalence of social-class endogamy could be a valuable index of the degree of openness of any given society; the lower the rate of endogamy, the more liberal the society.

Kalmijn successfully demonstrated that in modern industrialized societies, homogamy based on given attributes such as class origin was gradually giving way to *educational* homogamy. Mare (1991) further pointed out that people who went to university tended to find marriage partners on campus, so that the site of education could also have an important function as a marriage market.

Let us ask which is the most important factor governing choice of marriage partner in the Japanese case: class origin, or education? Watanabe and Kondō (1990) looked at marriage from a class association perspective, using the 1985 SSM survey data, and suggested that choice of marriage partner was not necessarily unrelated to class origin (family background). Shida *et al.* (2000) analyzed the 1995 SSM survey and found that class homogamy was on a downtrend across all age cohorts, concluding that "individual based marriage is on the rise" (p.166), with educational achievement now counting for more than class origin. I myself argued that the influence of educational achievement on marriage as a class association was no mere recent phenomenon, but had already been a significant factor for many decades (Shirahase 2005).

Yamada (1999) argued that the trend toward postponing or avoiding marriage was caused by a class mismatch between the sexes. Women who remained unmarried were mostly highly educated offspring of privileged households, whereas non-marrying men were mainly low-income workers with low educational credentials. The desire of women to marry up, and achieve a kind of social rebirth through marriage, means that the more privileged their upbringing has been, the higher is the standard of living they demand after marriage. This reduces the pool of eligible candidates and hence increases the likelihood that such women will remain unmarried. Meanwhile men who cannot provide women with a satisfactory standard of living tend to fall out of the marriage market without having found a partner.

In the days when arranged marriages were still the norm, matchmaking was often attempted, to balance the interests of the two houses involved in the marriage alliance. However, with the decline of arranged marriages and the growing dominance of love marriages, family lineage ceased to be an important factor in marriage decisions, and it became possible for any good-looking woman to marry into an elite family. Behind this phenomenon is the image of a marriage market predicated on love and therefore open to all. Glenn *et al.* studied female social mobility through marriage, and argued that since physical attractiveness and character are unrelated to class origin, women's social mobility, through marriage at least, is more independent of class factors than that of men, resulting in the formation of a freer marriage market (Glenn *et al.* 1974). Heath (1981) also found that women's marital mobility is more independent of class origin than man's intergenerational mobility through occupation (see also Chase 1975; Portocarero 1985).

According to the *13th National Fertility Survey*, carried out in 2002, only 6.4 percent of married people surveyed that year[4] said that theirs was an arranged marriage, with some 90 percent reporting love marriages (National Institute of Population and Social Security Research 2006). However, if we take a closer look at these love marriages, we find that couples who met each other in the workplace or through their work accounted for one third, with another 30 percent or so reporting that they were introduced to their partner by friends or siblings, indicating numerous cases in which marriage stemmed from an encounter in a place where there was a strong likelihood of shared lifestyles. Despite the apparent dominance of love marriages, there is still room for further study as to just how free the marriage market really is.

In the course of their discussion of the falling fertility rate, Shida *et al.* (2000) state that "great changes are coming over the Japanese marriage market" resulting in "increased imperfection of the market" (p.174). Shida *et al.* do not make it entirely clear what they mean by market imperfection, but we may surmise that the numbers of participants in the marriage market, and the kind of people participating, are not well coordinated. I therefore propose to move on to a discussion of the quantitative issue of who are the participants and how many of them there are in the marriage market, and the qualitative issue of who marries whom, in the framework of social class theory. I will then go on to examine the significance of class homogamy for social class structure, with particular reference to child-rearing. I will be looking mainly at marriages between people with similar educational credentials, dividing them into three groups according to educational level attained. I define completion of compulsory education as "low level," senior high school graduation as mid-level, and graduation from junior college, technical college or university as high level. Regarding the pattern of class homogamy, I will briefly look at the results of the 1985 and 1995 SSM survey data, since the 2005 SSM survey did not include the questionnaire item about class origin of the spouse.

Who gets married when?

We have already seen in Figures 3.2 and 3.3 that despite the trends toward postponement and avoidance of marriage, the great majority of Japanese people do still get married eventually.

First, let us take a look at trends in the proportion of each educational class group in the unmarried population. Figure 3.6 covers men and women in their twenties and thirties, comparing the proportion of each educational group in

Male

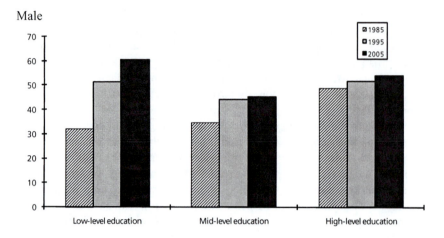

Female

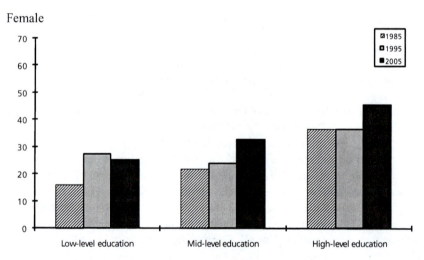

Figure 3.6 Trends in non-marriage rate by educational level (%)

Source: The SSM survey in 1985, 1995, and 2005 Note: Sample limited to those in 20s and 30s

1985, 1995 and 2005. Looking first at the men, the low-education group shows the highest rate of increase in non-marriage. In contrast, the high-education group shows the smallest rate of increase, climbing just 5.2 percentage points from 1985 to 2005. The mid-level group also shows a rise in the non-marriage rate, but with most of the increase coming between 1985 and 1995. From 1995 to 2005 this group showed the smallest increase of the three. The low-education group showed by far the largest retreat from marriage from the mid-1980s to the mid-1990s, although I should note here that this group constitutes a small minority – about 6 percent of male respondents in their twenties and thirties, and just 43 cases in the 2005 SSM survey. As such the data should be treated with some caution.

Now let us turn to the women. Here the pattern differs from the male cases in several important respects. First, the pattern changes sharply from 1985–1995 to 1995–2005. From 1985 to 1995 we see a high rate of increase in non-marriage in the low-education group. But in the following decade, that group shows a slight decline in the non-marriage rate, while the mid-level and high-level groups show large increases in non-marriage. As a result, the change in non-marriage rates for the whole period of 1985 to 2005 is roughly the same for all three groups. From the results displayed here we can confirm a clear gender gap in marriage patterns among Japanese in their twenties and thirties, which is revealed with the passage of time. The theory I mentioned earlier, that poorly educated men and highly educated women were the two groups with rising rates of non-marriage, is only half supported by the data here. Certainly poorly-educated males show a relatively high extent of increase in non-marriage rate from the mid-1980s to 1990s, but for women the trend away from marriage seems to have been fairly uniform across educational attainment groups.

Figure 3.7 presents non-marriage rate by class origin measured by father's main work. I compare the non-marriage rate of men and women in their twenties and thirties in 1985 and 1995 to see changes in the non-marriage rate by class origin. Class origin is divided into six categories, following the EGP class schema (Erikson *et al.* 1979). They are (1) professional-managerial, (2) routine non-manual, (3) urban self-employed, (4) farm workers (5) skilled manual, and (6) unskilled manual. First, focusing on men, class background significantly affects the chances of being single in 1985 and 1995. In 1985, men of the professional-managerial class and of the unskilled manual class are more likely to be unmarried than men from farming families. In 1995, men of farming origins continue to show the lowest non-marriage rate while men of the routine non-manual and skilled manual classes show the highest non-marriage rate. When we examine the change in non-marriage rate, we find that class categories which exhibited an increased non-marriage rate are the routine non-manual and the skilled manual classes. The unskilled manual class, though generally regarded to be the most unfavorable category, does not show a particularly large increase in non-marriage rate.

One possible reason why those who originated from the routine non-manual and the skilled manual classes show a relatively high increase in non-marriage rate is due to the change in the age distribution of the members of these class origins. The average age of men with routine non-manual and skilled manual class origins became younger, that is, from 31.6 in 1985 to 29.4 in 1995 and from 30.5 to 28.9, respectively. An increase in the non-marriage rate among those with these class origins is partly derived from the change in the age composition of these class members. Thus, the claim that men with an unfavorable family background are likely to be kicked out of the marriage market and show a particularly high increase in the non-marriage rate is not supported by our results.

Looking at the female non-marriage rate by class origin, there is no large difference between 1985 and 1995. Indeed, the extent of the difference in the non-marriage rate by class origin is smaller among young women than among young men. The difference in the non-marriage rate by class origin was not significant in

Male

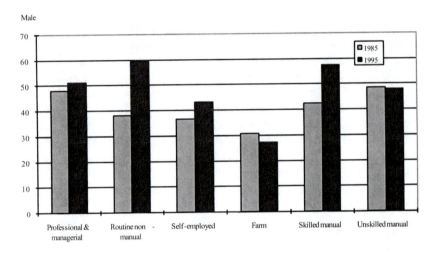

Female

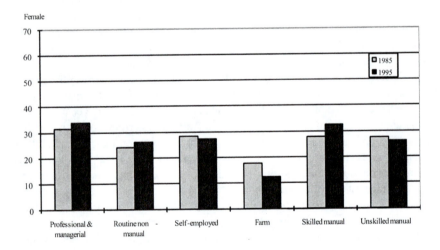

Figure 3.7 Trends in non-marriage rate by class origin (%)

Source: The SSM survey in 1985 and 1995
Note: Sample limited to those in their 20s and 30s

1985, but it became statistically significant in 1995. The association between the non-marriage rate and class origin among young women became significant over the decade. Women of the professional-managerial class and the skilled manual class show the highest non-marriage rate, while women of farming origins show the lowest non-marriage rates.

Why did the difference in non-marriage rate by class origin become significant recently among women? One reason would be due to the declining impact of social

Table 3.2 Mean number of years from leaving education to marriage, by education, 1985–2005

	1985	1995	2005
Men			
Low-level	11.671	13.012	14.448
Mid-level	8.452	9.507	10.145
High-level	5.745	7.269	7.188
Women			
Low-level	8.052	9.429	9.257
Mid-level	5.681	7.123	6.911
High-level	3.821	5.560	5.458

Source: SSM surveys, 1985-2005

norms regarding young women. The effect of class origin on female non-marriage rate was not significant in 1985 because the social norm calling for women to get married around the proper marital age, say 23 or 24, was still strong regardless of class origin. But by 1995, when the pressure on women to get married by their mid-twenties was reduced, the option of not getting married early became accepted, and the difference in non-marriage rate by class origin became apparent.

Marriage timing

Table 3.2 uses the same three time points to look at changes in the period from completing education to getting married. The clearest trend to be seen here is the lengthening of the period from completing education to marriage among men in the low-education group. Mid-level men also show a lengthening of that period, though not to as great a degree. As for highly-educated men, they actually showed a slight shortening of the period from graduation to marriage during the decade from 1995 to 2005.

In the case of women, all three groups showed a slight decline in graduation-to-marriage period from 1995 to 2005. Interestingly, at the same time that the proportion of people staying unmarried increased, those who *did* get married tended to do so more quickly.[5]

Table 3.2 shows years from leaving education to getting married, but of course it does not tell us how long people in the sample knew the person they eventually married. The 2005 survey tried to put that right by adding a question on that point. It allows us to estimate the mean number of years from first encounter to marriage for three age cohorts: those married in 1990–2005, in 1975–1989, and prior to 1975 (figure not shown). For the men, it is clear that the encounter-to-marriage period has been lengthening over the years, especially for those with low levels of education (1.2 years for the oldest cohort and 8.1 years for the youngest cohort). For the oldest cohort, the courtship period rose with level of education, but for the youngest cohort the courtship period among men with low levels of education was the longest. Among women the same trend may be observed to an even more dramatic extent, with encounter-to-marriage taking almost twelve

Table 3.3 Patterns of educational association of marriage partners

Wife's educational level	Husband's educational level			
	Low	Mid	High	Total
Low				
Observed value	457	227	29	713
Expected value	126.4	361.8	224.8	713.0
% of total	64.1	31.8	4.1	100.0
Standard residual	29.4	−7.1	−13.1	
Mid				
Observed value	283	1621	607	2511
Expected value	445.2	1274.2	791.6	2511.0
% of total	11.3	64.6	24.2	100.0
Standard residual	−7.7	9.7	−6.6	
High				
Observed value	12	304	701	1017
Expected value	180.3	516.1	320.6	1017.0
% of total	1.2	29.9	68.9	100.0
Standard residual	−12.5	−9.3	21.2	

Source: combined SSM data of 1985 to 2005

years for women with low levels of education in the youngest group against less than two years in the middle and oldest groups.[6]

Who marries whom? A study of educational homogamy

Let us now look at the relative levels of education of husband and wife among couples already married. Who marries whom? This will be the main research question for the rest of this chapter.

Table 3.3 displays matrimonial patterns for a sample divided into three levels of education. Here the null hypothesis is that educational level has no bearing on marriage, and standard residuals were calculated for the degree to which each group deviates from that hypothesis. The null hypothesis was rejected, with particularly large deviations recorded for the groups with low and high levels of education. In other words, there is a significant correlation between the levels of education of the two partners in a marriage, and that correlation tends toward educational homogamy.

Let us next ask ourselves whether the pattern of educational homogamy shows any change over time.

Table 3.4 displays patterns of educational homogamy for three age cohorts: those married in 1990–2005, 1975–1989, and prior to 1975. All cohorts show high degrees of educational homogamy, with especially high standard residual scores recorded for high and low educational levels among the most recently married cohort.

Table 3.4 Educational attainment of marriage partners by marriage cohort

Wife's educational level	*Husband's educational level*			
	Low	*Mid*	*High*	*Total*
1990–2005 cohort				
Low				
Observed value	25	25	3	53
Expected value	3.0	28.1	21.8	53.0
% of total	47.2	47.2	5.7	100.0
Standard residual	12.6	−0.6	−4.0	
Mid				
Observed value	42	469	203	714
Expected value	41.0	379.2	293.8	714.0
% of total	5.9	65.7	28.4	100.0
Standard residual	0.2	4.6	−5.3	
High				
Observed value	4	163	303	470
Expected value	27.0	249.6	193.4	470.0
% of total	0.9	34.7	64.5	100.0
Standard residual	−4.4	−5.5	7.9	
1975-1989 cohort				
Low				
Observed value	56	42	9	107
Expected value	12.0	55.4	39.7	107.0
% of total	52.3	39.3	8.4	100.0
Standard residual	12.7	−1.8	−4.9	
Mid				
Observed value	88	548	208	844
Expected value	94.5	436.7	312.8	844.0
% of total	10.4	64.9	24.6	100.0
Standard residual	−0.7	5.3	−5.9	
High				
Observed value	4	94	273	371
Expected value	41.5	192.0	137.5	371.0
% of total	1.1	25.3	73.6	100.0
Standard residual	−5.8	−7.1	11.6	
Pre-1975 cohort				
Low				
Observed value	371	158	17	546
Expected value	174.4	263.6	108.1	546.0
% of total	67.9	28.9	3.1	100.0
Standard residual	14.9	−6.5	−8.8	
Mid				
Observed value	151	592	192	935
Expected value	298.6	451.3	185.1	935.0
% of total	16.1	63.3	20.5	100.0
Standard residual	−8.5	6.6	0.5	
High				
Observed value	4	45	117	166
Expected value	53.0	80.1	32.9	166.0
% of total	2.4	27.1	70.5	100.0
Standard residual	−6.7	−3.9	14.7	

Source: combined SSM data of 1985 to 2005

Male

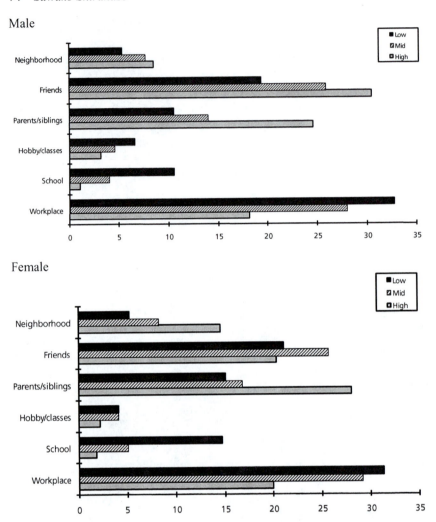

Figure 3.8 How/where spouse was met by academic level

Source: The 2005 SSM survey

Turning now to the two partners' occupation at time of marriage (Table 3.5), we find that cells on the diagonal that marks equality between the partners invariably have the highest standard scores. This clearly indicates residual tends to marry like, in terms of occupation as well as education.

The question then naturally arises as to why exactly people tend to marry partners of similar educational and occupational status. Figure 3.8 displays data on where married people met their future partner. For the highly-educated group, the workplace and school both scored highly. For highly-educated women, in particular, school clearly also served the function of a marriage market, with

Table 3.5 Husband and wife's occupations at time of marriage

	Husband's occupation				
Wife's occupation	Professional/ managerial	Low–level white collar	Agriculture	Blue collar	Total
Professional/ managerial					
Observed value	88	106	5	61	260
Expected value	39.6	104.2	12.9	103.3	260.0
% of total	33.8	40.8	1.9	23.5	100.0
Standard residual	7.7	0.2	−2.2	−4.2	
Low-level white collar					
Observed value	143	495	20	358	1016
Expected value	154.6	407.4	50.3	403.7	1016.0
% of total	14.1	48.7	2.0	35.2	100.0
Standard residual	−0.9	4.3	−4.3	−2.3	
Agriculture					
Observed value	2	7	41	23	73
Expected value	11.1	29.3	3.6	29.0	73.0
% of total	2.7	9.6	56.2	31.5	100.0
Standard residual	−2.7	−4.1	19.7	−1.1	
Blue collar					
Observed value	22	64	17	224	327
Expected value	49.8	131.1	16.2	129.9	327.0
% of total	6.7	19.6	5.2	68.5	100.0
Standard residual	−3.9	−5.9	0.2	8.3	

Source: The 2005 SSM survey

nearly 15 percent finding their future husband there. By contrast, people in the low-education group were relatively more likely to find future spouses in the neighborhood or through parental or sibling connections. Low-education men also showed a particularly heavy dependence on friends for introductions. Although all three groups showed a high degree of homogamy, the venues and occasions for encountering future spouses varied with educational attainment level. People with low levels of education tended to rely on connections of locality or kinship, resulting in a tendency toward homogamy. Among those with high levels of education, there is a tendency to meet marriage partners in the same higher education institutions, and hence they too tend to end up with a partner from a similar home background. We may observe that the same home environment that leads toward high-level academic attainment also shows up in marriage patterns. The data also shows that the workplace is an important marriage market, especially for the mid- and high-level educational groups.

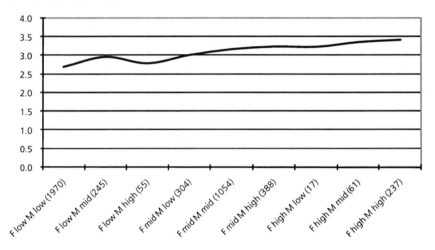

Figure 3.9 Self-reported standard of living at age 15 by parental education

Source: The 2005 SSM survey
Note: F=Father, M=Mother. The figures in the parentheses are the number of observations

The significance of matching educational credentials among married couples

Hitherto we have been looking at the sort of partners that get brought together in marriage, with the focus on educational homogamy. Finally, let us consider the practical significance of the educational matching between the two spouses, from a class perspective. Before we look at the educational credentials of marriage partners, let us consider what impact parental educational credentials have on self-reported living standards at the age of 15 (Figure 3.9).[7]

Figure 3.9 shows the correlation between the level of educational attainment by both the respondent parents, and self-reported living standards at age 15.[8] The highest self-reported standard of living was among respondents whose parents both had high levels of education, and the lowest was among those whose parents both had low levels of education. The question of how precisely to go about measuring class origins is an extremely important research theme. Suffice to say for now that this very rough-and-ready approach does at least allow us to guess that it is not just paternal educational achievement that determines awareness of living standards at the age of 15; maternal educational achievement also plays a significant role.

I have already mentioned that study of homogamy is one way of seeing just how crystallized social class structure is. If there is a strong tendency for people to marry partners of similar class origins[9] and educational attainment, that indicates that the basic units of class structure are homogeneous, and as a result class structure will tend to perpetuate existing patterns. Conversely, it has long been conjectured that if marriages between people of different class origins and levels of education increase, then the units of class structure will become more diverse,

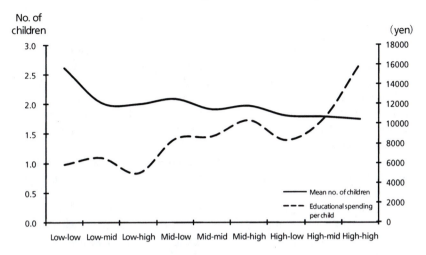

Figure 3.10 Mean number of children and per-child educational spending by husband and wife's educational level

Source: The 2005 SSM survey
Note: Sample aged 30-49

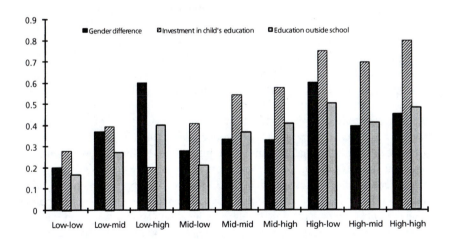

Figure 3.11 Attitudes to child-rearing by husband and wife's educational level

Source: The 2005 SSM survey
Note 1: Gender difference: "Boys and girls should be brought up differently."
Note 2: Investment in child's education: "Children should be given the most expensive education possible."
Note 3: Education outside school: "Children should be given extra education through a home tutor or after-hours crammer."

The level on the left is that of the respondent to the survey; the level on the right is that of the respondent's spouse.

leading to more fluidity in the stratification structure itself. However, there is still a shortage of rigorous theoretical and empirical analysis on the question of what exactly is the significance of a high rate of homogamy within a society. In an attempt to remedy this shortage, I have attempted here to analyze levels of investment in child-rearing and degree of awareness of the importance of child-rearing among married couples with varying combinations of educational attainment. This is because I take the bringing up of the next generation as a concrete activity that can perpetuate the class status of the parental generation or lead the children's generation to a higher level.

Figure 3.10 shows the mean number of children and per-capita spending on child-rearing against level of parental educational attainment.[10] Our results show that the number of children declines, and per-capita spending inversely rises, as parental educational level climbs. Couples where both partners had low levels of education had the most children and spent the least on bringing up each of them. In contrast, couples where both partners had high levels of education had the fewest children and spent the most on bringing up each of them. These results match those that relate household income to numbers of children (Shirahase 2008). Many people throughout Japanese society complain of the high cost of child-rearing. However, the content of child-rearing varies widely with income level and social class, and people of high socioeconomic class tend to have fewer children and spend more on each of them. Ultimately this signifies a more positive investment strategy to pass on high social class to the next generation.

Moving on to the topic of attitudes toward childrearing, Figure 3.11 maps the strength of various attitudes against parental educational attainment.[11] The figure shows results for three questionnaire items which showed statistically significant differences in child-rearing attitudes. The bar on the left of each cluster shows gender awareness in bringing up child(ren) – i.e. the degree to which couples saw it appropriate to apply different principles to the rearing of boys and girls. The very high results for couples where one parent had a low level and the other a high level of educational attainment are interesting, but must be read with care, since this kind of marriage is rare and there were only five cases with a low-level respondent and high-level spouse and five cases of the opposite pattern. Perhaps more significant is the relatively high level of gender awareness among couples where both partners had high levels of education. Highly educated Japanese people tend to be critical of the traditional gendered division of labor, but when it comes to bringing up their own children, it seems that their attitudes may not be quite as "gender-free" as one might expect. When we look at gender differences in attitudes toward child-raising, highly-educated women married to similarly highly-educated men are more likely to make distinctions based on the gender of their children than any other combination of gender and educational level. Another point which I like to emphasize in terms of our results here is that the questionnaire only asks if the principles to the rearing of children should be different, and it does not go on to ask in what way it should be different. Therefore, more positive answers on gender difference in child-rearing principle does not necessarily mean that the respondents have conservative gender attitudes towards child rearing. It may rather imply that highly-educated couples are more likely to be concerned about gender in raising their children, because they care more about gender as an important social issue that impacts on childrearing strategy.

A second question, on attitude toward investing financially in children's education, found an especially high level of positive responses among couples where both partners had high-level education. Among couples where the respondent had mid-level education, there was a distinct upward curve matching the level of education of the spouse, indicating that the educational level of one's marriage partner is a significant influence on one's own attitude to education. Overall, we find that where both partners have a low level of education they tend to pay relatively little attention to their children's education, whereas highly-educated couples tend to be very enthusiastic about educating their children. We may therefore confirm that the combination of educational levels in a married couple is indeed an important factor influencing the education of the next generation and the transmission and perpetuation of parental class status.

The final question, about attitudes toward sending one's children to cram schools or hiring private tutors for them, showed a similar pattern to the other two results. About half of highly-educated couples agree that their children should do extra-school work and receive supervision from private tutors. Highly-educated people are very much concerned about their children's educational achievement, regardless of the educational level of their spouse. It appears that they make extra effort to help their offspring to follow in their footsteps and inherit their advantageous social class position.

Conclusion

This chapter has sought to analyze Japan's aging society, characterized by a low fertility rate and the postponement or avoidance of marriage, from the perspective of social stratification theory. Who gets married? Whom do they marry? How is individual marital activity related to macro-level class formation? This research represents one attempt to get a handle on these issues. At present I cannot claim to have demonstrated more than a rudimentary level of analysis, but I hope to build on the findings presented here toward more thoroughgoing research.

The trend toward non-marriage was confirmed for men with low levels of education, and for women of all groups. A chronological division of the data into the two periods from the mid-1980s to mid-1990s, and from the mid-1990s to the mid-2000s, hinted at a possible qualitative difference between the two periods. Among Japanese men, the trend towards non-marriage appears to have leveled out in recent years among those with mid- or high-level education, whereas the non-marriage rate still seems to be rising fast for men with only a low level of education. For women, by contrast, the trend toward non-marriage seems to have come to a halt among those with low levels of education, while it has proceeded yet further among those with medium and high levels of education.

Looking at the eras covered by the SSM surveys used in this chapter, the 1985 to 1995 period was a rollercoaster, including the zenith of the bubble economy and its subsequent collapse, while 1995 to 2005 included a sizeable chunk of the so-called "lost decade" and was largely an era of economic recession. Throughout both periods, however, the average age at first marriage continued to rise for men and women alike, as it has done ever since 1980. However, marital behavior does come across as strongly gendered. For women, average age at first marriage rose steadily, irrespective of economic circumstances, whereas for men the pace of increase in age at first marriage eased off from 1990 to 2000. It is hardly surprising that the macroeconomic environment influences marriage behavior; however, that influence is far from uniform, and its significance was seen to differ between men and women.

For example, the rise in the non-marriage rate for low-education men seen in recent years is related to the rate of youth unemployment and the steady rise in non-standard forms of employment (Kosugi 2003). For young males who are expected to support a family as the main breadwinner, inability to find stable employment is a major obstacle to marriage. We may assume that the prolonged post-bubble recession was a particularly severe blow for men with low levels of education, already in a weak position in the labor market. In contrast, the rise in non-marriage among women after the recession set in during the mid-1990s was most pronounced among those with mid-to high levels of education. Looking at a pool of possible marriage partners whose wages were falling in response to the recession, many women refrained from marriage because they could not find what they considered a suitable partner. That said, the popular theory that declining marriage rates result from a mismatch between "poorly-educated men who cannot get married" and "highly educated women who won't get married," comes across as an over-simplification, since the high rate of homogamy in Japan means that poorly-educated men and highly-educated women are not necessarily competing in the same marriage markets.

In recent years we have seen a particularly noticeable narrowing of the gender gap in non-marriage rates among the highly-educated part of the population. This part of Japan's marriage market seems to be distinctly segmented from the rest of it, and within it the rate of non-marriage is much the same for men and women. We have also seen a closing of the gender gap in mean age at first marriage, with women's non-marriage rates rising in pursuit of men's within the same class. In that sense, women have gone further in catching up with men in the highly-educated class than in any other, and it seems fair to conclude that a substantial sub-class is developing among highly-educated men and women: a sub-class that never marries. In striking contrast, the low-education class exhibits a dramatic widening of the gender gap, with the non-marriage rate for men rising sharply in recent years. People with low levels of education are of course at a disadvantage in labor markets; our data suggests that they now also face higher barriers within the marriage market, particularly for the men. We also observe a striking increase among poorly-educated men in the proportion who never marry, suggesting that at the present point in time, trends in labor and marriage markets are moving in direct correlation with each other.

We also considered the significance of educational homogamy for social class structure and found clear evidence of class differences in the degree of enthusiasm for investing financially in nurturing the next generation. Highly educated couples showed high educational aspirations for their offspring, investing a lot of money in bringing up and educating a small number of children. Our analysis demonstrates that this could be characterized as a mechanism to pass on more certainly the parents' privileged social class to the children. At the same time, among homogamous couples, those with low levels of education showed the most negative attitude toward their children's education. Just as the highly educated couples effectively passed on their privileged class to their offspring, so, too, the relative negligence of the poorly educated couples would tend to pass on low class status to the next generation. To put it another way, it is not so much that the high incidence of educational homogamy we have observed here solidifies the social class structure as that the degree to which the parental generation is willing to work positively to defend the class of the children's generation tends to promote the maintenance and inheritance of the existing structure of class relations.

Acknowledgements

I am grateful to the 2005 Social Stratification and Social Mobility (SSM) research committee for the permission to use the SSM surveys. The 2005 SSM survey was supported by the Grant-in-Aid for Specially Promoted Research of the Japanese Ministry of Education, Culture, Sports, Science, and Technology (grant number 16001001). I would also like to acknowledge the support of the Grant-in-Aid for Scientific Research (S) of the Japan Society for the Promotion of Science (research project, "A Comprehensive Study Examining the Forms of Social Stratification in an Aging Society and Constructing Public Norms," grant number 20223004).

Notes

1 In the oriental calendar, the year of the fiery horse (*hinoeuma*) occurs once every 60 years. Girls born in that year are thought to grow up as intractable, self-willed women and so the fertility rate tends to drop sharply in that year, especially for baby girls.

2 South Korea is undergoing an even more drastic decline in the total fertility rate than Japan. As of 2005 over-65s accounted for only about 10 percent of the Korean population, but the pace of increase was ahead of Japan's. It is estimated that it will take only about 17 years for South Korea to increase its over-65 population from 7 percent to 14 percent of the whole (National Institute of Population and Social Security Research, 2007).

3 Defined as the percentage of the population that has never been married by the age of 50.

4 The respondents of this survey is wives aged 50 and under. The valid number of the sample for analyses was 6,836 (see the report by National Institute of Population and Social Security Research (2006) for further information on the survey).

5 A word of caution: the data here shows the mean period in years between completion of education and marriage, among people who are already married. In this era of increasingly postponed marriage, the fact that this data was calculated from people

already married (in their twenties or thirties) could be seen as introducing an element of selection bias.

6 The same caveat applies as for my discussion of Figure 3.6: the sample of young married people contains a very small number of low-education cases, 19 cases for women and 55 cases for men in the 2005 SSM, so the statistics should be taken as suggestive rather than authoritative.

7 This analysis is restricted to people who were still living with both their parents at the age of 15. The survey found 407 people (7.7 percent) had no father in the household at age 15, 72 (1.4 percent) had no mother, and 25 (0.5 percent) had neither.

8 Respondents assessed their standard of living at age 15 by choosing one of five options from "poor" to "affluent." These responses were then converted to a five-point scale for analysis.

9 The 2005 SSM survey did not include a question on spouse's father's main occupation, so we are limited to discussing homogamy in terms of educational attainment only for the present.

10 In order to control for age effects, this analysis was restricted to people in their thirties or forties.

11 This analysis was also restricted to people in their thirties or forties.

References

Atō, M. (2000) *Gendai Jinkōgaku: Shōshi-kōreika Shakai no Kiso Chishiki* [Contemporary Demography: Basic Knowledge on the Low Fertility Rate/Aging Society]. Tokyo: Nihon Hyōronsha.

Blau, P. and Duncan, D.O. (1967) *The American Occupational Structure,* New York: Wiley.

Chase, I. (1975) "A comparison of men's and women's intergenerational mobility in the United States." *American Sociological Review* 40: 483–505.

Erikson, R., Goldthorpe, J.H. and Portocarero, L. (1979) "Intergenerational class mobility in three Western European societies: England, France, and Sweden," *British Journal of Sociology*, 30: 415–41.

Glass, D. ed. (1954) *Social Mobility in Britain*. London: Routledge.

Glenn, N., Ross A. and Tully, J. (1974) "Patterns of intergenerational mobility of females through marriage." *American Sociological Review* 39: 683–99.

Heath, Anthony (1981) *Social Mobility*. Fontana Paperbacks: Glasgow.

Hiroshima, K.(2000) "Kin'nen no gōkei tokushu shusseiritsu no yō'in bunkai: fūfu shusseiritsu wa kiyo shite inai no ka?" [Decomposing factors in recent trends in the special fertility rate: Is the fertility rate among married couples not contributing?]. *Jinkō Mondai Kenkyū* [Research on Population Problems] 26: 1–19.

Iwasawa, M. (2002) "Kin'nen no kikan TFR hendō ni okeru kekkon kōdō oyobi fūfu no shussei kōdō no henka no kiyo ni tsuite" [On the contribution of changes in marriage and childbirth behavior among couples to changing trends in total fertility rate in recent years]. *Jinkō Mondai Kenkyū* [Research on Population Problems] 28: 14–44.

Japan Ministry of Health, Labor and Welfare (2007) "'Heisei 18-nen jinkō dōtai tōkei geppō nenkei (gaisū)' no gaikyō" [Outline of the 2006 annual digest of monthly dynamic population statistics (approximate figures)].

Kalmijn, M. (1991) "Status homogamy in the United States," *American Journal of Sociology* 97: 496–523.

Kaneko, R. (2004) "Shōshika katei ni okeru fūfu shusseiryoku teika to bankonka, kōgakurekika, oyobi shussei kōdō no sokutei" [Decline in the fertility rate among married couples, the delay in marriage, the increased level of education, and the measurement of fertility behavior]. *Jinkō Mondai Kenkyū* [Research on Population Problems] 60: 37–54.

Kosugi, R. (2003) *Furiitaa Toiu Ikikata* [Freeter as a Way of Life]. Tokyo: Keisō Shobō.

Lipset, S.M. and Bendix, R.(1959) *Social Mobility in Industrial Society*, Berkeley, CA: University of California Press.

Mare, R. (1991) "Five decades of educational assortative mating," *American Sociological Review* 56: 15–32.

Miyamoto, T. (1999) *Fukushi Kokka Toiu Senryaku: Sueden Moderu no Seiji-Keizaigaku* [The Welfare State as Strategy: a political-economic study of the Swedish Model] Tokyo: Hōritsu Bunkasha.

Myrdal, A. and Myrdal, G. (1934) *Kris I Befolkningsfrågan* [The Crisis of the Population Problem], Stockholm.

Nakanishi, Y (2003) "Takata Yasuma no jinkō riron to shakaigaku" [Takata Yasuma's population theory and sociology], in I. Kaneko ed., *Takata Yasuma Rikabarii* [Resuscitating Takata Yasuma]. Tokyo: Minerva Shobō: 110–29.

National Institute of Population and Social Security Research (2007) *Latest Demographic Statistics 2007*, Tokyo: National Institute of Population and Social Security Research.

—— (2006) *The 13th National Fertility Survey*, Tokyo: National Institute of Population and Social Security Research.

Portocarero, L. (1985) "Social mobility in France and Sweden: women, marriage and work." *Acta Sociologica* 28: 151–70.

Shida, K., Seiyama, K. and Watanabe, H. (2000) "Kekkon shijō no henyō" [Change in the marriage market]" in K. Seiyama ed. *Nihon no Kaisō Shisutemu 4: jendā/shijō/kazoku* [Class Stratification System of Japan 4: gender, market, family], Tokyo: Tokyo Daigaku Shuppankai.

Shirahase, S. (2005) *Shoshi Korei Shakai no Mienai Kakusa: Jenda, Sedai, Kaiso no Yukue* [The Unseen Gaps in an Aging Society: Locating Gender, Generation, and Class in Japan] Tokyo: Tokyo Daigaku Shuppankai.

Shirahase, S. (2008) "Kodomo no iru setai no keizai kakusa ni kan-suru kokusai hikaku" [International comparison of economic differentials among households with children]. *Shakai Seisaku Gakkai-shi* [Journal of the Social Policy Study] Vol. 19: 3–20.

Sugita, N. (2006) "Shōshika mondai to shakai seisaku: Myrdal to Takata Yasuma." Topic for free discussion, *Shakai Seisaku Gakkai-shi* [Journal of Social Policy Study].

Takata, Y. (1925) *Kaikyū Oyobi Dai-san Shikan* [Class and the Third View of History]. Tokyo: Kaisō-sha.

—— (2006) (originally published in 1926) "Umeyo ueyo" [Give birth and proliferate]. Reprinted in *Keizai Ōrai* [Economic comings and goings]. July edition.

Watanabe, H. and Kondō, H. (1990) "Kekkon to kaisō ketsugō" [Marriage and marital association], in H. Okamoto and M. Naoi (eds) *Nihon no Kaisō Kōzō 4: Josei to Shakai Kaisō* [The Japanese Stratification Structure 4: Women and Social Stratification], Tokyo: Tokyo Daigaku Shuppankai.

Yamada, M. (1999) *Parasaito Shinguru no Jidai* [The Age of Parasite Singles]. Tokyo: Chikuma Shobō.

Part II
Class sorting

4 From credential society to "learning capital" society

A rearticulation of class formation in Japanese education and society

Takehiko Kariya

Introduction

Japanese society has long been seen, particularly by Western observers (e.g. Cummings 1980) as an egalitarian society, with meritocratic philosophy and practices. Until recently, these images of Japanese society have been shared by most Japanese people as well. In various survey instruments designed to measure social stratification, the majority of people identify themselves as some variation of "middle class" (Naikakufu). Moreover, some studies (Tachibanaki 1998) show that the extent of income inequality through the 1970s and 1980s was much smaller than that found in other industrialized nations, such as the US or the UK. This data has led writers in both academic and popular literatures to define Japan as a "classless society" or "middle-class society" (*ichioku sō chūryū shakai*) (Murakami *et al.* 1978).

These images of egalitarianism and equality have been supported by an understanding of the educational system as a reliable, if demanding, mechanism of meritocratic achievement and social mobility. The phrase, "examination hell" (*juken jigoku*) has epitomized this rigorous competition. It has commonly been assumed that through academic achievment in this educational meritocracy, all students are offered equal life chances, regardless of their social origin or class background. While the social and personal costs of this severe competition are high, Japanese education has been perceived as having an overall positive effect on both the levels of academic achievement of the population as a whole and on the production of a comparably narrow range of social class positions, from top to bottom. Thus, some academics (Asō and Ushiogi 1977) have argued that despite an education system that allocates young people into different socioeconomic positions strictly on the basis of meritocratic achievement, Japanese society also has produced broad patterns of equality, a rather unusual resulting pattern. These representations of the relationship between society and education have captured the subjective experience of many Japanese within the system as well as the mainstream commentary in the popular literature (Asō and Ushiogi 1977, Ushiogi 1980).

However, recently, the Japanese media has begun to report changing perceptions of society. Polarization of income, lifestyles, "hopes," and educational achievement have been the focus of both media and academic attention. Over the last few years, there have been several bestselling books on social differentiation that document increasing inequality (e.g. Sato 2000, Yamada 2005, Miura 2005). Some of these arguments focus on the emergence of what is called a "class society," with reduced social mobility, more class closure and increased rigidity overall (especially in higher, non-manual positions) from one generation to the next. Others focus on patterns of expanding discrepancy in income, job security, consumption practices, and even educational achievement. Both groups often criticize neo-liberal reforms adopted by the current government as one of the factors that have produced or exacerbated the emerging patterns of inequality.

In this chapter, I focus on the patterns of differentiation in Japanese education in order to articulate and evaluate these claims of an emerging "class society." Education is a particularly privileged site to examine this dyanmic because differentiation in achievement and attainment among children is often influenced by their parents' socioeconomic-cultural status on the one hand, and linked to the students' future life chances on the other hand. Therefore, one advantage of focusing on differentiation within education is that we can isolate and predict future societal changes in connection with social class influences. I begin the chapter by asking a number of related questions. To what degree have patterns of inequality in education expanded? Have the dynamics of meritocracy in Japanese education changed? How much does social class background influence educational achievement and attainment? What societal mechanisms are behind those changes?

I will argue that we are seeing a shift from a previous pattern of Japanese meritocracy. That is, we are seeing a shift from what was once called a "credential society" (*gakureki shakai*) to a new society that I will call a "learning capital society." I will argue that this shift in the articulation of capital from credentials to competencies is contributing to the emergence of a new dyanmic of class cleavage. I focus especially on individuals' learning competencies, which are a combination of skills and attitudes, and include eagerness to learn, learning habits, initiation of active learning and the acquisition of facilitating skills. Then, I will analyze how these learning competencies are becoming central to the formation of a new type of human capital as Japanese society shifts to a more "flexible" labor regime, a knowledge economy in both education and employment, for the twenty-first century. Finally, by showing that these learning competencies are not equally distributed among schoolchildren, I will argue that this emerging regime will also lead to a newly configured class society, in which socioeconomic inequality is increasingly defined by and articulated through the unequal distribution of learning competencies, rather than simply levels of achievement and their documentation in credentials.

Japanese credential society as the pre-history of "learning capitalism"

To understand the recent changes in Japanese egalitarianism and meritocracy, social class and capitalism, it is instructive to begin by looking at how Japanese meritocracy has been transformed in the postwar period. During the 1970s and 1980s, *"gakureki-shakai-ron"* (translated as the discourse of "Japanese credential society") appeared in Japanese academic literature to describe the meritocratic characteristics of Japanese educational attainment and sorting within a particular social structure. More popularly, it became known as a distinctive and perhaps unique "J-mode of credential society."[1] In this regard, it could be said to have captured a "common-sense" acceptance of the relationship between education and society, particularly as it relates to career advancement in employment. *Gakureki-shakai* (hereafter called the "J-mode educational credential society")[2] was a commonly-used term and easily found in newspapers, TV news, books, and policy discussions in business and governmental councils.

This J-mode credential society is composed of two elements: on one side is schooling though which academic achievement and educational attainment are structured, and on the other is employment, where career attainment and advancement is based on the results of this educational sorting. The J-mode credential society is understood as the mechanism that generated the extreme academic pressure referred to as "exam hell," or the severe competition among students to pass entrance examinations for prestigious schools and universities. Because admission to both high schools and universities is organized through standardized entrance exams, students are stratified according to their academic achievement scores. Examinations are mostly objective tests of discrete pieces of information, often with a multiple-choice or short-answer format. In order to enter a competitive university, students are forced to prepare for these exams by cramming for years on end. Thus, competition for entrance to selective schools and universities pits students against one another, putting them under great pressure. According to many journalists, educators and policy makers (Rinji Kyōiku Shingikai 1985), the J-mode credential society is regarded as a primary cause of a variety of social problems within the school, including bullying and school violence, as well as a factor disrupting students' lives outside school, leading to student alienation and even suicide.

Furthermore, the curricular content that constitutes the vast majority of entrance exams is generally acknowledged to have virtually no bearing on any part of students' lives besides the exam-taking itself. Critics contend that the information that is taught in schools, especially that which is part of exam preparation, has little relevance to any future job requirements and virtually no connection to young people's lives outside a very narrow measure of academic achievement. Nevertheless, some degree of mastery of this exam knowledge is essential for the successful preparation for exams, and thus the tests are powerful tools that motivate students to work hard. While the relationship between intellectual ability and exam scores remains quite obscure, these scores are thought to measure the degree of commitment and sacrifice students are willing to make in order to secure educational credentials and eventual occupational advantage. Put in psychological terms, under the J-mode educational society, students study for the exams out of "extrinsic motivation" rather than any "intrinsic motivation" (Ichikawa 2001).

As educators and policymakers became increasingly aware of the variety of social ills associated with the J-mode educational credential society, it was diagnosed as a "disease," sometimes referred to as "diploma disease" (Dore 1976), despite the fact that educational reforms have long sought ways to abolish or at least diminish the deleterious effects of this J-mode credential regime. While the rhetoric of these reforms has often explicitly focused on the ill effects of this "disease" for many years, empirical evidence linking any negative academic or social effects to the J-mode educational credential society has been lacking. Thus, it has been quite difficult to measure the effectiveness of any particular reforms even if they did get implemented, and by the same token, difficult to systematically generate new reforms with any confidence. In fact, a review of some of these reforms suggests that in many cases, reforms that were designed to ameliorate these various dysfunctions may have often had the opposite effect of reinforcing or even exacerbating social inequality (Kariya 2001).

Under the J-mode credential society, graduates from highly selective universities are offered more chances to work for larger firms or public offices, which provide better economic and social rewards. These graduates are offered not only the chance to be employed by privileged workplaces, but also a better chance of being promoted after they secure employment. They receive positions that usually ensured higher levels of job security, especially under the assumption of "lifelong employment" a practice popular at the time. As a result of this link between education and work, these "winners" in the J-mode credential society, namely graduates from prestigious universities, are highly likely to enjoy much better career chances. These two components of the J-mode credential society are closely linked, mutually reinforcing the credibility of the educational sorting mechanism and its perception of the legitimacy of its results. In this model, it is considered obvious and "natural" that great rewards are given to winners, and so, getting into better schools is very advantageous to secure employment and life status. On the other hand, this perceived relationship makes competition to enter prestigious schools increasingly severe, more selective, and more competitive as the school becomes the final arbiter in determining life course.

However, recently the J-mode credential society regime is undergoing a transformation that appears to be mitigating the severity of the self-perpetuating selection system and reducing competition. There have been many new school policy initiatives attempting to introduce new curricula which emphasize learner-centered ideals of pedagogy. Also, the demographic decline in the number of students completing high school has also reduced pressure on students as they compete for university entrance. We will discuss both of these features in more detail below.

Second, on the employment side, rapid changes have taken place as well. Partly because of the economic recession of the 1990s and partly because of pressures to cut labor costs, the job market for new graduates and young people dramatically changed during the 1990s and early 2000s. The number of part-time jobs increased, job turnover rates increased, and the lifelong employment system was no longer assumed to function for young workers. Today, a much higher rate of fluidity and instability characterizes the youth labor market, with differing effects on the self-perception and subjective understanding of young people. The number of "freeter" (a neologism from the contraction of the English word "free" and the German word "arbeiter," meaning temporary or part-time employee) and NEET (a term originally used in British social policy, meaning those Not in Education, Employment, or Training) has greatly increased. Statistics indicate that there were about 3 million freeter between the ages of 18 and 35 in the early 2000s. While there is some appeal among young people to finding employment that does not bind them to a very demanding company for the whole of their lives, recently more of the negative features of this sort of employment are also being documented. Because most of these jobs are in the low-level service sector, these young people lack job security and earn substantially lower wages, with greatly reduced opportunity to learn valuable occupational skills while working (Genda 2001, 2005). In this climate of "flexible" labor, fewer companies are willing to invest in training any new labor, especially for those in the part-time sector (Ohki 2003).

At more elite levels of society, images of a new career trajectory have also emerged. Young entrepreneurs such as Mr. Mikitani of Rakuten or Mr. Son of Softbank, both presidents of fast growing IT companies, provide a new corporate image and model of career success for able young people. These young entrepreneurs opted out of large companies or public offices and launched their own businesses, amassing a great fortune from stock options. These new success models contrast with the former success model under the J-mode credential society, in which lifelong employment and status promotions within a large company were central to a successful career. The new model conveys the message, particularly to the younger generation, that they do not have to wait for many years to realize their talents as long as they believe in their own potential and are willing to take a risk in their careers. Clearly, degrees from highly selective universities are still correlated with better job opportunities, particularly at large firms. Nevertheless, even for many graduates of the most prestigious universities, there is increased uncertainty about job security. Large and famous companies like Sony have announced that they will no longer consider university names when making hiring decisions (although it is difficult to evaluate any change in actual practice that announcements such as this one might have generated). With an increased number of students ending up as "freeter" and NEET, if educational achievement cannot be reliably and predictably translated into desirable occupational success, we can say that the assurance of a smooth transition from school to work that was once a defining characteristic of the J-mode credential society has been called into question.

All of the changes detailed above indicate the nature and scope of the transformation of the J-mode credential society. However, it is not clear yet what direction this shift is taking. To predict the direction, we must focus on the accumulation and formation of human capital because changes in successful career trajectories are supposed to reflect changes in the process of human capital formation (Kariya 2008). I argue that these transformations of the J-mode credential regime show the emergence of a "new class society," where *learning competencies* are the core of the new types of human capital formation. In place of the exam-taking skills which were crucial to success under the J-mode educational credential society, the *ability to learn* has come to occupy the central place in the new class society.

Job competition model and trainability

To understand the importance of learning competencies and the ways that human capital formation are changing, an analytic model of "job competition" is useful. This model is provided by the American economist Lester Thurow (1975).Thurow suggests that a real labor market does not fit the so-called "wage-competition model" used by neo-classical economists, and in particular, by human capital analysts. In the neo-classical argument, workers are regarded as competitors for higher wages. Human capital, which is composed of skills and knowledge used in the workplace, is mostly learned before the workers enter the labor market.[3] Instead of this neo-classical model, Thurow introduces what he calls a "job-competition" model which proposes that workers compete for jobs, not for wages. The job competition model presumes that workers do not have fully valued vocational skills prior to entering the workplace, but instead learn many essential skills through on-the-job training, after being employed. Therefore, employers are more concerned with selecting workers who have the potential to learn skills efficiently. Unlike the wage competition model, in which employers seek workers who already have skills directly applicable to the jobs, the job competition model contends that employers seek workers who have higher "trainability" indicators because the skills needed by the employers will be learned on the job. "Trainability" is a concept that refers to one's competencies or readiness to be trained; workers with higher trainability indicators can learn skills faster and more efficiently than those with lower trainability indicators. Of course, this is important to employers because workers with higher trainability will involve lower training costs, and be more able to learn new skills as the nature of their work changes. As we will discuss later, a clear corollary exists between workers' trainability and learning competence. Thurow also suggests that employers use the job seekers' background characteristics – such as education, gender, and race – to predict their trainability.

The job competition model seems to fit the J-mode credential society well for several reasons. It fits with the Japanese discourse on credential society, in that graduates are hired not because they have learned any relevant skills or accumulated any particularly valuable knowledge by the time they leave schools to enter the workplace. That is, the job competition model does not assume that workers possess useful skills prior to entry into the labor market, but rather that firms will provide important training on the job after hiring the workers. As the job competition model assumes, the J-mode credential society also envisions a society in which long-term employment is desirable and able to be secured. This allows workers to use the skills learned on the job for a relatively longer period of time in the same firm, thereby offering the firm a better investment in the training of its employees.[4]

If we use the job competition model as our guide, we can see the J-mode credential society model as rationally organized and efficiently functioning during the high-growth postwar period. This would suggest that employers were capable of screening workers utilizing the names of the universities or high schools from which they graduated as an index of trainability. The entrance exams to get into university could then be understood to measure students' trainability (rather than simply achievement), and thus, even if the universities themselves did not teach their students any relevant skills or knowledge, graduating from a particular university would convey useful information to employers as they screened potential employees. Thus, even if Japanese schools and universities do not teach any relevant skills for future careers, the rank and reputation of the schools would still certify students' trainability.

However, under the conditions of the J-mode credential society, it is not clear how important trainability is in the explanation of workers' successful careers because trainability, opportunities to learn skills, and career paths all overlap in life-long employment and advancement processes. The ports of entry into jobs are determined by employers' decisions based on indexes of trainability, usually indicated by the rank of universities or high schools from which applicants graduated. In the J-mode credential society, career paths and opportunities to learn skills usually develop at the same time in ways that prevent us from being able to analytically separate them. Of course, both are strongly influenced by early career stages (Takeuchi 1995); the early career stages are affected by the ports of entry into jobs, which again are allocated based upon the schools and universities attended and graduated from. Afterward, the first positions assigned to the workers tend to link in a predictable way to future career trajectories.

Trainability is a form of learning competence, which is a combination of eagerness to learn skills and acquire knowledge, good learning habits, being able to initiate active learning, and having the ability to learn how to learn, so to speak. But trainability is strongly and deeply embedded in career structure in this J-mode credential regime. Even if workers do not explicitly know how to obtain training and improve their skills themselves, their career paths necessarily lead them to opportunities and structures of training. Thus, trainability is a latent factor in explaining career successes, but its influences are very difficult to isolate and its effects very difficult to measure. Moreover, one might say that in the J-mode credential regime, individual high learning competencies are not necessarily regarded as so important partly because trajectories and opportunities of both training and promotion are strongly correlated and therefore it is difficult to distinguish relative influence or causality, and partly because for both, subsequent opportunities for training to enhance learning competences and promotion are greatly influenced by the entry jobs.

The narrow definition of "trainability" is one aspect of the larger and more generalized concept of "learning competencies." In order to better understand the transformations that are going on in today's market, we need to focus on this wider "learning competence." Like human capital theories, Thurow's job competition model also implicitly assumes that valued skills and knowledge are structured and provided by employers in a form that can be easily and regularly accessed by workers, and which employers can call upon to provide and structure training. But this is no longer the case in Japan. Particularly, as life-long employment disappears, firms are no longer providing long-term training for entry-level workers, and thus we cannot assume that firms will be able to develop these competencies in their workers. Instead, today it is the responsibility of the workers to accumulate these skills and knowledge and thus develop these competencies on their own.

In the contemporary Japanese context, not only can the company no longer be assumed to be the source of training but the very nature of competencies must be reevaluated. A much broader and more flexible concept of learning competencies becomes necessary in today's flexible and fluid labor markets. What is called for is a much more general and self-reflective notion of learning competencies that will include the ability to learn, adapt and improve by recognizing and exploiting disparate resources (including those not provided by the company at all). "Learning" in this new context requires competencies that go beyond the ability to be trained for a particular job or position. In the "knowledge economy,"or "high skills society" (Brown *et al.* 2001), skills and knowledge required for a job change so rapidly that workers cannot acquire them fully within the context of their job experience. Without high learning competencies, which enable workers to find and develop suitable and appropriate skills wherever, however and whenever they are required, workers will be unable to exploit the full range of learning situations to their own advantage and, eventually, will miss the chance for career advancement.

Finally, it is no longer the employers who make the effort to train employees; indeed, it is not considered the employer's responsibility to do so. Instead, it is now the workers who are required to shoulder the risks and responsibility for developing and improving their own skills. These changes are transforming the representations and practical formation of human capital in the Japanese labor market today. More flexible ways of human capital formation have become more important than ever before. Workers must have not only the knowledge and skills to be trained, but also the learning competencies to know how to learn in innovative and self-directed ways in order to fully participate in, and contribute to, this rapidly changing knowledge-based economy. Successful workers must move from being "trainable" to being more generally competent if they are to be of value to their employers, as well as if they are to thrive or even survive in this new fluid market as their career trajectory takes them from one employer to another. Thus, transformation of the J-mode credential society emphasizes, beyond trainability, the significance of learning competencies, which are a combination of eagerness to learn, good learning habits, initiating active learning, and learning how to learn. Today, all of these tasks must be understood as the worker's own responsibility.

Educational reforms and learning competencies

As social and economic needs shift, new skills and new competencies are necessary, not only in Japan, but also in all industrialized societies. Brown *et al.* (2001) contend that in a "high skills society," the new set of skills involve greater emphasis on problem-solving, cooperation, collaboration, and the like. They insist that under a new and more flexible paradigm of employment, skills required for professional and managerial jobs shift from "Fordist" to "Post-Fordist" skill sets. In Japan, too, borrowing the idea of "knowledge worker" from Drucker, one Japanese management consultant characterizes the importance of new styles of learning as follows:

> Knowledge workers are individuals with more autonomous resources, who properly fit within the new knowledge economy. Regardless of age, these workers make attempts to solve problems in changing environments through continuously developing new potentials and exploiting new knowledge.
>
> (Yamazaki 2000)

These discursive shifts, emphasizing the importance of learning, have very different implications from those in the former J-mode credential society regime. Under the credential regime, achievement in school was measured by the individual's ability to take in large amounts of intrinsically irrelevant knowledge for the sake of entrance examinations. On-the-job training under long-term employment was the primary mode of skill transmission but was often seen as lacking flexibility. Knowledge and skills learned on the job were limited in scope and thus ended up being obsolete quite quickly. Advocates of learning competency insist that the J-mode credential society must adapt to the knowledge economies of the twenty-first century. This pattern has been echoed in the educational literature as well. In education discussion as early as the 1980s, two lines of argument emerged: one was to reform educational practices at the level of classroom pedagogy in an effort to push Japan out of its exam-oriented education mode. The other was to proceed towards a "life-long learning society."

In the late 1980s, the *Rinji Kyouiku Shinjikai*, the Prime Minister's Ad-hoc Council for Education Reform, was set up by Yasuhiro Nakasone, and began a series of reports that were very critical of the J-mode credential society regime. According to the council, Japan had finally caught up with Western industrialized societies, and therefore the education system should shift its emphasis from just cramming in knowledge to more creative and independent learning practices. "Creativity" (*sōzōsei)* and "individuality" (*kosei*) were the keywords in the reforms.[5] The Council also proposed that *gakureki-shakai* (the credential society) should shift to a "life-long learning society" (*shōgai gakushū shakai*) in which people are given more chances to develop their own potential throughout their lives, in school and beyond. Unlike in the J-mode credential society, where learning is organized around the passing of university entrance exams during adolescence, the proposed new style of learning would continue throughout one's life. The

Council insisted that second and third chances to learn after schooling should be given to all, and that the new school curriculum must be organized around a longer perspective. Thus, creativity, individuality, and expanding opportunities for lifelong learning were seen as the means to develop young people's and the nation's full potential. These factors were all thought to be necessary for Japan to survive in the twenty-first century under a knowledge-based economy.[6]

Since then, many reform plans have been proposed and some parts of them implemented. So-called "room for growing" educational reforms (*yutori no kyōiku*) have been implemented in the following ways: to transform the cramming in of knowledge into learner-centered education; to reduce onerous demands on children; and to establish multiple criteria to measure students' achievement. All of these emphasize the importance of learning competencies. Below is a brief summary of these reform ideals, how they were manifest in policy rhetoric, and an outline of the actual effects.

Since the early 1990s, a new perception of academic achievement/ability (*atarashii gakuryoku kan*) has been introduced. This new pedagogical philosophy emphasizes the importance of students' self-learning competencies for critical discovery and problem-solving instead of teacher-centered education, in which learning is manifest usually as rote memorization of information and facts.[7] While difficult to actually pin down in any specific programmatic statements, the key words surrounding educational discourses of this period shift from a focus on the content of teaching to the styles of learning, and particularly to self-learning (*mizukara manabu*). "Life studies" (*seikatsuka*), a new subject that combines social studies and sciences, was introduced in the revised national curriculum in 1989 for first and second graders in elementary schools. Life studies is designed to integrate a set of skills and concepts that fosters children's intellectual growth by calling upon their own experiences, thereby motivating them to find and develop their own interests. In the same line of thought, integrated learning across subjects (*sōgōteki na gakushū no jikan*) has been introduced for all students from third to twelfth graders. This new subject area asks teachers to design a curriculum particularly suitable to the students at each different school. It is thus suggested, even demanded, of teachers not to teach in the former teacher-centered style of pedagogy but rather to support and stimulate students in ways that encourage students to learn for themselves. One of the famous slogans from this period is "shidō yori shien wo" ("from guidance to support"), indicating a new student-teacher orientation as well as a new pedagogical goal and style to reach that goal. Thus, not only do these reforms demand new types of curriculum and pedagogy, but also new forms of social relations between teachers and students, all designed to promote students' active exploration of self-learning through the school curriculum.

Secondly, to remove pressure from students – especially in test-oriented education – the contents of national curricula have been reduced by about 30 percent, with classes no longer being held on Saturdays. "Return children to communities and families" is the phrase capturing the ideal, and it is also supposed to give more "room for growing" to all children. Unfortunately, when the reforms were implemented, many local communities lacked sufficient funding to provide any educational replacement programs on Saturdays, and less wealthy families did not have enough resources to provide meaningful activities for their children.

Third, multiple criteria to measure students' achievement have been introduced both for daily teachers' evaluation and entrance examinations. Thus, students are no longer evaluated simply on their exam scores, but instead, admission procedures also include letters of recommendation, student essays, and some systematic review of other non-academic skills or strengths in order to have a fuller picture of each student's ability, potential and achievement. In daily teachers' evaluations, students' interests, motivations, and attitudes are regarded as integral parts of academic achievement and reported in school transcripts and report cards (*tsūshinbo*). Some high schools and universities now place more emphasis on student achievements reported in school transcripts and accept students on the basis of recommendation by their high schools instead of only through the regular entrance examination procedure.

Thus, in contrast to the J-mode credential society, this new set of educational reforms is designed to serve as the foundation for the development of a lifelong-learning society that can provide all people with the opportunity to continue learning after leaving school by developing their own individual potential through "self-learning," "learning how to learn," "learning by doing," and "learning through the community." Expanding learning opportunities was and still is expected to increase chances to learn, chances beyond the period of university entrance exams, thereby providing second and third chances to develop oneself, as well as to reduce pressures at the point of entrance exams.

But reformers tended to ignore the fact that the discursive shift and set of policy initiatives through which this new lifelong learning society was generated could also create a strong social norm, a set of expectations that would compel everyone through a particular learning route throughout their lives, whether or not they desired it, whether or not they had the material support, whether or not they had the outside opportunities to take advantage of this route. In other words, one can never stop learning; in order to enrich his/her life economically, socially, and culturally, but also to maintain one's status as being productively employed and secure occupational status, he/she has to continue learning and improving, adapting and exploiting new opportunities. Thus, reformers put into place a set of expectations that could easily develop into a norm requiring everyone to learn forever in the lifelong learning society.

Demographic decline and market shifts

In addition to these reforms, demographic changes have also reduced entrance examination pressures. The numbers of 18 year-olds have declined significantly since the 1990s, decreasing from more than 2 million in 1992 to 1,260,000 in 2008. Thus, independently of any educational reforms introduced, college admissions have become much less selective. As a result, except for highly ranked universities and top rank high schools and private junior high schools, the most severe competition for admission has disappeared. Nearly half of new students entering post-secondary and higher education institutions now do not take competitive entrance examinations (MEXT 2008).

Changes in the labor market also have hastened the transformation of the J-mode credential society. Due to the increasing number of part-time and temporary jobs, particularly for young people, the labor markets have become divided more clearly and severely than before, into a primary or core labor market, and a secondary or peripheral labor market. This "dual labor market" has also weakened the J-mode credential society by placing more importance on learning competence. The numbers of jobs which require high skills are limited and difficult to secure, while there is an increasing number of temporary and part-time jobs that require low skills offering only limited opportunities to develop learning competencies. Once workers, particularly young ones, are allocated into the secondary labor market, few can improve their learning capacities or upgrade their skills sufficiently to allow them to move up into jobs within the the primary labor market. These shifts have a number of different effects.

Opportunities to learn skills are no longer provided automatically by the workplace. The coordinated trajectories among learning opportunities, career success and the formation of human capital, once characteristic of the J-mode credential society with lifetime employment, have now become disaggregated within the new economy. The skills, knowledge and technology required by employers that must be mastered by employees is changing faster than even personnel and management can often keep up with. Accordingly, what employees learn becomes out of date much more quickly. Individuals are required to renew skills and update knowledge, and to obtain new skills and develop new familiarity simply to keep the jobs that they have, let alone transfer to better ones. Finally, employers are no longer willing to wait for a return on their investment in employee training; they need to see demonstrable outputs in a much compressed time frame. They want to see more results more quickly and thus, demand that workers learn skills quickly and work more efficiently. Employees have to adapt themselves to the changes in this very fluid market more rapidly or face relegation to an even less secure secondary market.

Diminishing job security and long-term employment means that workers must pay their own training costs, costs which had been paid at least in substantial part by the employer in the earlier, more stable markets. Responsibility for human capital accumulation has shifted to the workers themselves. Self-development (*jiko-kaihatsu*) and self-education (*jiko-keihatsu*) are today commonly used words that capture this shift of responsibility to the individuals for their own working lives. This new and more dynamic definition of learning competencies over and against the anachronistic "on-the-job-training" (*shanai kyōiku*) of the J-mode credential society becomes all the more important in such a fluid and insecure labor market that is especially precarious for young people.

The rise of learning capital society

As discussed above, the labor market bifurcation has developed into more distinctive tracks in recent years. The initial ports of entry into jobs determine not only workers' economic rewards but also future opportunities to learn skills and to improve learning competencies. In the primary labor market, job security is higher, opportunities to learn skills are greater, and there are more chances to improve learning competencies as well. In contrast, in the secondary labor market, usually the "dead-end jobs" of part-time or temporary work, opportunities and resources to learn skills are limited and scarce. The divide between these two labor markets explains why it is so difficult for workers to transfer from secondary to primary labor markets. Different opportunities to learn skills are a key factor here.

By nature, any sort of learning is an incremental process, and this includes self-learning. Learning competencies are developed and expanded through learning itself. The more one learns, the more one's learning competencies improve, and the more one is able to learn. With higher learning competencies, one can recognize learning resources and opportunities more proficiently and exploit them more efficiently. Given the same availability of learning resources, those with higher learning competencies will be able to utilize the resources more efficiently, and thus learn more than others. On the other hand, in a context where there are fewer available learning resources and fewer learning opportunities, or where learning competencies are of uneven or compromised quality, a vicious circle develops. In such a case, even if individuals have good initial learning competencies, their competencies diminish over time if they are not continuously exposed to and engaged in active learning opportunities. As a result, human capital not only fails to develop, but can spiral downward and end up being "devalued" or even obsolete in this quickly-changing market if and when a job is secured. We would expect that the greater the segmentation of the dual labor markets becomes, the more divergence in the distribution and development of individual human capital between those two markets. If this premise is correct, differences in learning opportunities not only produce differences in acquired vocational skills, but also create gaps in learning competencies. This results in individual differences in learning efficiency as well as in the social structural characteristics associated with the dual labor markets.

Furthermore, if learning competencies acquired through school education become used as a screening device to allocate different people into the primary or secondary labor markets, it will be increasingly difficult to move from the secondary into the primary markets. If this happens, the way learning competencies are distributed in relation to individuals' socioeconomic and cultural background will become an important question because the differentiation of learning competencies that occurs in the early stages of life will be crucial to the shape of one's occupational trajectory and life chances.

In sum, through different learning processes and contexts, human capital is formed differently. With better opportunities and resources, and higher learning competencies, learning creates more learning, and thus more human capital.

And the opposite is equally true: for those who are in disadvantaged learning situations, their diminished competencies will continue to compromise any future chances. Once learning competencies become a key factor in the formation of human capital, opportunities to improve learning competencies become crucial in determining life chances. With higher learning competencies, individuals' investment in their own human capital becomes more efficient. Thus, insofar as learning competencies are the core of human capital development, we can call it a form of "learning capital." High learning competencies, as in other forms of capital, continually increase in value, and can be transformed into other forms of capital, such as human capital, cultural capital (through a richer learning environment in the family, for example), social capital (through the development of a wider and more effective social network) and financial capital (through expanded occupational opportunities). Here we also find a mechanism, embedded in the transformation processes of the J-mode-credential society, of how learning capital divides people into two separate worlds: haves and have-nots. Therefore, as in other capitalist societies, a learning capital society is one where the unequal distribution of capital leads to social inequality, and its reproduction over time. This is the dynamic we will examine in the next section.

Social class differences in learning competencies

This line of discussion raises a question: what is the effect of the shift from the J-mode credential society to a lifelong learning society on different segments of society? Has this transformation of capital facilitated or even promoted the development of a society in line with egalitarian ideals? As learning competencies are becoming more important for everyone's ability to survive in society as a whole, the opportunity to develop adaptive and marketable learning competencies at younger ages becomes all the more crucial for each individual's life chances. This raises a second and related question linked in important ways to education: are learning competencies distributed equally regardless of individuals' socioeconomic and cultural background? We have seen that educational reforms are ostensibly aimed at establishing and developing learning competencies necessary for individuals' market survival and the development of the market as a whole. If chances to learn these skills in employment are harder to acquire in any systematic way for some segments of the population, then our schools must take responsibility for developing learning competencies at early stages in young people's development. But if schooling fails to do this, and instead *expands* the unequal distribution of learning competencies, ideals of lifelong learning represent a betrayal to its egalitarian ideal – one primary ideal that educational reformers set for themselves. The final section of this chapter examines the effect of these educational reforms and their implications under today's quickly changing labor market and wider society.

It has been argued that schooling is vital in the development of learning competencies and crucial for future learning and future life chances. If learning competencies are unequally distributed at an earlier stage of life, differentiation in the processes of incremental accumulation of human capital may be irreversible. If some children are exposed to fewer or lower quality learning chances, the effect of this differential exposure will retard initial development, and have lifelong effects. If lifelong competencies are linked in this way to early exposure, it cannot be convincingly argued that subsequent failures to develop such competencies by an adult is attributable to individual irresponsibility. Rather, in this case, the development of competencies would have to be considered the effects of systemic unequal exposure to learning situations in childhood. That is, systemic effects institutionalized through the very school system educational reforms have targeted as the primary site to develop learning competence in every child.

Are different social classes of young people being systematically exposed to different learning situations in ways that demonstrate a clear difference in the ways they develop learning capacities? This is an important question because of the way that the school channels young people into the dual market. But more enduringly, it is important because it points to an issue that educational reformers have often ignored in their attempts to make schooling more adaptive to shifting conditions in the labor market and society: the school's role in the development of social class inequality. It seems that the educational reforms assumed that if every child had his/her own interests in learning and every school and teacher could develop individual students' interests appropriately, no such class differentiations would appear. If every child were acting in her or his own best interest, and if all schools and teachers were able to promote and support students properly, a truly meritocratic system would emerge, one where the full range of distributive talent, ability and drive would be rewarded regardless of the differences in socioeconomic or cultural background of students.

In reality, not all schools and teachers are able to provide learning opportunities and resources sufficient for all students to develop in this way. When the schools fail to realize this goal, it is the most vulnerable students who are most adversely affected. Especially students from disadvantaged families, those who have the least support from their parents and home environments, are more likely to fall behind in developing learning competence as well as basic skills. Since methods to nurture these new competencies are not yet well developed in actual classrooms, even well-intentioned practices may actually hurt these students. From both students' and parents' points of view, it is not easy to find concrete ways to develop these competencies when the school fails them. In sum, although the ideals of education reforms seem clear, real classroom pedagogy designed to allow students to acquire those goals is still not fully developed and is unevenly practiced. Eventually, students with the least support from their families may be more likely to miss out on important opportunities to develop these learning competencies, and thus never develop the mechanism of lifelong human capital formation.

Survey instrument

It is not easy to measure individuals' learning competencies, in part due to the fact that it is best considered an ability to adapt to a number of different stimuli that develops over time, rather than a set of discrete degrees of achievement, such as could be measured in entrance exams. Nonetheless, we can observe the development of these competencies indirectly by examining individuals' learning attitudes. On the behavioral level, learning competencies can be indicated by students' learning attitudes. We attempted to develop an instrument that would allow us to measure these attitudes as reliable indicators of leaning competencies. In our survey, we conducted two basic tests of Japanese language and mathematics. The survey was conducted in 16 public elementary schools and 11 public junior high schools in Japan in 2001. In total, 921 fifth grade students and 1,281 eighth grade students were surveyed.[8]

We ran a factor analysis with variables of students' learning attitudes. Factor analysis allows us to construct an underlying unobservable factor (which we call "learning competency") from the observed variables. Students were asked to indicate among the following variables which ones accurately characterize their own in-class behavior.

"I always take notes in class."
"I often raise my hand and give my opinions in class."
"When I don't understand, I ask my teacher."
"When I make a mistake in exams, I always correct it afterward."
"I actively engage in research in class."
"I am often a leader in group-work activities."

The variables above are designed to measure students' degree of active participation and their perception of themselves as taking responsibility for their own learning. These were judged to be central to the main construction of "learning competencies," that is, of being able to "learn how to learn." Because "learning competence" includes the ability to recognize and exploit learning situations, we tried to specify those paradigmatic situations relevant to the students' immediate situations that would offer them this sort of chance, and then to measure self-perceptions of performance in those situations. It should be noted that the last two questions were designed to measure students' attitude toward the set of recent educational reforms that focused on "New Perceptions of Academic Achievement/Ability" (MEXT 1993). We assumed that the higher a student's score, the more positive his/her learning attitudes were, and therefore, the higher his/her learning competence would be. Based on the results of these tests, we organized the respondents into three groups: a Higher LC ("learning competence") Group, a Middle LC Group, and a Lower LC Group, each of which was composed of one-third of the students sampled.

In order to use this sample to address the issue of students' social class position, we examined the data to determine correlation between levels of LC and family background. Because we have no data on parental occupation, education or income, in order to test the influence of family background on LC, we ran a factor analysis with variables from the students' family cultural variables. These variables presented a gradient from "culturally rich" to "culturally poor" based on indicators from students' home life, such as if their family regularly "watches news on TV," "owns a computer at home," "takes trips to museums," "read books to me when I was young," and "baked sweets at home." Using the frequency of each of these activities, a one-dimensional statistical measurement was created by factor analysis, and students were grouped into the following three categories: High Cultural Group (HCG), Middle Cultural Group (MCG), and Low Cultural Group (LCG), each of which consists of almost one-third of the sampled students. In this analysis, we used these variables as indicators of social class background, reflecting students' socioeconomic position.

To see the relationship between students' learning competencies and the standard measures of academic achievement, we compared the mathematics and Japanese language mean test scores. Figure 4.1 (for fifth grade students) and Figure 4.2 (for eighth grade students) both show that the higher the LS, the higher the achievement test scores. Correlatively, the lower LC group students show the lowest test scores; the high LC group students have the highest scores. Thus, we can conclude that learning competencies are positively related to students' conventional academic achievement. The same result is confirmed by regression analyses with test scores of eighth graders as dependent variables (Table 4.1). Even after controlling for gender, the grades students received on report cards in elementary school, and cram school attendance, students' learning competencies have a significant positive effect on test scores.

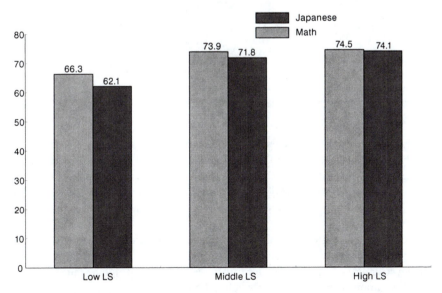

Figure 4.1 The mean of test scores of students with different learning competencies (5th grade)

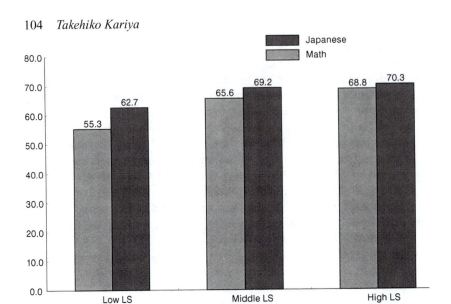

Figure 4.2 The mean of test scores of students with different learning competencies (8th grade)

Table 4.1 Regression analyses for test score (8th grades)

| | Mathematics | | | Japanese | | |
	B	Beta	Sig.	B	Beta	Sig.
Constant	39.797		0.000	50.931		0.000
Male dummy	−3.425	−0.070	0.008	−9.008	−0.239	0.000
JUKU attendance	17.194	0.353	0.000	7.694	0.204	0.000
Grades in elementary school	4.792	0.235	0.000	4.913	0.311	0.000
Learning competencies	4.184	0.173	0.000	1.961	0.105	0.000

How are learning competencies distributed? Figures 4.3 and 4.4 show the results of cross-classifying students' learning competence groups and their family background as measured in LC groupings. As the figures indicate, it is obvious that those students from families with higher cultural status are more likely to have higher learning competencies. This is true for both fifth and eighth grade students.

Next, we ran a regression analysis for learning competence scores with family background, cram school attendance, and gender as independent variables. As shown in Tables 4.2 and 4.3, both for fifth grade students and eighth grade students, the two dummy variables of family cultural background have significant effects. Those from lower cultural background groups tend to have lower LC scores. On

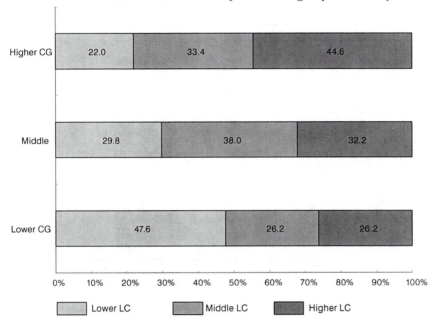

Figure 4.3 Cross tabulation table: family background by students' learning competencies (5th Grade)

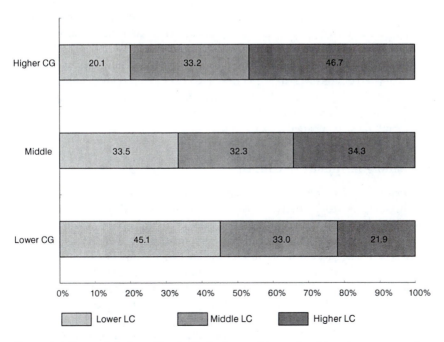

Figure 4.4 Cross tabulation table: family background by students' learning competencies (8th grade)

Table 4.2 Regression analysis predicting learning competencies (5th grade)

	B	Beta	Sig.
Constant	−0.059		0.374
Male dummy	0.051	0.026	0.451
JUKU attendance	0.076	0.035	0.298
Cultural–low	−0.287	−0.136	0.000
Cultural–high	0.362	0.166	0.000

Table 4.3 Regression analysis predicting learning competencies (8th grade)

	B	Beta	Sig.
Constant	−0.172		0.005
Male dummy	0.264	0.132	0.000
JUKU attendance	0.070	0.035	0.219
Cultural–low	−0.294	−0.136	0.000
Cultural–high	0.333	0.155	0.000

the other hand, the higher the cultural background of the students, the higher the LC scores, after controlling for other independent variables. In other words, learning competencies are distributed unequally among students from different family backgrounds, even after controlling other variables.

The findings indicate a number of disturbing patterns: first, learning competencies are distributed unequally; second, this unequal distribution is strongly influenced by students' family background. In fact, as early as fifth grade (11 years old) these patterns are already manifest. We can speculate that differences in cultural capital and social capital embedded in family background contribute to the gaps in learning competence. Therefore, if schools fail to develop the learning competencies of these disadvantaged students, then those who have the least support from families eventually face the most severe challenges in developing those competencies later in life.

Expanding inequality in education

The analyses so far indicate that learning competencies are distributed unequally among students from different social backgrounds. In this sense, education reforms in Japan do not seem to have been successful. Thus, it is difficult to see any positive effect in terms of learning competencies, which was, after all, what the educational reforms were supposed to bring about. For all of the policy rhetoric of "individuality" and "creativity," of taking greater initiative for one's learning, etc., it would be impossible from this data to identify any positive educational effect. In fact, it appears that social class background is actually reproduced in relatively regular and efficient ways in both learning attitudes and academic achievement. Not only is there little evidence to suggest that these sets of educational reforms improved anything at all, in fact, there are some indications that they have actually made the situation worse, at least for some segments of the population.

Over the duration of these reforms, there is evidence of expanding inequality in students' academic achievement, in a traditional sense. Due to a lack of comparable data sets from the past, it is not easy to test whether students' social class backgrounds are having a stronger influence on patterns of academic achievements now than they did before. We do not have appropriate data to chart any correlation between students' social class background and their academic achievement over time. However, the survey mentioned above includes the same 16 public elementary schools in which a similar study was conducted in 1989. Both surveys included comparable data on mathematics and Japanese achievement. Also, although the survey in 1989 did not include exactly the same questions about students' family cultural backgrounds, both surveys did have exactly the same questions about students' daily habits, and a series of questions was asked on both surveys about students' daily habits and relations with family members. These focused on a domain one might call "self-discipline." Questions included:

"Do you have breakfast and brush your teeth every morning?"
"Do you use conventional greeting ('tadaima') to your parents when you arrive home?"
"Do you arrange your school satchel the night before?"
"Do you have a fixed bedtime?"

Based on the responses to these questions, we categorized fifth grade students into three groups: Upper Scored Group, Middle Scored Group, and Lower Scored Group. We then correlated these groupings with the test scores for mathematics and Japanese. The distributions of the test scores correlated with the "self-discipline" grouping are shown in Figures 4.5 and 4.6. Both mathematics and Japanese test scores are perceptibly more polarized in 2001 than in 1989. In other words, differences in "cultural capital" seem to be growing. Moreover, these differences appear to have had a greater effect on school achievements in 2001 than in 1986, before the education reforms began. If we consider the "self-discipline" score an indirect indicator of students' social class background, class inequality in traditional academic achievement shown by test scores seems to be expanding under the educational reforms.

Conclusions

We have found that learning competencies are unequally distributed among students, and that social class represented by family cultural background is strongly related to this pattern of inequality. Note that variables here include elements of new academic competencies (and not simply measures of academic achievement), features that were emphasized by the new set of educational reforms, and cast doubt on the efficacy and even suitability of these reforms. Of course, there are limits to the range of claims we can make from this data: we do not know whether

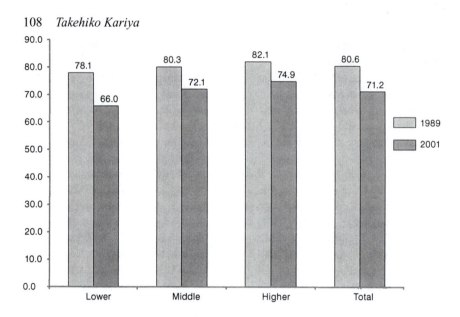

Figure 4.5 Mathematics test scores by students' daily habits (5th Grade)

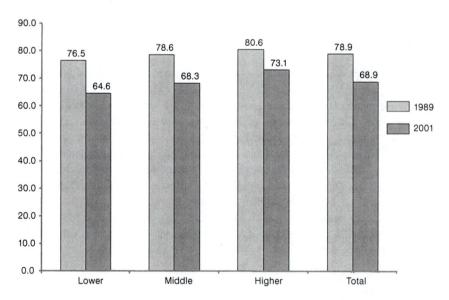

Figure 4.6 Japanese language test scores by students' daily habits (5th Grade)

patterns of emerging inequality are actually created by the educational reforms in question or if they are more general effects of the transformation of the J-mode credential society into today's lifelong learning society. That is, it is not easy to identify the relevant effects of each of our variables. Nevertheless, from these findings we can evaluate the attempt by educational reformers to establish an effective and measurable regime of lifelong learning. We can evaluate the effect of reform on the development of more flexible learning competencies that are both responsive to the new knowledge economy and more able to develop the innate potential of each individual student across the spectrum of social class. The evaluation is negative.

Under the J-mode credential society regime, the goals for success in education were very clear and the rules were very obvious: achieving higher scores in examinations was a clear target and unambiguous goal for everyone, in large part because it was understood as a path to educational, occupational and social success. This widespread agreement among students, teachers and parents supported the assumption that linked educational aspirations and the meritocratic pursuit of socioeconomic success, regardless of social origins. As we saw in the last section, the discrepancies in traditional academic achievement among students with different "self-discipline" scores were smaller before the reforms began. This distressing trend can be attributed to a number of features, as outlined above, and have a number of different possible implications.

Under the new constructions of academic achievement, students are evaluated by teachers on their attitudes, behaviors, interests and learning competencies. Thus, the methods of evaluation have changed from an objective, one-dimensional gradient of test scores to being largely based on teachers' subjective evaluations of a whole range of subtle factors that are very difficult to quantify. Moreover, consensus on the best way to set and attain academic goals also have become less clear because the measurement of students' competencies is more subjective and involves multivariate criteria. While these new forms of evaluation might be more detailed, even more thorough, they also are less likely to point in a single direction, and less likely to generate any unambiguous expectations or desirable practices at either home or school to realize these expectations.

Just as importantly, the collective understanding of how the school is oriented to external goals for success is similarly becoming less clear. Success in school is no longer a guarantee of success in career or life. As a result, the incentives for working hard are less clearly defined. Especially for those at the bottom of the school hierarchy, the high probability of relegation to the secondary tier of the dual labor market could very well signal the futility of hard work to many. Once young people begin to question the possibilities of transferring from the secondary to the primary labor market, it may be difficult for them to maintain high aspirations and motivation to work. Thus, just as an "incentive-divide" (Kariya 2001, Kariya and Rosenbaum 2003) appears to be taking place in the labor market, we would expect to see it also trickle down into secondary schooling.

Of course, the deterioration of a discernible J-mode credential society did not eradicate everything that came before. Learning competencies must have been important even under the former credential society, as discussed above. And in fact, we would expect that learning competencies would have been unequally distributed under that regime, too. But in the previous regime, which stressed the concrete result of academic achievement, from a personal perspective it was thought that through effort and hard work one could overcome a compromised family cultural background. From a more systemic perspective, higher levels of academic achievement were one of the established mechanisms for social mobility over and above the reproduction of family-based inequality. In fact, previous empirical research indicates that there were achievement gaps among students from different socioeconomic family backgrounds even in the era of the credential society (Kariya 1995).Although the gaps were relatively stable until the end of the 1980s, they began expanding during the 1990s and the early 2000s (Kariya and Shimizu 2004). In other words, until the 1990s, the differential among different social classes as measured in conventional academic achievement levels was smaller than it is today.

The shift from the credential society toward a "high skill society" has ushered in new labor requirements and types of human capital. These changes have resulted in shifts into a more clearly visible dual labor market that today divides people not only according to their performances, but maybe even more significantly, according to their general ability, and their ability to continue to learn in this new market structure. What we have called "learning competencies" have thus emerged as a new form of capital, which like other forms of capital, are not equally distributed. The situation appears to be getting worse, and it is not clear that the most recent spate of educational reforms are improving the situation[9]. We do not have any data showing changes in students' learning competence differentiation during the 1990s and into the 2000s, but based on other data that indicate patterns of increasing class-based differentiation of academic achievement measured by conventional tests, we can speculate that the distribution of learning competence is also falling out according to class lines and exacerbating these patterns.[10] If this is the case, we can expect to see other societal and economic changes accompanying the transformation of the J-mode credential society to generate increasingly severe conditions for those students who are from home and school situations that limit their exposure to learning opportunities, and thus their development of adaptive, efficient and successful learning competencies. As the formation of human capital has become less structured through employment, opportunities to improve learning competencies in the workplace have become more limited and less clearly defined. Therefore, differentiation of learning competencies at the early stages of schooling places disadvantaged children in more severe positions than similarly placed students in the J-mode credential society regime. This differentiation seems to be exacerbated, rather than ameliorated, by the present state of schooling, which is characterized by the introduction of a series of educational reforms with very little positive impact.

It is a bitter irony, of course, that neither educational reformers nor advocates of "knowledge workers" intended these reforms to increase patterns of inequality in learning competencies. Rather, they tried to remove "useless" learning that was generated by what they saw as excessive emphasis on the preparation for exams. They attempted to introduce more "authentic learning," both in education and employment, under the banner of "lifelong learning." It was supposed that every student or worker would have his/her own interests, motivation and ability to learn to develop into a more fully-realized learning competence. It is possible that if there existed truly open and universal accessibility to potential learning opportunities, this intention might have proved correct. But in practice, the unrealistic idealism, one that ignored the pre-existing differential distribution of these all-important learning opportunities, has worked in exactly the opposite way. In fact, "learning competencies," understood as a product of the shift in market structure and human capital formation characteristic of this new "knowledge economy," are proving to be just as strongly correlated to class divisions, and may very well prove to be even more so over time, than the older notion of academic achievement and occupational training.

Where has the J-mode credential society gone? Our answer is found in today's "Learning Capital" society. As discussed above, learning competencies are the core engine that structures and runs the accumulation and distribution of this new form of human capital. Given better learning competencies, individuals are able to utilize learning resources and opportunities more efficiently and more meaningfully (and even more enjoyably). Employers look for those with higher learning competencies and give them better learning opportunities. Of course, inequality in learning competence expands through different patterns of exposure in the workplace, but it begins in the school.

Is this a new type of class society? So far as learning competence is unequally distributed among children from different social class families, this is certainly not any more of an egalitarian society than what preceded it. Thus, we can call this class society a new form of human capitalist society, namely, a "Learning Capital Society," where social and class inequality is manifest between those with high learning competence and those without. As reformers intended, the J-mode credential society has indeed been radically transformed, and in some ways, eradicated altogether. But the lifelong learning society that has replaced it has brought upon us a potentially more divisive, even polarizing "Learning Capital Society," an outcome that few reformers would have foreseen.

Notes

1 Ishida (1993) summarizes discourses which characterize such distinctive nature of Japanese educational credentialism.
2 The term "J-mode" was used by Kaneko (2007) in a different context, in which he characterized relationships between higher education and occupation in terms of knowledge formation.
3 Human capital theories do not deny that new skills are learned after hiring, but the initial hiring decisions are still mainly based on academic achievement, a measurement of human capital that is constituted by the skills and knowledge obtained through schooling.
4 Some sociologists of education in Japan have borrowed Thurow's idea to propose a "Company Competition model," which resembles Thurow's original idea. The difference is that in this adaptation, competition is for a place at a particular firm rather than for a particular job (see Kobayashi 1985).
5 "Creativity" (*sōzōsei*) is used often in phrases such as "Japanese people lack creativity due to their cramming style of learning in school," or "Because we lack creativity,

Japan has a smaller number of Nobel Prize winners." "Individuality" (*kosei*) is another key word in education, with the usual suggestion that it is something that Japanese lack compared with Westerners. However, the contents of these two terms are not well-defined and the methodologies designed to nurture them are not well articulated in the educational policy reform rhetoric.

6 See the arguments made by Honda (2005).
7 Of course, not all learning and teaching were rote memorization of knowledge and facts even in the 1980s (see Lee, Graham, Stevenson 1996).
8 For details of the survey, see Kariya and Shimizu (2004).
9 In 2008, the Ministry of Education released a new national curriculum. The Central Council of Education, which generated the revision, admitted that the education reforms in the 1990s and 2000s are not working well and decided to increase the contents of curricula and class hours. Additional resources were necessary, but the government has not yet approved budget increases sufficient to implement these revisions.
10 Results of PISA indicate that influences of socioeconomic background on students' PISA-type learning competence, which is supposed to be the type needed in the twenty-first century knowledge economy, are moderately expanding (OECD 2007).

References

Asō M. and Ushiogi M. (eds.) (1977) *Gakureki Kōyō-Ron* [Studies on Effects of Educational Credentials], Tokyo, Yuuhikaku.

Brown, P., Green, A. and Lauder, H. (2001) *High Skills: globalization, competitiveness, and skill formation*, Oxford: Oxford University Press.

Cummings, W. K. (1980) *Education and Equality in Japan,* Princeton, NJ: Princeton University Press.

Dore, R. (1976) *The Diploma Disease: education, qualification, and development*, Berkeley, CA: University of California Press.

Genda, Y. (2005) *A Nagging Sense of Job Insecurity: the new reality facing Japanese youth*, trans. Jean Connell Hoff, Tokyo: LTCB International Library Trust, International House of Japan.

Honda, Y. (2005) *Tagenka suru "Nōryoku" to Nihon Shakai* ["Ability" to Diversify and the Japanese Society], Tokyo: NTT Shuppan.

Ichikawa, S. (2001) *Manabu Iyoku no Shinrigaku* [Psychology of Learning Motivation], Tokyo: PHP Publisher.

Ishida, H. (1993) *Social Mobility in Contemporary Japan: educational credentials, class and the labour market in cross national perspective*, Stanford, CA: Stanford University Press.

Kaneko, M. (2007) *Daigaku no Kyōiku Ryoku* [Educational Power of Universities], Tokyo: Chikuma Shobō.

Kariya, T. (1995) *Taishū Kyōiku Shakai no Yukue* [The Rise of Mass Education Society], Tokyo: Chuoukoronsha.

——— (2001) *Kaisōka Nihon to Kyōiku Kiki* [Expanding Stratification and Crisis in Education in Japan], Tokyo: Yūshindo.

——— (2008) *Gakuryoku to Kaiso* [Academic Achievement and Social Class], Tokyo: Asahishimbun Shuppansha.

Kariya, T. and Rosenbaum, J.(2003) "Stratified incentives and life course behaviors" in *Handbook of the Life Course* edited. by Jeylan T. Mortimer, Michael J. Shanahan, London: Plenum Publishers, pp.51–78.

Kariya, T. and Shimizu K. (eds.) (2004) *Gakuryoku no Shakaigaku* [Sociology of Academic Ability], Tokyo: Iwanami Shoten.

Kobayashi, M. (1985) "Rōdōshijō no kōzō to senbatsu riron [The labor market structure and the theories of selection]," *Kōtō Kyōiku Kenkyū Kikō* [Bulletin of Institute for Higher Education] 4: 59–73.

Lee, S., Graham, T. and Stevenson, H.W. (1996) "Teachers and teaching: elementary schools in Japan and the United States," in T. Rohlen and G. LeTendre (eds) *Teaching and Learning in Japan*, Cambridge: Cambridge University Press.

MEXT (Ministry of Education, Culture, Sports, Science and Technology) (1993) *Atarashii Gakuryokukan Nitatsu Kyōiku Katei no Sōzō to Tenkai* [New Perceptions of Academic Achievement/Ability and Creative Development of School Curricula], Tokyo: Tōyōkan Shuppansha.

—— (2008) *Kokkousirhitu Daigaku Tankidaigaku Nyūgakushasenbatu Jissijoukyō no Gaiyō* [Summary of Implementations of Admissions for New Students by 4 year and 2 year Colleges], http://www.mext.go.jp/b_menu/houdou/20/09/08092911.htm

Miura, A. (2005) *Karyū Shakai* [Downstream Society], Tokyo: Kōbundō.

Murakami Y., Kishimoto S. and Tominaga K. (1978) "Debate on the New Middle Class," *Japan Interpreter* 12 (Winter 1978): 1–15.

Naikakufu (Cabinet Office), (each year) *Kokumin Seikatsu nikansuru Ishiki Chōsa* [National Survey of People's Life], http://www8.cao.go.jp/survey/index-ko.html

OECD Programme for International Student Assessment (PISA) (2007) *PISA 2006: Science Competencies for Tomorrow's World: Volume2: DATA*, Paris: OECD.

Ohki, E. (2003) "The characteristic of the investment activity for the education and training in corporation and the regulation factors," *Nihon Rōdō Kenkyū Zasshi* [The Japanese Journal of Labour Studies], 514: 4–14.

Rinji Kyōiku Shingikai (Ad-hoc Council on Education) (1985) *Kyōiku Kaikaku nikansuru Dai 1 ji Tōshin* [The First Proposal for Education Reforms], Mombujiho, Monbusho, Tokyo: Gyōsei

Sato, T. (2000) *Fubyōdō Shakai Nippon* [Japan as Unequal Society], Tokyo: Chūō Kōron Shinsha.

Tachibanaki, T. (1998) *Nihon no Keizai Kakusa* [Economic Inequality in Japan], Tokyo: Iwanami.

Takeuchi, Y. (1995) *Nihon no Meritocracy* [Meritocracy in Japan], Tokyo: University of Tokyo Press.

Thurow, L. C. (1975) *Generating Inequality: mechanisms of distribution in the U.S. economy*, New York: Basic Books.

Ushiogi M. ed. (1980) *Yureru Gakureki Shakai* [The Shifting Educational Credential Society], Tokyo: Shibundo.

Yamada, M. (2005) *Kibō Kakusa Shakai: "make gumi" no zetsubōkan ga nihon wo kirisaku* [Society of Hope-Disparity: the tearing of Japan by the sense of hopelessness among the 'losing side'], Tokyo: Chikuma Shobō.

Yamazaki, H. (2000) "Nihon kigyō wo sosei suru knowledge keiei [Knowledge management to revitalize Japanese enterprises]," *NRI Research News*, March 2000. HTTP: www.nri.co.jp/opinion/c_news/2000/pdf/rn20000304.pdf

5 Social class and economic life chances in post-industrial Japan

The "lost generation"

Mary C. Brinton

Introduction

The reproduction of social class across generations has been a salient topic for Japanese sociologists for many decades, much as it has been for sociologists in Western industrial societies. The optimistic "thesis of industrialism" popularized by modernization theorists in the 1960s predicted that with increasing industrialization, universalistic criteria such as education would come to outweigh social class origins in determining a person's social class position and economic fate (Kerr *et al* 1960; Levy 1966; Treiman 1970). But as empirical analyses of intergenerational class mobility accumulated in the 1970s and 1980s, it became clear that people's social class origins remain an important influence in their adult lives. While the inheritance of social class may diminish as societies industrialize, eventually a plateau seems to be reached (Erikson and Goldthorpe 2008; Grusky and Hauser 1984). Studies comparing intergenerational class mobility in various industrial countries have demonstrated that the idea of an ever-evolving trend towards greater intergenerational mobility across class boundaries is (unfortunately) not borne out.

Japan is no exception to this generalization (Ishida *et al.* 1991; Ishida 1993). Despite the widespread perception both inside and outside Japan that it is a "credential society" where education is the key to socioeconomic success and, likewise, hard work is the key to education, Japan is actually quite *unexceptional*: opportunities for intergenerational mobility via educational attainment in Japan are no more open than in other societies. Ishida's landmark comparative study (1993) of intergenerational social mobility in Japan, the U.S., and Great Britain effectively shattered any conception that access to higher education in Japan is more open to individuals of varied social class backgrounds than in those two societies. Moreover, Ishida found evidence that the effect of social background on higher educational attainment in Japan increased across the cohorts coming of age between 1930 and 1975.

How about the effects of education and social class background on an individual's social class destination? Here as well, Ishida demonstrated that Japan is similar to other industrial societies: a person's social class background exerts an independent effect, irrespective of its effect via educational attainment, on one's social class position in adulthood. This is further supported by the updated findings in Ishida's chapter in this volume. In short, we can comfortably assert that social class reproduction is as alive and well in Japan as it is in other advanced industrial societies, despite the prevailing popular conception in Japan – at least until very recently – that anyone can overcome lowly class origins if they exert enough effort.

This chapter takes up the broad question of how Japan's "lost generation" will experience the economic effects of their social class origins as their adult lives progress. The "lost generation" refers to Japanese who finished school and tried to begin their working lives during the recession of the 1990s. Much has been written about the difficulties this generation experienced as companies cut back on hiring new graduates in an effort to reduce costs and survive in the difficult "post-bubble" economic environment (Genda 2001; Honda 2005b). But few people have addressed whether social class has had much to do with *which* young people were the hardest hit in this tough labor market (Genda 2007). Are there reasons to think that youth from lower social class backgrounds have been more negatively affected than others by employers' changing hiring and employment strategies? I think there are.

I will suggest in this chapter that Japanese youth in the lower strata of the class structure have become especially economically vulnerable in the past 15 years. Their opportunities for securing a stable income over their life cycle are being strongly thwarted by the fact that they have reached young adulthood at a historical moment when Japanese employment relations are undergoing transformations that work to their disadvantage.

Does this mean that social class background is generally becoming a more significant factor in determining Japanese individuals' labor market success? That is the second large question I wish to raise in this chapter. The answer rests on whether recent Japanese labor market transformations are permanent or have instead been a temporary adjustment to the recessionary economic circumstances in Japan in the 1990s and beyond. If it is the former, then we can expect a widening disparity in the economic life chances of Japanese in their twenties and an increasing role of social class background to be harbingers of things to come – the beginnings of a secular trend of widening economic inequality and greater economic repercussions from intergenerational class reproduction among members of each successive cohort. This would mean that the current cohort represents a turning point. But if instead, recent changes in employment relations are mainly the result of Japanese employers' adjustment to economic recession rather than to more fundamental changes in the post-industrial domestic and global economy, then a more appropriate view of the current generation should be as a "lost cohort" or "lost generation" sandwiched between prior cohorts and future ones. This latter view would rest on the assessment that Japanese employment relations have only *temporarily* become less stable due to economic recession and that social class background advantages and disadvantages only became temporarily salient for this generation.

This is a crucial issue, and one that we cannot yet definitively resolve. Its resolution depends not just on gathering more data (which would be the social scientist's "easy way out" of such a dilemma) but also on what one views as the most important underlying causes of the current generation's widening economic outcomes. My view is that the current generation is indeed best viewed as "lost" in the sense of being sandwiched between cohorts who came of age during prosperity and those who will come of age in a moderately restored Japanese economy where many employers will pass over the thirty-somethings who could not gain a toehold in the labor market when they should have. I return to this crucial issue of "historical turning point" vs. "lost generation" later in the chapter, once I have sketched the empirical outline of how the labor market position of the current generation of less-advantaged youth compares to prior generations.

Before beginning my analysis of this question, I want to distinguish between social class and economic life chances. We can think of economic life chances as encompassing the material resources to which one has access, including capital assets (e.g. in the form of land ownership, stocks, dividends, etc.) as well as the wages one obtains through working. These are generally correlated to social class but they are not the *same* as social class, as evidenced for instance by the contrast between a small business owner who employs other workers (and is thereby a capitalist by virtue of owning the means of production) and a much higher paid white-collar employee.

The aspect of economic life chances with which this chapter is concerned is success in the labor market, i.e. wage- and salary-earning success. I consider whether greater economic differentiation between individuals who will or will not succeed over their lifetime in the context of the Japanese labor market may be increasing substantially for the present generation. If earnings differences – economic life chances – are increasing across classes of workers, then whether or not social class is being reproduced across generations more strongly than before, the *economic implications* of that reproduction may be substantially greater for the present generation than for prior ones. That is, I am not necessarily arguing that social class reproduction itself is strengthening, but that its economic consequences are becoming more stark. My aim is to prod the reader to consider a variety of evidence suggesting the possibility that the old mechanisms of social class reproduction are generating newly severe economic consequences in the context of postindustrial Japan in the early twenty-first century. This context is marked by the fundamental restructuring of employment relations, the reshaping of the sites and processes through which skills are acquired, and the concomitant dramatic changes in how young Japanese move from school into the world of work.

In what follows I will explore the relationships between individuals' social class backgrounds, educational attainments, social class positions as adults, and their economic life chances in Japan, and suggest how these relationships seem to be changing for the current cohorts coming of age. My central contentions are that the economic life chances of young Japanese are becoming more divergent than those of recent prior generations, and that this is due to how employment restructuring chances in postindustrial Japan is altering the already complex relationships among social class, education, and wages in Japan.

My object of analysis is a moving target, so to speak. The cohort that has reached adulthood since Japanese employment relations began to be seriously restructured in the 1990s is not old enough yet for us to know definitively how their early work experiences are going to affect their labor market fortunes as their lives play out. Moreover, systematic work-history data on a sizable enough number of Japanese in their late twenties or early thirties have not yet been collected by either Japanese or foreign social scientists; we cannot truly even understand the relationship between what happened to them when they entered the labor market several years ago and what they are experiencing as they move into the life stage where normatively speaking they should have settled into stable employment. The empirical data I will draw on in the chapter thus comes from a variety of sources rather than from one definitive data set.

In the first section, I draw heavily on Ishida's meticulous examination of the interplay among social class background, education, social class destination, and income in the labor market in his 1993 comparative study of Japan, the U.S., and Great Britain. I use some of Ishida's findings to establish what one might call a baseline understanding of the processes of intergenerational social class reproduction and its economic consequences in twentieth-century Japan. This baseline is what we will have in mind as we explore in the remainder of the chapter the possible implications for youth of the dramatic changes in employment relations in the last decade of the twentieth century and the first decade of the twenty-first century in Japan. Changes in labor demand and in employment relations have rendered "getting one's foot in the door" much more difficult for this generation, especially for high school graduates. Given the strong association between social class origin and education in Japan (as in other industrial countries), the increased difficulties faced by young high school graduates are likely to widen the gap between their economic life chances and those of their university-educated counterparts who generally come from higher social class backgrounds.

Social class and its economic consequences in Japan

While there are various class schemas, one common way of conceptualizing classes is by their relationship to the means of production and to labor. Within the worker or employee class, people are further distinguished by the nature of their work and the degree of skill involved (Ishida 1993). Employers are at the top of the class structure and the non-skilled working class is at the bottom. The probability that an individual will move out of a particular social class background to a different class position as an adult is conceptualized as the probability of social class mobility.

While the level of intergenerational class reproduction is not markedly different in Japan than in other postindustrial societies, there is nevertheless some variability across societies in how permeable the boundaries are between adjacent classes. Ishida's comparative study of the U.S., Japan, and Britain used data collected in 1975 for national samples of men to examine cross-national commonalities and differences in the class structure and its reproduction (Ishida 1993). These 1975 data are particularly suitable here as a reference point because the dominant features of the Japanese employment system (including hiring practices, rewards systems, and a labor market segmented by firm size) were firmly established by this period.

In assessing the probability that a man would move into a different class category than his father, Ishida found a significant boundary between the non-manual (white-collar) class and the skilled working class (blue-collar) in Japan and Britain but not in the U.S. This boundary was particularly marked in Japan, such that "Crossing the 'collar-line' appears to be more difficult in Japan than in Britain, and *the Japanese skilled and non-skilled working classes together appear to form a blue-collar mobility regime where the tendency for reproduction among the blue-collar classes is strong*" (Ishida 1993: 192; italics mine). In contrast, Ishida found no class boundary between the professional-managerial class and the non-manual class in Japan. Strong boundaries between the non-manual and manual working classes were absent in the U.S. (in contrast to Japan) and also did not exist between the professional-managerial and the non-manual working class (similar to Japan). The comparison of Japan and the U.S. suggests that Japan is more rigid in terms of the intergenerational reproduction of blue-collar workers.

Given that the overall degree of social class reproduction in Japan is not lower than in the U.S. and other Western postindustrial societies, and that the degree of reproduction of the manual working classes is relatively strong, why has this not been more visible to the Japanese public? As the editors of this volume note in their introduction, social class has come to the fore only recently in Japanese society, with the publication of books such as Sato Toshiki's *Japan as an Unequal Society* in 2000 that argued that the managerial class has become more closed in recent years.

Three things have probably rendered social class reproduction less striking in Japan than in the U.S. (if we take the U.S. as a case in point). First, social class and race are not as visibly and strikingly intertwined in Japan as in the U.S. As a proportion of its total population, the U.S. has much more sizable minority groups, and the social class distributions of whites and African-Americans in particular are markedly different. The relationship of race to class undoubtedly gives greater visibility to social class reproduction in the U.S.

Second, young Japanese who are unable to support independent households are more likely to live in their parents' households than is true for their American counterparts. This renders the reproduction of low socioeconomic status across generations less starkly visible than when the younger generation is living independently and in poverty.

Third, and most important for us here, wage differences *across* social classes are larger in the U.S. than in Japan. Table 5.1 draws on data presented in Ishida's book that shows men's mean (average) individual income by social class in the two countries. Here, I set the mean income of the non-manual working class at 100 and calculated the mean income for each of the other classes.[1] Men in the employer class clearly have an earnings advantage over the other classes in each country, particularly in the U.S. The situation of the petty bourgeoisie – small shop owners and farm owners – is less advantageous in Japan, partly because this category in 1975 was still comprised of many farmers due to Japan's later industrialization than the U.S. But the comparison of the remaining four class categories across Japan and the U.S. is what I would particularly like to emphasize. Men in the Japanese managerial and professional class have a strong earnings advantage over men in the three categories of the working class, especially the non-manual and the skilled. When we use the average income of a non-manual working-class male as the benchmark, the average Japanese managerial-professional worker earns 36 percent more, compared to 18 percent more for his American counterpart. Skilled working-class and semi- and non-skilled working-class men in Japan reap the same earnings with each other on average, whereas men in the semi- and non-skilled working class in the U.S. reap substantially lower earnings than any of the other classes.

What do these findings signify? First, they show that even in the context of a strong class boundary between the Japanese non-manual working class on the one hand and the skilled and semi- and non-skilled (manual) working classes on the other, the difference in average earnings between non-manual workers and the bottom group – semi- and non-skilled manual workers – is small. Stated differently, we could say that the earnings consequences of intergenerational reproduction in the *lowest* level of the working class in Japan do not appear to be as negative as in the U.S. In contrast, the drop in earnings for the semi- and non-skilled working class in the U.S. relative to skilled blue-collar workers and low-level white-collar workers is quite substantial. This baseline from the 1970s is important to keep in mind when we turn shortly to the experience of the most recent generation.

Second, the earnings gap between low-level white-collar (non-manual) workers and professional/managerial workers appears to be higher in Japan than in the U.S. As Ishida points out, this could be because professional/managerial workers tend to be older in Japan and therefore have more seniority. This brings us to the issue of how various worker attributes contribute to earnings in Japan, and to what has been distinctive about the Japanese earnings regime.

Table 5.1 Mean individual income by social class: Japan and the USA

Social class	Japan	USA
Employer class	169	248
Petty bourgeoisie	98	135
Managerial and professional class	136	118
Non-manual working class	100	100
Skilled working class	88	99
Semi- and non-skilled working class	88	77

Source: Adapted from Table 7.1, Ishida 1993: 213

The effects of social background, occupation, education, and labor force experience on earnings: Japanese distinctiveness

The comparative income data from Ishida's study of social class mobility can be supplemented by studies by labor economists, whose principal focus tends to be wages rather than social class and its reproduction. Tachibanaki and his colleagues (1998) compared the determinants of individual wages across eight countries (Japan, the U.S., Canada, Korea, Australia, the U.K., Germany, and France). Their findings on "occupational wage differentials" (how wages vary across occupations) are consistent with those of Ishida. The rank ordering of occupations by their wage levels is very similar across countries. But the *importance* of occupation in determining wages differs across countries. Among the eight countries they examined, Japan stands out as one of the countries where occupation is least important; that is, occupational wage inequality is low in Japan relative to other countries. As Tachibanaki points out, it is well-established in the social science literature that education and occupation are highly correlated in country after country, so the finding that occupation does not strongly determine wages in Japan is indicative also of the smaller role of education in Japanese wage determination.

Table 5.2 shows the relative effects of social background, education, and labor force experience on individuals' earnings in Japan, the U.S., and Britain, drawing once again on Ishida's comparative study. Social background has a large effect on an individual's earnings in each country, trumping the effect of acquired human capital in the form of education and labor force experience. But what is striking about Japan is that the relative effects of education and labor force experience are the *reverse* of what they are in the U.S. and Britain; that is, *the effect of education pales in comparison to the effect of labor force experience on Japanese earnings.*

The relatively small effect of education on earnings in Japan is very striking, given Japan's reputation as a "credential society." Compared to the U.S. and Britain, education is not as important in Japan in determining an individual's earnings as labor force experience. This has been documented in other studies as well, and is consistent with research showing the relatively small white-collar/ blue-collar wage gap in Japan compared to many other countries, including the U.S. (Brown *et al.*. 1997; Hashimoto and Raisian 1985; Kalleberg and Lincoln 1988). Along with this, it has been noted that Japanese blue-collar workers are

Table 5.2 Relative effects of social background, education, and labor force experience on individual income: Japan, USA, Britain

	Japan	*US*	*Britain*
Social background	39%	37%	44%
Education	19%	32%	38%
Labor force experience	42%	31%	18%
Total	100%	100%	100%

Source: Adapted from Table 4.2, Ishida 1993: 90. The proportion of income explained by education in Britain was rounded by me from Ishida's original figures.

distinguished from their counterparts in Western countries by the similarity between their age-earnings profiles and those of white-collar workers (Hashimoto and Raisian 1985; Kalleberg and Lincoln 1988; Koike 1983). Whereas blue-collar workers in most Western economies do not exhibit steep age-earnings profiles, Japanese blue-collar workers in large firms do. This observation is reflected in Koike's now-classic phrase "the white-collarization of Japanese blue-collar workers." Blue-collar workers in Japan, if they are able to enter a large firm upon school graduation, typically receive on-the-job training and subsequent seniority wage increases as they move through their career in the firm.

An important characteristic of the large "labor force experience effect" on Japanese workers' earnings is that firm-specific experience makes a particularly important contribution to earnings. Thus we can think of labor force experience as having a double-barreled impact on Japanese workers' life-cycle earnings, through the sheer impact of continuous years of work experience plus the added boost contributed by work experience accumulated in a specific firm. This added boost of firm-specific experience holds across workers in firms of different sizes, and is especially large for workers who have spent their careers in firms with over 1,000 employees. In the U.S., by contrast, the effect of total work experience on workers' earnings in mid-career is much lower, the proportion of that effect that consists of *firm-specific experience* is much lower, and the differences across these figures by firm size are much lower (Hashimoto and Raisian 1985).

Several statements can summarize the relationships between social class background, occupation, education, and earnings in Japan that have been traced out in studies by sociologists and labor economists through the 1990s. For simplicity, we can use the U.S. as a counterpart in these statements:

1   The intergenerational mobility barrier between the manual and non-manual working classes appears to be larger in Japan than in the U.S.
2   But an individual's inheritance of a low-level (semi-skilled and unskilled) working class position has not necessarily led to economic consequences that are as negative for the individual in Japan as in the U.S.
3   One reason is that labor force experience is a more important determinant of earnings in Japan, whereas education is more important in wage determination in the U.S. (and Britain). If a young Japanese worker can just "get his foot in the door" to stable employment after graduation, then his earnings prospects are likely to be quite good, regardless of whether he has a post-secondary education or not. Stable employment in Japan has conventionally meant employment in a large firm, and since the 1960s this pathway has been open to new high school graduates (in blue-collar jobs) as well as university graduates (Honda 2004). Large-firm employment is important for Japanese workers' lifetime earnings because the risk of being laid off is lower than in smaller firms, and because age-earnings profiles are steeper than in smaller firms.
4   The contribution of firm-specific experience to lifetime earnings is particularly important in Japan, again in contrast to the U.S. This contribution

is the highest in firms of over 1,000 employees, and it applies to blue-collar (high school-educated) workers as well as to white-collar workers, who are generally university graduates.

This outline sets the stage upon which the younger generation stepped when Japan entered the 1990s. Did young men of lower social class origins continue to enter blue-collar work and accumulate full-time employment experience that would bring them wages that were not too far below those of non-manual workers? Below I describe the changes in labor demand and in employment relations that have rendered getting one's foot in the door so much more difficult for this generation, especially for high school graduates who do not go on to higher education.

Economic recession and labor market transformation: 1990s Japan and beyond

With the onset of its most severe economic recession in several decades, Japan entered an extended period of depressed labor demand in the early 1990s. The causes of this recession are well-known and are documented elsewhere, having to do with the overvaluing of land and other capital assets in the late 1980s. Labor demand plummeted throughout the 1990s, with the ratio of job openings to job seekers falling precipitously. Because Japanese employers have traditionally concentrated their recruitment of new workers so heavily on brand-new graduates rather than on mid-career recruits, the brunt of the decline in labor demand was shouldered by young people rather than by mid-career workers. Moreover, at the same time that labor demand fell, the *nature* of labor demand and labor supply changed in ways that have particularly disadvantaged the least well-educated among Japanese youth – precisely that population that tends to be from the lowest social class origins.

First of all, the Japanese manufacturing sector, which had steadily employed over one-third of the labor force since the 1960s, began to decline in importance after 1992. This decline occurred considerably later than it had in Europe and the U.S., which had experienced employment declines in the manufacturing sector since the 1970s (Honda 2005a; OECD 2001). The impact of this decline was hardest for high school graduates (not university graduates), who had been Japanese employers' main source of labor for manufacturing jobs since the high-growth 1960s. While the ratio of job openings to job applicants fell for new graduates from all educational levels in the 1990s, the drop was especially dramatic for high school graduates. The ratio of job openings for new high school graduates to job seekers rose from 1.07 in 1985 to a peak of 3.08 (or three jobs for every job-seeker) in 1992, then shot downward to one-sixth that level (.50) in 2003. It had recovered slightly by 2005, to .69 (Ministry of Health, Labour, and Welfare 2005).

A second major change is on the labor supply side: rates of higher education attendance increased by about half between 1990 and the early twenty-first century, reaching more than 45 percent (and considerably higher if two-year post-secondary schools, *senmon gakkō*, are included). Thus, significant educational upgrading occurred among the youth labor force. This too has further constrained the job opportunities for youth who do not go on from high school into post-secondary education.

Third, the nature of Japanese employment relations began to change in the 1990s as employers suffered under the large wage bill of their middle-aged male employees, to whom "lifetime employment" and the concomitant seniority wages had been promised when they were hired during Japan's high-growth period from the late 1960s onward. Faced with the challenge of finding cheaper and more flexible labor to supplement the labor provided by these mid-career high-wage employees, employers increasingly turned to hiring part-time and temporary workers. This was not news for certain categories of workers, notably married women, who have had high rates of part-time employment over the past few decades. But it has been an almost entirely new phenomenon for other categories of workers, notably the young.

In order to understand how young people have been affected by employers' efforts to create a larger buffer of temporary and part-time employees around their core male middle-aged employees, we need to revisit what has conventionally been required for a good lifetime earnings trajectory in Japan: entry into a full-time job straight after graduation, and the accumulation of long work experience, preferably in a large firm. How common are these experiences in the current generation compared to the cohorts that immediately preceded them? In particular, how are individuals of low social class origins and low educational backgrounds faring? It is necessary to look at data from a variety of sources to investigate these questions.

Figures 5.1 and 5.2 show the change between 1990 and 2003 in the percentage of male and female workers who work in a part-time capacity. The line in each figure shows the increase in the part-time rate across all age groups, and the other lines show the rates for workers age 15–24 and 25–34. For men (Figure 5.1), the overall rate doubled between 1980 and 2003, increasing from 6.1 percent to 13.7 percent. The level and the extent of increase was lower for workers age 25–39, but for young workers (age 15–24), the rate of part-time employment more than tripled, reaching nearly 30 percent by 2003. As shown in Figure 5.2, rates of part-time employment for women are much higher (with the overall rate highly affected by the fact that many middle-aged married women workers, in contrast to middle-aged men, are in part-time positions). The increase among young women mirrors that for men, with 35 percent of young female workers in part-time jobs by 2003.

In addition to the dramatic rise in part-time employment among youth, unemployment rates also increased sharply. The unemployment rate for youth age 20–24 more or less doubled in every region of Japan between 1990 and 2003, and more than tripled in some (Statistics Bureau, Japanese Ministry of Public Management). While 1990 regional unemployment rates for this age group ranged between 3.7 to 6.3 percent, 2003 regional rates were nearly double that

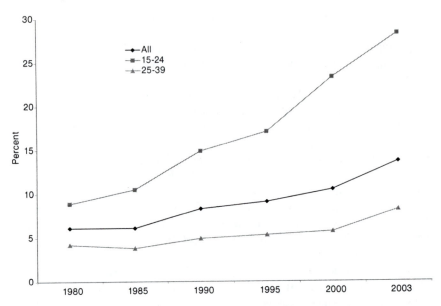

Figure 5.1 Male part-time workers as a percentage of all male workers, by age group

Source: Statistics Bureau, Japanese Ministry of Public Management. *Annual Report on the Labour Force Survey*, various years.

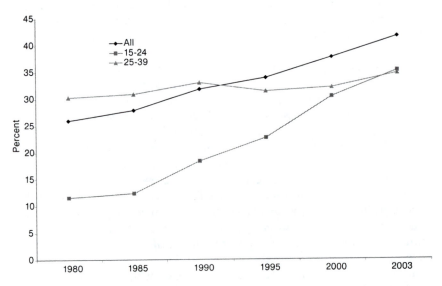

Figure 5.2 Female part-time workers as a percentage of all female workers, by age group

Source: Statistics Bureau, Japanese Ministry of Public Management. *Annual Report on the Labor Force Survey*, various years.

level (ranging from 6.1 to 13.3 percent). Unemployment rates for the younger age group – age 15–19 – are quite a bit higher than for people in their young twenties (as is true across post-industrial societies), and had reached 20 percent or higher in several regions by 2003 (notably Tohoku, Hokuriku, Shikoku, and Kyushu).

Of equal or greater concern in Japanese policy circles has been the increase in rates of idleness among Japanese youth over the past decade and a half, with idleness defined as being neither in school, in the labor force, nor actively searching for work. Idleness rates have increased considerably for the 20–24 year age group and have increased even more sharply for the youngest age group (15–19), rising to over 25 percent in a number of regions.

Is the situation really as bad as it appears? And what if anything does it have to do with social class? Is there reason to suspect that youth of lower social class origins are particularly strongly affected by changes that have occurred in the level and nature of labor demand and supply? If we consider the U.S. as an example, educational upgrading (higher rates of university attendance) and the loss of manufacturing jobs in the 1970s and 1980s did lead to a significant bifurcation of wages between high school and university graduates (Blau and Kahn 2002; Freeman and Katz 1995; Juhn *et al..* 1993). Most of the research on this increase in wage inequality has been undertaken by labor economists rather than sociologists, and hence the traditional sociological emphasis on social class has not been a central feature of the research. But given the strong relationship between social class origin and education, it is likely that as the impact of education on wages has increased in the U.S., the relationship between social class origins and wages has also increased. Are the trends in Japan similar? Is there increasing economic bifurcation between the haves and have-nots among Japan's youth, as the impact of social class background insidiously works its way through the new dynamics of the postindustrial labor market?

We might try to take solace in a few additional statistics from Japan. For one, we can check the entry-level wages for new high school graduates vs. new university graduates over time, to see if the gap is widening. Actually, this gap has remained surprisingly stable in Japan over the past 12 years; new high school graduates consistently earn about 80 percent of what new university graduates earn. This figure also holds when one compares the entry-level wages of high school and university graduates who enter firms of the same size, i.e. the figure holds whether one looks at small firms of 10–99 employees, medium-size firms of 100–999 employees, or large firms of more than 1000 employees (Ministry of Health, Labour, and Welfare 2003). That would seem to bode well for the continuing ability of Japanese high school graduates to gain a return in the labor market from their education.

However, one must remember that these figures presume that graduates *were able to get jobs*. Moreover, as I discussed earlier, one of the key features of the Japanese earnings regime is that earnings increase steeply with years of labor force experience, especially experience in the same firm. So figures on the entry-level wages of high school and university graduates do not pick up very much of what is going on in the Japanese youth labor market at present (as described so far in this chapter), where large numbers of youth are not landing jobs at all, let alone full-time jobs. Although not shown here, it is also important to note that rates of job turnover have increased for younger cohorts, suggesting that fewer and fewer young people are going to accumulate long years of experience in the same firm compared to earlier cohorts.

To assume the role of devil's advocate for a moment more, we can try to interpret some additional figures in a positive light. We know that there are traditionally quite a few high school graduates who fail their attempt to enter the university of their choice and decide instead to spend a year as *rōnin*, studying for the next year's university entrance exams. Given the bad labor market conditions and the educational upgrading of the labor force, perhaps more and more young Japanese have recently been deciding that they will sit out a year after high school and study harder to get into their first-choice university. This would be a more positive way to explain the increased rates of youth idleness, rather than assuming that it is youth from lower-class backgrounds who are idle. This is because the youth who become *rōnin* are generally those whose parents have the economic resources to support them for an extra year – youth who do not need to immediately enter the labor market for economic reasons. In the next section I turn to the analysis of which Japanese youth seem most likely to be idle.

Japanese high school graduates: an assessment of idleness rates upon graduation

To take a closer look at which Japanese young people are idle – neither working (at least not in a full-time job), in school, nor looking for work when they graduate from high school – I gathered school-level data on the more than 200 general (non-vocational) high schools in Kanagawa prefecture.[2] Table 5.3 shows the immediate post-graduation destinations for the senior graduating classes between 1997 and 2003.

This table speaks to the great increase in Japanese rates of matriculation to university immediately following high school graduation – from just under 20 percent in 1997 to nearly 34 percent in 2003. In contrast, rates of matriculation to junior college have slightly declined (from 14 to 11 percent) and rates of entry to other post-secondary training schools have remained stable (at about 23 percent).

Table 5.3 Immediate post-graduation destinations of public general high school graduates in Kanagawa Prefecture, 1997–2003†

	1997	1999	2001	2002	2003
University	19.8	20.2	27.3	31.5	33.5
Tandai (junior college)	14.4	15.0	13.4	11.9	11.1
Senmon gakkō (specialized schools)	23.3	23.2	21.9	22.4	22.5
Job	11.7	10.8	9.3	8.7	8.4
Idle	30.8	30.8	29.1	27.7	26.6
Total	100.0	100.0	100.0	100.0	100.0

† The unit of analysis is the high school

The proportion of graduates moving directly into jobs has declined from about 12 percent to 8 percent. The residual "idle" category includes *rōnin* (students who are studying for the next year's university entrance examination) as well as students who are neither continuing directly on to higher education nor have been hired by an employer to begin a post-graduation full-time job. This latter group includes students for whom the highly structured school-work system (Rosenbaum and Kariya 1989) has failed, for they were not placed into either a full-time job or a higher educational institution by the time of graduation.

In order to estimate the "true" percent of high school graduates who eventually go to university, we should somehow add *rōnin* to the number of graduates who go directly to university. Likewise, to estimate the "true" percent idle, we should somehow subtract *rōnin* from the "idle" category. To do this, I performed the following calculations:

True university = university + [university / (100 – idle)] * idle

True idle = idle – [university / (100 – idle)] * idle

where "university" is the reported (observed) percent directly entering university and "idle" is the reported percent idle in the data set. These calculations result in an upward revision of the percent going to university, as *rōnin* are now incorporated into that figure. Likewise, the percent "idle" declines but now more accurately reflects the "true" percent idle.

I then recalculated the "true" percent idle for each general high school in Kanagawa prefecture. These figures are added to Table 5.3 to produce Table 5.4.

The estimated figures reveal a number of interesting things. First, the "true" percent going to university rises to 45 percent by 2003, which mirrors the official Japanese government statistic for university matriculation in Kanagawa prefecture. The rate for "true" idle (hereafter called "idle") goes down, as we have

Table 5.4 Immediate post-graduation destinations of public general high school graduates in Kanagawa Prefecture, 1997–2003†

	1997	1999	2001	2002	2003
Original figures					
University	19.8	20.2	27.3	31.5	33.5
Tandai	14.4	15.0	13.4	11.9	11.1
Senmon gakkō	23.3	23.2	21.9	22.4	22.5
Job	11.7	10.8	9.3	8.7	8.4
Idle	30.8	30.8	29.1	27.7	26.6
Figures from estimation					
"True" university	30.2	30.9	38.8	43.6	45.3
"True" idle	20.5	20.3	17.2	15.1	14.0
Max. value, "true" idle	48.1	48.1	46.0	46.3	44.1

† The unit of analysis is the high school

now subtracted out from this figure those graduates who are likely to be *rōnin* (and who eventually enter university). The mean percent idle per school is fairly static, around 17 percent, but fully half of Kanagawa's 14 school districts have idleness rates for new high school graduates of 19 percent or higher (not shown in the table). The highest percent idle at any school is close to 50 percent across the period – meaning that nearly *one-half* of the graduating class of the school was neither proceeding directly or eventually to post-secondary school nor had a full-time job in hand at the time of graduation.

From which high schools is the largest proportion of idle youth coming? High school quality can be measured by the score on the prefectural standardized high school entrance exam required for entrance into each high school. Table 5.5 shows the zero-order correlations (relationships) between a school's quality and the proportion of its graduates who go on to different destinations. As would be expected, there is a statistically significant positive relationship between the quality of the high school and the proportion of its graduates who proceed to university, either immediately after graduation (row 1) or at any point after graduation (row 6). There is no change in this relationship over the years shown in the table. The relationship between school quality and the proportion of graduates going directly into the job market has not changed over time either; it is negative and statistically significant, indicating that the lower a school's quality, the higher the proportion of its graduates going directly into the labor market.

It is the relationship between school quality and the proportion of idle graduates that is of greatest interest. While there was a statistically significant *positive* correlation between this proportion and school quality in the late 1990s (.52 in 1997, .59 in 1999), this relationship has disappeared in recent years. That is, we can no longer reliably use a high school's quality to predict how many of its graduates will neither have a job nor an immediate post-secondary educational destination as they leave school. Prior to 2000, one *could* use school quality to predict this because the "idle" category was still largely measuring *rōnin*. This changed by 2001. The negative relationship between school quality and the proportion of its graduates who were "truly" idle increased from the late 1990s

Table 5.5 Correlations between school quality and post-graduation destinations of students from Kanagawa public general high schools†

	1997	1999	2001	2002	2003
University	0.92*	0.95*	0.93*	0.93*	0.93*
Tandai	-0.11	-0.45*	-0.05	-0.12	-0.16
Senmon gakkō	-0.81*	-0.86*	-0.73*	-0.75*	-0.70*
Job	-0.80*	-0.73*	-0.83*	-0.82*	-0.81*
Idle	0.52*	0.59*	0.03	-0.02	-0.04
"True" university	0.92*	0.96*	0.95*	0.95*	0.95*
"True" idle	-0.66*	-0.74*	-0.82*	-0.84*	-0.84*

† The unit of analysis is the high school; * $p < 0.01$

into the twenty-first century, showing that it has become more and more the case that the "worst" high schools are producing the largest numbers of idle graduates.

Given the relationship between social class origins and education in Japan, this can be taken as tentative evidence that individuals from lower class origins are the most likely to be populating the ranks of the idle in Japan, neither going on from high school to higher education nor entering the labor force. Their inability to secure post-graduation employment and to begin accumulating work experience, which is so important in Japan for increasing one's earnings, signals a widening economic disparity between youth of different social class origins.

Still, our story is not complete – there remain some important missing pieces. Is there a relationship between Japanese young people's social class background and the quality of the high school they attend? Many high school teachers report that there is, based on their own observations.[3] But one could object that these observations do not constitute rigorous data. Japanese sociologists have demonstrated that there is a relationship between social class background and educational attainment (i.e. university vs. junior college, two-year training school, or high school), but have not generally looked at high school quality. An exception is Seiyama and Noguchi's study (1984), which found a significant effect of social class background on the rank of the high school a student attended, even after taking into account middle school academic performance.[4]

Data collected by Kariya in 1996 on 1,804 seniors across thirteen high schools in the Tokyo metropolitan area can be used to look at the relationship between students' social class origins and the quality of the high school they attend.[5] My analysis of these data show that social class background (measured by whether an individual's father is in a white-collar occupation or not) and ninth-grade academic performance affect whether youth go to vocational or general high schools. Higher-performing, middle-class youth are much more likely to go to general high schools. Both social class and ninth-grade performance are also related to the quality of the high school attended (measured by the minimum standardized exam test score required for high school entrance), similar to Seiyama and Noguchi's findings. Because the relationship between social class and academic performance in ninth grade is so strong, this appears to be the main way in which social class affects the quality of the high school one attends. That is, social class has an indirect effect on high school quality via its relationship to academic performance in middle school. As attested to in other studies, both social class and high school performance affect whether high school seniors go on to university or not.

These results suggest that students from lower social-class backgrounds are more likely to end up in high schools at the lower end of the quality hierarchy, and that the main mechanism is via the relationship of social class to academic performance in middle school. It is beyond the scope of this chapter to further examine why social class and academic performance are closely related; this is taken up by Kariya's chapter in this volume. Instead, I contend that the worsening fates, especially idleness, of graduates of low-ranked high schools show that social class is mattering more and more for the labor market outcomes of the present generation.

Conclusion

It is well-established that there is an overall similarity between the extent of social class reproduction in Japan and other industrial societies. Japan is no more "open" or "closed" than other societies in its intergenerational mobility patterns. But intergenerational class reproduction and mobility in Japan needs to be viewed in the context of the relatively stable labor market institutions that existed across the second half of the twentieth century. Throughout that period, Japan had a system in which the most certain pathway to economic success in the labor market involved getting a full-time job immediately after graduation and establishing long tenure in one firm. The school-work transition system was especially stable for high school graduates (Rosenbaum and Kariya 1989). With dramatic changes in the institutional context, the mechanisms of intergenerational reproduction of social class may also change, and may do so in ways that affect some social classes more than others. To state it differently, parts of the class structure may rigidify in the sense that it will become more and more difficult for a substantial number of individuals to achieve a stable toehold in the labor market.

I contend that Japan is at just such a historical moment. The system of employment relations within which postwar cohorts came of age is undergoing dramatic change. The cohort that reached adulthood in the mid-1990s has faced a dramatically changed environment, not just in terms of the lowered demand for their labor but in terms of the upgraded skills that are required and in terms of how employers structure the employment relationship.

To be sure, youth throughout advanced industrial economies fared badly in the labor market in the 1990s. Japan is not exceptional in this regard, but it *is* unusual in several ways: first, the pathway for young adults into a stable earnings trajectory was highly normatively determined in Japan throughout the second half of the twentieth century – entering a large firm directly after graduation was *the* way to stable employment and a steady upward earnings trajectory throughout one's working life; second, this pathway was open to some proportion of both high school and university graduates. This meant that even though social class background traditionally has had a strong influence on educational attainment and on whether one becomes a white- or blue-collar worker in Japan, the ability to attain stable employment and earnings was not limited to the highly-educated – nor to individuals of non-manual class origins. My perception is that this is now changing.

In closing, I note that a striking feature of the current discourse in Japan on whether the labor market will improve is a focus on whether hiring will pick up for young workers in *future* cohorts. While this is an important question, it ignores the fact that some proportion of the cohort of people who came of age during the post-bubble economic recession in Japan may have missed out on the opportunity to gain a toehold in stable employment *for good*. That is, even if one favors an optimistic scenario predicated on two assumptions – that the Japanese economy experiences a good recovery and that companies revert to the traditional model of recruiting large numbers of new school leavers – this leaves unresolved the question of what will happen to the cohort of people who "missed the boat" in the late 1990s and early twenty-first century and did not secure a stable job. Articles in a recent special issue of the quarterly publication of the Japan Institute of Labour Policy and Training point to the impact of the fundamental realignment of family, education, and work in Japan on current youth's employment and transition to adulthood (2005). In previous work I have discussed Japan's unique human capital development system, or the ways that educational institutions and firms share the training of individuals (Brinton 1988, 1993, 2005). This is now changing, with firms offering the promise of on-the-job training and long-term employment to fewer and fewer young workers. There is substantial evidence that firms are diversifying their hiring and reward practices, with many firms making a substantial number of their hires on a part-time and contingent basis as they try to hold onto the "Japanese model" of long-term employment for an ever-smaller core of male workers.

The younger generation discussed in this chapter has been caught in the transition away from the old model of long-term employment and relegated to a more marginal sector of the labor force. But if Japanese-style reform is "incremental" rather than a whole-scale change to a different model that puts priority on a vigorous external labor market (Vogel 2006), then Japan's gradual economic recovery may well mean that the standard and venerated practice of recruiting workers straight from school will be readopted by many employers as new cohorts enter the labor market. If that is the case, the "lost generation" is best viewed as such, rather than as a generation that ushered in a dramatic new phase in Japanese capitalism. How will this generation be able to plug their lives back into the system as the economy recovers? What will be their stock of work experience at that point? How many Japanese employers will be interested in hiring workers in their mid-thirties with spotty work experience, rather than young entry-level workers straight out of school? If, as it is beginning to appear, the members of the "lost generation" who have not had stable employment experience are disproportionately from lower social class backgrounds, we can expect the impact of social class on their economic life chances in adulthood to be quite strong. It is in this sense that they are a generation who is lost and who will potentially have harder lives than either the cohorts immediately before them or those that immediately follow them.

Notes

1 Note that Ishida combined the managerial and professional classes in this table.
2 In other work I have examined these figures for general academic and vocational high schools separately; this is not reported here, as the primary focus is not on high school type.
3 In interviews with teachers at sixteen public high schools in Kanagawa prefecture in the mid-1990s, many teachers told me that the relationship between social class background and school rank was very clear to them. However, the sensitivity of this issue is such that securing data on students' social class background is very difficult (see LeTendre *et al.* 1998 for a discussion of this issue).

4 In their study of the high school-work transition, Rosenbaum and Kariya reported that *within* a high school, there was no correlation between the social class background of workbound students and the status of the occupation they entered after graduating (Rosenbaum and Kariya 1989). But this research compared students' destinations once they had entered the same school, and then looked only at those students who found jobs, so its relevance for our question is limited.

5 I am grateful to Takehiko Kariya for providing me with access to these data. The data were collected by Kariya with funding from the Ministry of Education. A previous paper using the data was published by Kariya et al. in 1997, "The Rise of Uncertain Future Plans Among Japanese High School Students," in *Bulletin of the Graduate School of Education*, University of Tokyo, Vol. 37, pp. 45–76.

References

Blau, F.D. and Kahn, L.M. (2002) *At Home and Abroad: U.S. labor market performance in international perspective*, New York: Russell Sage Foundation.

Brinton, M.C. (1988) "The social-institutional bases of gender stratification: Japan as an illustrative case," *American Journal of Sociology*, 94: 300–34.

—— (1993) *Women and the Economic Miracle: gender and work in postwar Japan*, Berkeley: University of California Press.

—— (2005) "Education and the economy," in N.J. Smelser and R. Swedberg (eds) *The Handbook of Economic Sociology*, 2nd edn, New York: Russell Sage Foundation.

Brown, C., Nakata Y., Reich, M. and Ulman, L. (1997) *Work and Pay in the United States and Japan*, New York: Oxford University Press.

Robert Erikson and John H. Goldthorpe. 2008. "Trends in class mobility: the post-war European experience." in David B. Grusky, *Social Stratification: race, class, and gender in sociological perspective*, 3rd edition. Boulder, CO: Westview Press.

Freeman, R.B. and Katz, L.F. (eds) (1995) *Differences and Changes in Wage Structures*, Chicago: University of Chicago Press.

Genda, Y. (2001) *Shigoto no Naka no Aimai na Fuan* [A Nagging Sense of Job Insecurity], Tokyo: Chūō Kōronsha.

—— (2007) "Jobless youths and the NEET problem in Japan," *Social Science Japan Journal*, 10(1): 23–40.

Grusky, D.B. and Hauser, R.M. (1984) "Comparative social mobility revisited," *American Sociological Review*, 49: 19–38.

Hashimoto, M. and Raisian, J. (1985) "Employment tenure and earnings profiles in Japan and the United States," *American Economic Review*, 75: 721–35.

Honda, Y. (2004) "The formation and transformation of the Japanese system of transition from school to work," *Social Science Japan Journal*, 7(1): 103–15.

—— (2005a) "'Freeters': young atypical workers in Japan," *Japan Labor Review* 2: 5–25.

—— (2005b) *Wakamono to Shigoto: "Gakkō keiyu no shūshoku" wo koete* [Young people and Employment in Japan: beyond the "school-mediated job search"], Tokyo: Tokyo Daigaku Shuppankai.

Ishida, H. (1993) *Social Mobility in Contemporary Japan: educational credentials, class and the labour market in cross national perspective*, Stanford, CA: Stanford University Press.

Ishida, H., Goldthorpe, J.H. and Erikson, R. (1991) "Intergenerational class mobility in postwar Japan," *American Journal of Sociology*, 96: 954–92.

Juhn, C., Murphy, K.M. and Pierce, B. (1993) "Wage inequality and the rise in returns to skill," *Journal of Political Economy*, 101: 410–42.

Kalleberg, A.L., and Lincoln, J.R. (1988) "The structure of earnings inequality in the United States and Japan," *American Journal of Sociology*, 94: S121-S153.

Kariya, T., Tsuburai, K., Nagasu, M. and Inada, M. (1997) "Shinro mikettei no kōzō: Kōsotsu shinro miketteisha no sekishutsu mechanism ni kansuru jisshōteki kenkyū [The rise of uncertain future plans among Japanese high school students]," *Tokyo Daigaku Daigakuin Kyōikugaku Kenkyūka Kiyō* [Bulletin of the Graduate School of Education, University of Tokyo], 37: 45–76.

Kerr, C., Dunlop, J.T., Harbinson, F.H. and Myers, C.A. (1960) *Industrialism and Industrial Man: the problem of labor and management in economic growth*, Cambridge, MA: Harvard University Press.

Koike, K. (1983) "Workers in small firms and women in industry," in T. Shirai (ed.) *Contemporary Industrial Relations in Japan*, Madison, WI: University of Wisconsin Press.

LeTendre, Gerald, Rohlen, Thomas, and Zeng, Kangmin. (1998). "Merit or family background? Problems in research policy initiatives in Japan." *Educational Evaluation and Policy Analysis* 20 (4): 285–297.

Levy, M.J. (1966) *Modernization and the Structure of Societies: a setting for international affairs*, Princeton, NJ: Princeton University Press.

Ministry of Health, Labour, and Welfare (MHLW). (2003) *Basic Survey on Wage Structure*, Tokyo: Ministry of Health, Labour, and Welfare.

—— (2005) *White Paper on Labour*. Tokyo: Ministry of Health, Labour, and Welfare.

OECD. (2001) *Labor Force Statistics 1980–2000*, Paris: OECD.

Rosenbaum, J.E. and Kariya, T. (1989) "From high school to work: market and institutional mechanisms in Japan," *American Journal of Sociology*, 94:1334–65.

Seiyama, K. and Noguchi, Y. (1984) "Kōkō shingaku ni okeru gakkōgai kyōiku tōshi no kōka [Extra-school educational investments and the opportunity of entering a higher ranking high school]," *Kyōiku Shakaigaku Kenkyū* [Sociological Research of Education], 39:113–26.

Statistics Bureau. (Various Years) *Annual Report on the Labour Force Survey*, Tokyo: Ministry of Internal Affairs and Communications.

Tachibanaki, T. (1998) *Wage Differentials: an international comparison*, New York: St. Martin's Press.

Treiman, D. (1970) "Industrialization and social stratification," in E.O. Laumann (ed.) *Social Stratification: research and theory for the 1970s*, Indianapolis, IN: Bobbs-Merrill.

Vogel, S.K. (2006) *Japan Re-Modeled: how government and industry are reforming Japanese capitalism*, Ithaca, NY: Cornell University Press.

Part III

Class socialization

6 The "new working class" of urban Japan

Socialization and contradiction from middle school to the labor market

David H. Slater

Introduction: the "new working class" of urban Japan

Tomo was a first-year and Keiko a third-year student at Musashino Metropolitan High School,[1] a working-class high school in western Tokyo. This chapter begins with two snapshots from those first years that illustrate some features of family background, survival strategies, and career trajectories that these two students share with many working-class youth all over Japan. Working from this point, the first part of this chapter sketches how class and culture are interrelated within the context of Japanese secondary education. The second part focuses on the ways different class groups navigate the transition from middle to high school. The third part focuses on the sorts of orientations, goals, and strategies that characterize school culture at Musashino High, a place where working-class culture takes institutionalized form through practice. The final part of the chapter traces these young people's trajectories into the bottom rungs of the service labor market.

Tomo's mother is pleading with her son's teacher, trying to do what she can to keep her son in school despite his having been caught smoking, again. Tomo was very involved in his middle school homeroom and club activities, at least until the end. Now, having failed to get into any school other than Musashino, he is in school but demoralized. He has been caught smoking twice before and suspended once half a day. His tone varies from simmering resentment to feigned unconcern. He points out that there are almost three smoking cases a day at this school, so his getting caught only twice in the first year is not so bad, "on the mathematical average." While bright, at Musashino High, Tomo has stopped following most of the lessons and is beginning to think that maybe he is not "cut out for" school at all. His mother asks his teacher about his participation in the baseball team, a widely accepted index of school integration, especially for a student struggling academically. The teacher turns to Tomo, who replies deadpan: "Didn't you know? Everyone has quit because all the teacher wants to do is drill." (This is true – the baseball team does not have enough players to field a team.) His mother has reassured him that if he would just come to school, he could graduate and then maybe play baseball when he gets a job. Tomo's reply to his mother is a sarcastic indictment: "You mean, so I can get a job like Dad?" The teacher asks

Tomo's mother about her husband's job at the discount electrical shop in the area. She mumbles something that sounds like agreement, but in fact, she does not know what sort of work Tomo's father is doing these days because after he was laid off, from what was a temporary job anyway, he has not lived with them for many months.

Like many working-class youths who end up at Musashino, Tomo is somewhat bewildered at how he got to this place or where to go from here. The same is true for his mother. There is no particular suggestion of school or anti-education culture in their household or neighborhood, and his mother fully expected Tomo to graduate and get a job. She makes another appeal: "But Sensei, as his homeroom teacher, how do you think it is best for Tomo to return to the regular flow of the class," a question that rests on the assumption that success in high school relies on, or at least begins with, one's contribution to the school as a moral community. The teacher labors under no such illusions, as he takes out the school rulebook to show Tomo and his mother the chart that clearly shows the punishment for missing classes or breaking rules – three suspensions and then withdrawal. Flustered, his mother protests that this is premature. "Tomo is kicked out already?" The teacher shakes his head and calmly replies, "I just wanted you to know how students move through the school." All three of them stare blankly at the chart in the rule book.

Keiko was a senior when I first interviewed her formally, and like most students who make it to their final year at Musashino, if they have learned anything, it is the art of survival by withdrawal from the school as a social and emotional center (a lesson the struggling Tomo had never learned by the time he dropped out). She is averaging just above 30 percent on her term tests from two classes, but as she points out, there is really nothing to worry about:

> School is fine. I stay out of the headlights of the teachers and I guess I am not rude, and also, I have good looks. Let's face it, I could be a fashion model if I were not in school. I *might* be a model, afterwards. Anyway, they don't want to fail me. They don't really want to think about me at all. Sometimes, a teacher will wake me up in class, and ask why I am so tired, and I say "homework." This is funny to them, big laugh because everyone knows that no one is doing much homework here, but what can they say? I can pass these tests, if I take them enough times.

Keiko was never part of the school routine, even in middle school, when she spent her time smoking and drinking with an older boyfriend. Now, in high school, she works two part-time jobs – one on the weekend at a neighborhood fast-food restaurant where her mother used to work before she got sick. The other is at a place called "Twilight Snack," a sort of hostess bar where high school girls wear nice school uniforms (not from their own schools), serve drinks and chat with the male customers ("and nothing else," as she points out) for good money between the end of school and 8 or 9 pm. She says that she first thought of this because her father worked as a freelance accountant in a similar place once. She does not tell her mother about this job, because she knows that she is treading close to the line of respectability. She has told me since on a number of occasions that she never stays overnight, never misses the last train (about midnight), and never sleeps at her workplace or in a club. She tells me that she knows some other girls who end up in Ikebukuro (a Tokyo entertainment district) all night, and "you never know what happens to them. They usually drop out of school pretty soon after. That is not me. I always go home. I will be in school until I graduate. I promised my Mom."

When Musashino students get jobs, usually they are of short duration, with little security and few if any benefits. They go on to do the work that every society needs to have done – cleaning, serving, delivering, cooking, entertaining. Tomo never graduated. He enrolled in a trade school to get a certificate in computer repair, but did not finish that either. He kicked around at various delivery jobs until he began planning and managing the routes for the bicycle delivery carriers of a Tokyo newspaper. His status is that of a part-time worker, with no prospects of any more stable employment in the future. When asked about Musashino, he recalls it with bitterness, as the result of his abrupt and unjust relegation to the bottom of his middle school class, once things got difficult heading into high school. After graduation, Keiko did not become a fashion model but instead worked in a number of clubs and bars, where by her own reckoning, she often crossed the line of respectability she had kept during high school, but for much better pay. Today, she waitresses in a dank hostess bar in a nearby neighborhood. She, too, works what amounts to full-time hours (as many as 60 per week) but is paid by the hour with no offer of any promotion. She looks back on Musashino with much more affection, as a time of play with friends and being indulged by her teachers, but also points out that she would probably be doing what she is doing now whether or not she had gone to high school.

Tomo and Keiko are *ochikobore*, a term which might literally be translated as "fallen student" or even "dropout," but is in fact used to identify a student, still in school, who has dropped down to any school as low as Musashino. All regular schools in Tokyo are divided into districts and Musashino is distinguished from other schools in the district by being at the very bottom in terms of its student body.[2] As a school at the bottom of its district, it is in the same position as all of the other schools at the bottom of their district rankings all over Tokyo and other urban centers of Japan. It is also an important link in the channeling of young people from mostly working-class backgrounds into working-class jobs, and in teaching the skills, aspirations and strategies that allow working-class youth to get by in the city. Musashino is a bit lower in selectivity than the those schools at the bottom of the districts around the new towns to the south and west, but usually higher than those at the bottom of the "old towns" in eastern Tokyo, the traditional working-class area of *Shitamachi* manual laborers, shopkeepers and small business owners (see Bestor 1990). Vogel (1971) and Murakami (1977), among others, use the term "new middle class" for the white-collar salaried men and their families that were supposed to become the norm in urban Japan. Neither Tomo's nor Keiko's parents graduated from college (although Keiko's father did have certificate in accounting, she says), nor did they have regular jobs in an office. Yet, neither were they doing regular manual labor, as the term "working class" might have suggested to earlier generations. Very few Musashino parents work in the sorts of jobs that offer full-time, lifetime employment with benefits and stability, the sorts of jobs that were once thought to characterize both white- and blue-collar jobs in Japan (see Rohlen 1983, Cole 1971). Since many of these manufacturing jobs were outsourced to cheaper markets abroad over the bubble period and even in the early 1990s, full-time, life-time (*seishain*) jobs are increasingly hard to come by. Instead, Musashino High School caters to the children of what we might call the "new working class": those working in service-oriented jobs, with little stability and few benefits, jobs that characterize the bottom of the Japanese labor market as in many other post-industrial economies.

Depending upon the year and class, as few as between 6 percent and 15 percent of Musashino students had at least one parent with some college experience. Across the whole school, there were as many as 25 percent with divorced or separated parents, and based on my interviews concerning their relatively fluid home life, more than half had one parent not regularly at home for some part of their school life.[3] About 85 percent of the students' mothers worked outside the home in some capacity. Fewer than 5 percent of Musashino students had a room of their own for study. No Musashino students went regularly to any high-powered cram school during high school, and not more than 15 percent had remedial home tutoring. One or two students per year would get into a four-year college, but these were not competitive colleges. Those students with parents able to pay the tuition for *senmon gakkō* (training schools) might put off entry into the labor market for a year or two. This option increased in popularity from almost none in 1990 to almost half of the total class in 2005. In 1990, 25 percent got a regular (*seishain*) job upon graduation. Between 1995 and 2000, the figure was closer to 15 percent. And in 2005, there were only two students (out of a graduating class of 150). The ratio of part-time jobs had also shifted: in 1990 almost half the class got part-time jobs, usually at local stores and small firms.[4] The most common way for these students to enter the job market was to begin sounding out the supervisor at their part-time job to see if increased hours might be offered once they graduated – if they graduated. (Between a quarter and a third of the students who enter Musashino High never finish.)[5]

For much of the postwar period, students like Tomo and Keiko were under-represented in the academic literature in both English and Japanese as theorists rushed to capture the rise of the bright and shiny middle-class society of postwar Japan, something that such students were not really part of. More recently, as the academic and popular focus has shifted to the "flexibilization" of the labor market in this post-bubble, neoliberal moment, these students have once again been lost in our focus on the fracturing of middle-class identity and labor patterns. But this working class, old and new, is as important in today's post-industrial economy as it was in the high-growth economy of postwar recovery and bubble affluence. And the systematic sorting and socialization of their children to fill the places in the shifting bottom of this economic miracle has unravelled. It is the school's compromised and often contradictory role in this process of sorting and selective socialization into the labor market that is the focus of my chapter.

Culture and class: unity, differentiation and contradiction

Class formation, and its reproduction, is not only an economic fact, but a social and cultural fact as well. To the extent that cultural forms guide the participation and secure the consent of individuals, the perceived legitimacy and the hegemonic force of class formation depends upon the cultural forms deployed in the representation of these mechanisms and their results. (This roughly corresponds to Level 2 in Katznelson's terms; see Chapter 1 of this volume.) Class analysis thus must include not only the charting of stratification (or the articulation of class structure), but also must identify the differential distribution of these cultural forms and the ways in which they are deployed, manipulated and transformed by institutions and individuals at different places in social space in ways that explain and obscure, legitimate and naturalize, these structural differences. These cultural forms are not internal to the logic of capital itself, but are selected and combined from a pool of cultural forms that are specific to a particular time and place, a particular society at a particular historical moment. So, at one pole we have the relatively universal economic workings of capitalism (Katznelson's Level 1), while at the other, we have a very specific set of Japanese cultural forms through which capitalism takes shape and efficacy. Class formation is thus situated between these two poles: between the economy and the culture, between the universal and the particular.

As argued in the introduction to this volume, for much of the postwar period, the social scientific literature on Japan has stressed the importance, even distinctiveness, of a shared "middle-class culture" that has somehow bound Japanese society into a single coherent order in ways that have resisted the formation of distinctive or oppositional class cultures. And yet, Ishida (1993 and this volume) has demonstrated that the reproduction of social inequality is just as regular and just as effective in Japan as it is in other capitalist democracies; the chances of social mobility and class closure in Japan are roughly consistent with the UK, US and France. What are we to do with these divergent and possibly contradictory patterns, one that points toward culture cohesion and social unity, and the other toward structural differentiation and class divergence? More specifically, how can there be class formation without class culture? How can young people be reliably sorted into a highly differentiated labor market and still show so few of the signs of class identity or class consciousness thought to characterize capitalism? If we cannot speak of distinct class cultures, what are the mechanisms of class sorting? What are the structures and contradictions of differential class socialization? What constitutes the experience of class formation?

In Japan, as in many other so-called "middle-class" societies, the deployment of cultural forms does not necessarily result in the coalescence of any "tangible" (Hall and Jefferson 1976) sets of symbols that mark out some bounded population into a discrete "class culture." Like the notion of culture itself, which has undergone such thorough critique (see, for example, Gupta and Ferguson 1997), we need to rethink class culture. We need to recognize that "class cultures" rarely resemble anything like bounded subcultural groups as imagined on the model of ethnic enclaves with distinct "class codes" (Bernstein 1977). As Voloshinov (1973) reminds us, classes do not form single distinct sign communities. Rather, different classes draw from much the same symbolic resources as the dominant culture in their attempt to make sense of their material situation in ways that often lead to contradiction. And depending upon their place within social space, different groups will draw upon different signs in different ways, experience even shared processes as differentially meaningful, as generating different options and leading to different patterns of practice. In this way, the deployment of cultural forms outlines the boundaries of struggle as much as the flow of seamless reproduction (see Ezawa and Borovoy in this volume for similar approaches). This approach requires a level of analysis that moves away from the abstraction of "Japanese Culture" as something shared by the whole society but still does not settle into the notion of bounded "class cultures." Instead, I attempt to identify those specific institutional mechanisms that are most responsible for the differential distribution of the cultural forms that generate, organize and legitimate class practices, that allow and obscure individual understanding and movement through this process.

In Japan, the educational system has probably been the primary institution most responsible for *both* of these functions. That is, schooling is the primary site for the development of shared patterns of representation and whole-culture forms so central to the integrity of adult culture and social cohesion, and at the same time, it is the primary mechanism for the social and cultural differentiation of different segments of the population into distinct class trajectories which is central to the reallocation of young people into a highly diversified labor market. We should not imagine these two processes to be at odds with one another; in fact, it is only because school is so effective in the socialization of whole-cultural values that it is an effective mechanism for what is largely understood as legitimate differentiation. Reproduction of inequality and whole-culture socialization are always already occurring together.[6] In a country where 98 percent of the students attend high school, where high schools supposedly share the same curriculum, *and* where virtually the entire adolescent population is reallocated (from comprehensive middle schools to finely-ranked high schools) into ranked streams, education is one of the privileged domains in which to examine class formation.

The rich ethnographic literature on Japanese education provides us with a detailed image of the primary cultural forms as they are manifest in society through school. In class analysis, this work must be extended and recontextualized; the goal of class analysis is not to construct a cross-national comparison of cultural forms in order to capture "*The* Japanese School" or even "*The* Japanese High School" (Rohlen 1983) as different from another nation's school, as is often the case.[7] As necessary as these sorts of studies may be as a preliminary stage, they work by essentializing some common cultural core at the expense of noting the internal differences among schools. The goal of an ethnography of class formation is to demonstrate how hegemonic cultural forms are differently distributed and deployed to different ends at schools of different levels, and then, to show if and how these forms are linked backward to family class profile and forward to job and future life course trajectories. The ethnography of social class is still essentially comparative, although the level of analysis is not at the distribution of these forms *among* different societies, but *within* each society. That is, we need to understand how core cultural forms are differentially distributed in ways that allow different class groups to recognize, participate in, represent, and legitimate the shared functional requirements of sorting and socializing young people into different places within a complex class structure.

Just as often, this distribution of cultural forms generates patterns of contradiction rather than seamless reproduction, and the deployment of these same forms often leads to a denaturalization of the process that results in young people (and their parents) questioning their own flow through the system. "Group living" (*shuudan seikatsu*) is one such key cultural form.

Group living: models of self-making and institutional management

Much of the primary and early middle-school curriculum is largely based on a model of socialization that has been called "group living" (*shuudan seikatsu*). Unlike some incipient undercurrent buried in the "hidden curriculum," group living is the articulation of a moral community that is very much part of the formal curriculum as manifest in textbooks and teachers' manuals, and as evident in everyday school life. It begins with students' acknowledgment of the legitimacy, even primacy, of collective school goals. Realization of these collective goals often requires hard work, dedication and sacrifice, but also offers a place of secure membership, warm acceptance and "wet" indulgence. The idiom of wetness implies high levels of the emotional and largely unstructured involvement characteristics of an enduring relationship of belonging and even identity, and is most often contrasted with what might be called an instrumental relationship one enters into for personal advantage, or a "dry" relationship. Full participation in group living requires restraint (*enryo*) of one's own personal desires, both as a way to support others with feelings of empathy and mutual dependence, but also as a precondition that allows others to support you. In this way, an individual demonstrates fitness to be a member of a collective. In its more developed form, participation comes to imply a taking of personal responsibility for these collective goals, for others and for the cultural project of developing a self that is connected to and supportive of others. Thus, rather than setting individual goals against collective goals, group living becomes the foundation for individual development of self, a channel through which self can develop and mature. In Japanese institutions, you make your self insofar as you contribute to others within an institutional context.

But this alignment also enables group living to function as the foundation of institutional management or more generally, governance (Rose 1989). It is as much about the management of individuals into governable form as it is a structure that allows for those individuals to develop at all. It is as much a site of social order as it is one of social control. Group living demonstrates this capacity for governance in its representation of legitimate power as "soft authority," a diffuse set of priorities represented as naturally emanating from the collective needs of the group, rather than from the station or office of a superior such as a boss or a teacher.[8] In this way, group living aligns the individual and the collective in mutually constitutive processes of self-making and institutional governance.

Until recently, group living in Japan was not something that young people grew out of and left behind in primary school. In fact, it is the educational manifestation of roughly isomorphic patterns of collective order and control found in a wide range of adult social institutions. Some variant of group living is present in most sites of middle-class participation: club, university and professional academic associations, sports teams, company training practices, and most importantly, in virtually all corporate white-collar and blue-collar contexts. Stability, mobilization and productivity of adult institutions, especially work groups, are often structured through these principles. On the other hand, failure to secure such a place in one of these corporate groups risks relegation to spaces of largely anomic social relationships, ordered by "dry" criteria of contact, a world with ordered assumptions of distinct identities and divergent interests. The learning of group living in school is thus an important lesson for participation in and belonging to adult middle-class society. Where social identity is bound up with the full participation in institutional membership, learning the routines and ethos of the moral community of group living is a primary function of school socialization in whole-culture values.

Academic maximization and class sorting

This group living model of whole-culture socialization orders the daily routines of primary school and the beginning of middle school, but is marginalized as middle school students begin to be sorted and streamed into finely stratified high schools. Middle schools, like primary schools, accept students in their immediate residential area, and thus reflect the diversity of their neighborhoods. Urban neighborhoods are said to be more diverse in Japan than in many countries, so that each school demonstrates an internal heterogeneity more or less similar to the internal heterogeneity of the next middle school.[9] During elementary and early middle school, the curriculum is substantially uniform across schools and focuses on the various forms of social relations that are needed to form productive and coherent school cultures, that is, group living. But at the end of middle school, all students are reallocated to high schools on the basis of their achievement test scores. The best students in each district are streamed into the most selective high schools, and the low-achieving middle schoolers end up at the bottom-ranked high schools. In order to facilitate this reallocation, the middle school curriculum becomes increasingly academic, ensuring that students are sorted into a reliable array of academic streams that find formal articulation through high school entrance exam scores (*hensachi*). This is the most obvious juncture of class sorting in a young person's lifecourse, a transition from class heterogeneity in middle school to class homogeneity in each of the strictly stratified high schools.

This redistribution of students is broadly predicative of future educational, occupational, and lifecourse trajectories, as well as being closely coordinated with family background. It is the first instance of, and maybe the clearest image of, the class structure of the whole society, held up for all to see just at the moment it first emerges as an institutionalized fact.

Whole-culture socialization, as embodied in group living and practices of class sorting manifest through school reallocation, works in contrasting ways to produce different school cultures, different sorts of institutional order and control, and different sorts of identities. Rather than the whole culture curriculum of group living that stresses contribution to a collectivist moral community, entering into a desirable high school depends upon a development of individualistic achievement strategies, the outcome of which is measured in the minute relative differences among students. This collective moral order comes into direct conflict with the larger capital imperative of sorting and socializing students for different places within the highly diversified labor market. New goals and strategies for reaching these goals develop: rather than contributing to a warm and wet moral community, middle school becomes more of a competitive market, in which we see a rearticulation of individual values based on a narrow criterion of academic success. Group living that once served as the foundation for constituting a coherent and meaningful self is juxtaposed with the imperative of developing coherent and effective maximization strategies. In fact, the group living strategies learned in primary school not only have little value; indeed, they often retard success within this new academic curriculum. Individual priorities, peer relations and deployment of institutional authority all shift accordingly. Some students are better able to negotiate this shift than others.

In the next section of this chapter, I argue that students from different class backgrounds are caught in this transition in different ways; they have different resources to call upon and different class-specific goals that lead to different survival strategies. For students from richer families, this transition is an all-important moment which they start preparing to exploit years before. For those students from more working-class families, those students who end up at high schools such as Musashino, like Tomo and Keiko the transition is one that is intellectually confusing and often emotionally draining, as they fall out of the community that once supported them (and which they once supported) to an isolating place at the bottom of an academic hierarchy that did not even exist when they entered middle school. While young people from more elite families are already learning maximization strategies through cram school, for example, many working-class students do not even recognize the significance of this moment until it is already past. One way we can examine the complexity of class formation and the cultural reproduction of inequality is to see how different class groups recognize, navigate, and strategize through this important period of reallocation.

Middle school sorting

We often imagine class formation to function somehow beyond the recognition of individuals, often because it is obscured by ideas of race (Ogbu 1992), gender (Willis 1977), or other more accessible forms of identity. But because the process of class differentiation that occurs during Japanese middle school is the result of a relatively harsh disjuncture between group living and a more maximizing ethic of academic achievement, both are denaturalized and very much available as objects of explicit reflection, at least temporarily.[10] Interviews and fieldwork revealed a high awareness of the workings and significance of this sorting process, even if it was rare to find any students able to articulate the link between school sorting and the larger class implications that it carried. More obvious was how differently students from different class trajectories understood and represented this process. By juxtaposing the experience of those students who ended up at the elite schools with the experience of students like Tomo and Keiko from Musashino, we can begin to sort out the ways in which class formation is experienced.

Sara, a first-year student who entered one of the well-known elite high schools in Tokyo, explained:[11]

> I knew that getting into this school was important for me, for my future, because this puts you on the track. And if you are not on the track, well, I don't know, but you don't get where you are trying to go. You cannot just go to any high school and then get into a good college.

She continued: "My middle school was pretty good, I guess, and some of the teachers really helped you, but they could not make everyone ready [for high school] because we were all going to different sorts of high schools. It's not the teachers' fault – it's just impossible because lots of the kids just did not care about studying."

Sara's parents did what more than 90 percent of the parents of the students in her homeroom class at her elite high school did: had her attend cram school in a regular and strategic way to maximize her chances.

> The cram school was close to my house. My father used to joke that we moved houses so we could be near the cram school, but I don't know. Actually, he also said that the cram school was so expensive that we could not afford to pay train fare to some other cram school, so I had to go there. [This was offered and accepted as a joke by all the students present, humorously juxtaposing the relatively small train fare to the large tuition her father must have paid.] I went every day, with no commuting time back home. That was the key I think. Some of my friends commuted an hour or even 90 minutes each way to cram school. But for me, no time spent sleeping on the train. I could just go home, take a short nap and then work again. Or even skip my nap.

It would be temping to say that academic success is less the result of talent and hard work than it is bought and paid for in the urban market of secondary school in Japan, and in some sense this would not be untrue. The ability to allocate family economic resources to cram schools only provides opportunity; it does not secure success. Parents' money cannot buy success for children without the creation of a maximizing subjectivity, one that depends upon the definition of self as a possessive self, one defined by what can be accomplished, by the scores that can be generated. The matter-of-fact calculation of commuting time and study results was a common topic among Sara and her elite classmates. Sara seemed very bright and her narrative speaks of hard, directed effort over an extended period of time – just what she or any other student would need to get into the elite school she got into – but we see that this effort must be directed through particular institutional channels, in this case, cram school.

In contrast, Tomo explained his path through middle school to Musashino with a sense of confusion, even bewilderment, rather than strategic intent:

> I know that we were supposed to work hard in middle school, really, that's all we were doing. Studying for tests and taking tests. One after another. It was so sudden. The things that I liked to do [science projects, anything outside of the school classroom] we just did not do. And if you were going to pass these tests, you couldn't even do sports.

In middle school Tomo was active in class affairs and a real contributor to his homeroom for festivals and class projects, patterns of participation that embody the best ethic of group living. But he appears never to have caught up with the curve into more academic focus as it developed in middle school. Tomo's mother told me in an interview that "really, in middle school, Tomo worked hard, spent all of his time in school, so I thought he would be okay." She did not think that cram school was necessary as long as he worked hard, "because I thought his teachers would help him out more." Another day she explained, "I'm not sure where we could have found any money to pay for cram schools. Not for middle school. Maybe for high school, if he continues to struggle." In comments like these, we see both economic disqualifications, but also a set of priorities over the allocation of discretionary income within a family budget. Neither Tomo nor his mother were engaged in a strategy to maximize his chances and did not see school as an opportunity to do so. Like so many of the Musashino narratives, their narratives were grounded in a rhetoric of getting by, developing compensation strategies, and covering up.

Tomo and Sara both went to public comprehensive middle schools that streamed young people into the full range of high schools, public and private. Tomo, and other students who ended up at Musashino, not only did not make the cut for the desirable high schools due to their low levels of achievement, but in some fundamental way, did not realize the scope and significance of the academic shift during middle school. We can assume that smart and able young minds are probably distributed across the spectrum of class positions in roughly even patterns. To be sure, there are instances of students who enter good high schools and good colleges without going to cram school, but these are the exception to the rule – for example, fewer than 10 percent of Sara's classmates at her elite school. Class practices might best be seen in the larger orientation to and awareness of this pivotal moment. Coming from his family background and without the sort of cram school that Sara attended, Tomo had little in the way of systematic preparation in terms of both test taking skills or the larger discipline of competitive strategies (including those that extended all the way down to the precise calculation of the impact of train time on study). This transition found Tomo, and many others at Musashino, ill-equipped and unprepared. Less than any particular low test score, it is more the lack of awareness of and systematic preparation for this shift that captures the key feature of Tomo's working-class trajectory.

Kento, a classmate at Sara's elite high school, explained middle school this way:

> I enjoyed my [middle school] classes and my homeroom teacher was great. She was always giving me extra work, until I became too busy with cram school. I learned all sorts of things [in middle school], but not that much of what I learned ended up on the entrance exams for high school. We took all sorts of "mock tests" and I did very well on these, but they were just something that the teachers made up themselves. My teachers at cram school *actually had the tests* that the different high schools gave [from previous years] and they had figured out the techniques to help us pass. I knew that our regular [middle school] teachers could never do that. It was just a different thing.

Tomo and most of his first-year classmates at Musashino reported very negative feelings toward schoolwork, and their middle school teachers in particular, who in their minds were mostly pushing them into, even punishing them through, test taking. They had no luxury of distance and their narratives were as emotional as they were wet. Narratives of being ignored and abandoned, even betrayed, point to a representation of teachers as failing to live up to expectations. These expectations do not involve any transmission of useful knowledge or test-taking strategies, but pastoral care and even personal guidance, traits that appear to be mostly generated from representations of group living. As long as they were part of the school community, working-class students often reported being locked into relationships of conflict with their teachers over their poor test performance.[12]

Tomo recalled his middle school this way:

> [The teachers] stopped caring about the students and we never did anything except tests. The only time we ever did anything as a homeroom was once a week when we had to, and even then, we usually used that time to study vocabulary lists or something. They would keep on complaining about each test. They would read out test scores to the whole class, or post them on the wall, and everyone knew who got what. They all knew that I was at the

bottom, and dragging the class average down. I said, "Hey, everyone below the middle is also pulling it down," but I was always blamed. They always went after the bottom dwellers. Like me. After a while, you see what is going to happen and there is nothing you can do. Nothing to do about that. You have to give up. But I hated it. I always hated it.

This is not to suggest that group living is completely extinguished in middle school. In fact, there is still a framework of group living, albeit challenged and embattled, that rearticulates the macro-level contradiction between moral community and achievement in more immediate form within the daily life of the school. As one teacher at Sara's elite high school explained,

> When students focus too much on the cram school, it pulls them away from participation in [middle] school. Even if they are physically here, when their future is focused on results that come from cram school, they become selfish and start putting their personal things ahead of classroom things. It becomes very hard to teach a class like that anything but the textbook. I guess this is understandable – it's the reality of [middle] school – but nevertheless, it's a problem for us when so many students are spending time in cram school.

While Tomo felt torn and conflicted between these divergent possibilities, students like Sara quickly learned how to balance them in ways that satisfied both by compartmentalizing. Sara explained that as she progressed in middle school, she would spend as much time on her school lessons as was required for her to pass and as much time on her club activities as was available, but first allocated the time and energy necessary for success at cram schools. She knew that the path to success did not pass through her middle school classroom, and this distance from the school as a sorting mechanism allowed her to avoid some of the contradictory tensions that characterize middle school, enabling her to keep a generally positive, although rather dry, relationship at her school. As with her high school teachers, her relationship with her middle school teachers might be described as positive or negative, friendly or unfriendly, as the case may be, but rarely was there much emotion or complexity. There did not seem to be much at stake in these relationships, which is what we would expect given their tangential relationship to her larger instrumental goals.

Sara and her classmates who entered the high-level schools reported little conflict between the requirements of cram school and middle school. Successful maximization strategies almost always included the ability to move back and forth between these two spheres with ease and fluency. Sara explained, "My time was somewhat flexible [since she lived close to the cram school], but there were also times when I just had to leave. Sometimes the teacher understood that I just could not always be around after school."[13] Sara's classmate Kenji explained, "I enjoyed my other activities at school, but everyone knows that you don't get into a good high school by spending all of your time cleaning up the classroom or being good at club activities. Some kids do that, but not the students who go to cram school."

For Tomo, middle school was an arena of conflict and struggle. He did not experience the shift and increase of student attention to cram school as a balancing between responsibilities and spheres of belonging (to some moral community) and achievement (in the physically displaced academic market defined by the cram school industry). Rather, for him and many students who end up at Musashino, there are processes of betrayal by teachers and alienation from peers.

> When things first got difficult, I was able to get help from some of my friends, but this didn't last. They abandoned me. I guess they were busy at first, but then they started to spend more time with the others who were also going to cram school. Cram school. That was all they talked about. How interesting it was, their teachers, what good friends they had there.[14] At first, I wanted to go, but I began to see that it's just more study. No reason to do more of that if you don't have to.

It is not uncommon for students to strike out at teachers and classmates for violations of collective commitments to one another, at one time the foundation of the school's moral community. This is balanced by self-blame for failure to keep up with the curriculum. Self-chastisement about how much work they should have done in middle school is also another familiar theme if students get to the second year of high school. (During the first year, they are usually still too angry to blame or bewildered to shoulder any of the responsibility themselves.) Many become *ochikobore*, or those who fall to the bottom, like Tomo. Some remove themselves from the school, like Keiko. But unlike Sara and her elite classmates, the working-class students have no alternative mechanisms for advancement, such as cram school. So for Keiko and other working-class students, removal from the middle school community (not talking to the teachers as much, not socializing with classmates, or in more extreme situations, skipping school) meant jeopardizing any chances to advance to a desirable high school, and thus, ending up at schools such as Musashino. So, whether they leave middle school full of anger and resentment, or have already emotionally removed themselves from the contradictions of middle school, few enter high school with very high expectations.

High school socialization

High schools in metropolitan Japan are fully class-sorted, with each school having a thin segment of the student population of the district. Thus, while middle schools most immediately confront students with the often rending process of internal stratification and sorting, high school confronts students with the result of that sorting process. If the primary purpose of middle school is to differentiate a heterogeneous population, the high school's purpose is to solidify a homogeneous one. The curriculum plays a large part in this process.[15] More than around any philosophy of education or development of community, the days, weeks and months of high school are structured around the achievement of certain curricular goals. This is not much different from high schools in other national systems, but the structure of this curriculum is somewhat distinctive, resulting in different school cultures and different ways that class groups make sense of them. Usually, class theorists of education assume a sort of functionalist correspondence (e.g. as outlined by Bowles and Gintis 1976) between a curriculum and the future occupational requirements of students in the school. Thus, for example, a curriculum focused on abstract reasoning, synthetic problem solving, and leadership will be found at elite schools that prepare students for future positions of authority and responsibility, while working-class curricula stress execution and repetition, the ability to follow orders. The Japanese school is based on the memorization of non-synthetic pieces of information, a high degree of fragmented knowledge, largely devoid of any analytical or synthetic operation, characteristic of what is often called a "deskilling" curriculum considered most suitable to manual labor (see Apple and Weis 1983 for a review). But unlike in many national education systems, this is the same national curriculum to which all Japanese students are subjected. The national curriculum in Japan is not differentiated into high and low tracks that work according to different principles, and while there are differences in pedagogy, it is probably high-level high school students who must spend the most time mastering this "deskilled" curriculum in order to pass the tests to enter the most prestigious universities. While some have pointed to this fact as evidence of equality, even democracy (Cummings 1980), others have argued (Horio 1988) that this form and the amount of work required to master it encourage adherence to rule and repetition, and engender attitudes of docility and uncritical receptivity across society. In any case, class differences do not seem to be primarily encoded in the formal curriculum.

In order to find how class differences are encoded into symbolic and social capital, we need to look at the way this curriculum is embedded in different, class-specific institutional contexts. As we have already seen, through cram school, elite students far more often develop strategies for maximization which improve their chances of high exam scores. In this case, class privilege is reproduced less through the informal conversation of home cultural capital than it is valorized through in-school evaluation. In Japan, economic capital is not converted in the strict sense into another form, but simply spent: spent on cram school where the knowledge of future tests and the strategies for passing them are gathered and sold by pedagogy specialists in the cram school industry.[16] In fact, the highly segmented form of the curriculum lends itself to this form of purchase far better than the abstraction of "class codes" (Bernstein 1977) or *habitus* (Bourdieu 1977), both of which may be rather too complex for reliable transmission in most school settings.[17] In this way, a curriculum that appears to be class-neutral (that is, in no way corresponding to differential patterns of home-culture capital form) actually becomes an even more efficient, if prosaic, vehicle for the reproduction of inequality.

This formal curriculum thus does not demand understanding (how do you "understand" a multiplication table or a list of the longest rivers in Europe?), but it does require hard work strategically directed at and justified by the promise of passing entrance exams. Sara's classmate explained the thinking of many students at elite schools: "What we study is not really something you can 'understand' (*rikai*). You just memorize. That's okay because if we had to understand it all, we could never pass the exams." High school is a means of moving to another level, to college for elite students such as Sara, and mastery of the seemingly arbitrary bits and pieces of the exam curriculum is the means to that end. Maximization of this opportunity by students is not easy but important and necessary for success. Sara's classmate continues: "It is hard work, tons of work, but if you don't do it, you won't get anywhere. And then, why are you in school?"

Working-class high schoolers preparing for college entrance exams never to be taken

The situation at low-level high schools such as Musashino is dramatically different because virtually none of the students will even be taking college entrance exams. And if they are not going to take entrance exams, then what are they doing in school, which is built around these exams? At a bottom-level school such as Musashino, few students find any more meaning than realistically possibility to master the high school curriculum because where they go after Musashino will be very little affected by what they do at Musashino. It is not just that what is taught at these schools is unrelated to their university curriculum or the skills required by the world of work. It is that in order to enter the institutions that they enter (trade schools or the workplace) no exams are required. This is not a mystery to Musashino students, who see their elder siblings, friends and school *sempai* drifting into the low-level service sector of the economy. They quickly realize that they have very little chance of translating good school performance into a desirable job.[18] And this situation has not changed much recently. Despite the years of deregulation of education and reduction of required courses (*yutori kyōiku* and *jiyūka*), supposedly to allow each school to more sensitively cater to the particular needs of their own student body (see Kariya, this volume), this has not made the curriculum any more relevant or suitable to the students at Musashino. Said one teacher,

> Our students have always been so far below any sort of national standards that those sorts of policies have no meaning for us. When they stopped having classes on Saturday all it meant was less suffering for us and the students. We are not trying to meet any standards. The only thing that we try to do is finish whatever textbook that we ask the students to buy. They don't like to spend money on books that we don't finish, and I can understand that.

If there has been any consistent pattern of change to which teachers at Musashino point, it is less a function of any Ministry of Education reforms than it is to do with the reduced preparation of the students entering high school and their reduced learning. One older Musashino teacher explained, "While we hear about other schools increasingly teaching exam-oriented lessons, the real change for schools at the bottom is that we are being forced to accept lower and lower standards of passable work."

To cite one example, Keiko told a story from her 2nd-year English class. The test was a translation from English into Japanese about Australian culture. All of the students were taught the Japanese passage and its English translation, and were given a copy of each to study. When the day of the test arrived, they were given the English and asked to translate it. The teacher recorded their grades, and those students who did not get a passing grade had to take the test again, and then again, and then again, until they could produce enough of the Japanese to get a passing grade. This took a couple of weeks, as some of the students' scores went down in their subsequent attempts. Finally, the teacher began to give partial tests – where a student was tested on only a part of the passage at a time. This sped things up, finally allowing the last few stragglers to complete the passage one sentence at a time. They would stand out in the hall memorizing the Japanese sentence and then rush into the teachers' room, and often without even looking at the English, scrawl the memorized sentence as fast as they could before it slipped away. The teacher was embarrassed about this compromise, but defended his approach this way:

> I know that they don't learn the English in this way, not really. In fact, most of them don't understand the Japanese [that they translate into]. I also know that they don't need to study English. But they need to pass because they need to graduate, and if memorizing the lesson bit by bit will allow them to do that, that's okay with me. It's all in pieces anyway, so it's not really very different [from the rest of the lessons]. For a school like Musashino, it's what we have to do. Otherwise, everyone in the class fails. For students like ours, that means they cannot get a job. They at least have to graduate. I'm not going to fail them.

Clearly, students did not expand their understanding of the subject matter. They were also not working for some personal advantage. They were not maximizing anything, like their more elite peers. They had no stake in the outcome and thus no stake in the process. And the teachers, of course, were not deluded enough to imagine that they did.

But the students were learning something that did prepare them for their future: a form of work that was both distinct to their low-level, working-class school, and in some way "prepared" them for their next step. They did not learn logical reasoning nor did they have to take any responsibility for their own learning, in the way we might associate with elite jobs. Nor did they learn the unquestioned obedience to authority one might associate with an ethic of factory work in Western theorizing on working-class culture in industrial capitalism. The cultural forms that often characterize class trajectories are not replicated in today's Japan nor are they meaningful to the ways in which these young people are situated within the Japanese service economies. What's more, the students did not learn something more distinctively "Japanese" about collective responsibility or the moral community of group living. Instead, Musashino students learned how to perform clearly demarcated tasks, not for some meaningful if remote goal, but for the sake of completing it because they were asked to. Not in an oppressive atmosphere of strict obedience or conflict, but a sort of going through the motions of what we might call "dry" living. One very experienced female teacher characterized her students and what they learned in this way:

> You watch the kids coming to school, going to their classes, talking to us and to each other. Of course, they learn to do the things that they're supposed to do, and they do most of what we ask them to do. We don't have much verbal fighting and no actual school violence [like my schools in the 1970s and 1980s]. But that's because violence would take too much energy. They call the US school a "shopping mall" high school, right? Well, this is more like a "convenience store" high school.[19] We should have them punch in the time clock and wear a 7/11 logo. Some people say this is not what school is supposed to be like. But here, at Musashino, that is what school is like, and we are luckier than we were before.

When students were asked to comment on this characterization (school as a convenience store), some pointed out that "there are some differences: you can't sleep when you work the way you can in class." When one student said that you do get money from working, and you have to pay to be in school, another pointed out, "Yeah, but it's not much money in either place." On the whole they thought the comparison was quite apt.

The vacuum of authority and the politics of its delegation

Group living is a cultural context that shapes individual subjectivities in line with the moral and practical expectations of adult society, and as such, it is an important part of whole-culture socialization, an important part of learning how to participate in a wide range of institutional contexts. But as noted above, it is at the same time a management strategy, a form of governance that allows social control to be legitimately secured. The importance of securing order is clearly an important consideration for teachers at any high school. But more than that, the sort of order and control, the representation of legitimate authority and consent, provides a context within which students learn how to define themselves, their peers and those around them.[20]

In the more elite institutions, somewhat paradoxically, an ethic of utilitarian maximization and the displacement of the high school by the cram school as the primary terrain of competition enable the school to be a more manageable and relatively conflict-free zone. Students do not have to depend upon their teachers or compete with their peers as much as those students who are less able to access cram school. Still, the assumed importance of academics, and maybe more significantly, the relatively unquestioned patterns of participation that structure the practices of schoolwork support willing cooperation in an orderly classroom.

Elite schools are able to secure sufficient legitimacy to order and facilitate the various non-academic parts of the school. At most elite high schools, most students show up at sports day, participate to some extent in coordinated club activities, and allow teachers to maintain sufficient institutional authority to control the class. Musashino teachers cannot assume the same level of willing participation or cooperation from students. Neither the instrumental value of grades nor the academic orientations apply in the case of Musashino students. By definition, these students are those who failed to demonstrate such abilities and orientations – otherwise they would not be at Musashino in the first place. This is combined with the virtual meaninglessness of an academic curriculum, leaving working-class high schools without any coherent center. Missing is the primary mechanism that establishes daily routine, motivates students, and helps teachers establish their authority around some model of orderly social control, some pattern of legitimate governance. When students have no reason to be in school, making their time in school meaningful is quite difficult.

When the more abstract problem of "why the students are in school" finds no real consensus among teachers at the bottom-level schools, they have the more immediate problem of how to secure order and functional respect. A mid-career teacher, who lamented being transferred down from a much more elite school, commented:

> My students [at Musashino] see us as babysitters, or entertainers, or cops. There's no link between what we do [teaching] and how the students respond to us. They might like me or not, but it's sort of a personal thing, completely separate from what we're doing here – education. If they like me, they'll usually behave well. If they don't like me, then I have problems.

We see continuity from middle school: working-class students seem more likely to seek out personal rather than instrumental relationships with their teachers, whether they are rewarded if they find them or frustrated and angry if they do not. The wet relationship with teachers is echoed in each condemnation as well as each tribute. Musashino students in fact depend upon teachers to help them in all sorts of important ways, besides keeping them from failing out of school: pregnancies, police trouble, drugs, family violence. Teachers are thus important people in many of their students' lives. Nevertheless, this sort of closeness, even intimacy in a way, does not help teachers turn the school into a coherent place of social order and control. After all, daycare, stage shows, and jails (those places where babysitters, entertainers and cops are found) are not necessarily appropriate places for high school adolescents. Teachers at working-class schools must turn elsewhere for models of order and authority. While the predicament is rather distinctive to working-class schools, the ways of dealing with it vary. One important variable is the political orientation of the teachers, a fact that reminds us of the way that class sorting is never separated from its political implications.

At Musashino, I saw two options that were familiar to most teachers as present, in some form, at most schools. The first one is defined by the teachers who were active members of the teachers' union. Almost 70 percent of the teachers at Musashino in the early 1990s were active members (a figure that was to drop to a dysfunctional rate of almost 10 percent in a few short years).[21] Musashino was once considered a "union castle" (Rohlen 1977), a problematic school at the bottom where many of the more troublesome union teachers were sent in order to "contain the problem," as the vice principal of Musashino once explained to me. If these teachers could organize a voting block or critical mass, they would be able to run the more important committees in the school. Ideologically, this group saw postwar education as *kanri kyōiku*, or managed education, that was too focused on the control of education, control of both what students were taught and how teachers taught it. Some teachers argued that these practices violated both groups' human rights (Horio 1988). The union teachers were critical of group living models as methods of control, and instead were committed to an education that was more consistent with principles of individual liberty both in the content of their lessons and in the management of their classes. Pedagogically, these teachers were very critical of the Ministry of Education curriculum and its implementation. In theory they advocated a more open, even dialogical style in the classroom, more problem-solving tasks rather than tests, collective group projects rather than individual evaluation. In the words of one student, "lots and lots of discussions – no matter what, we would have a discussion." These teachers often attempted to remove themselves as the source of authority, and at times, as a target of student resistance, in ways that resembled a variation on "soft authority." As one union teacher explained, "Unless the students know why they're doing what they're doing, it doesn't have any meaning. They must come to some understanding." These classes generated little direct conflict with students, although other teachers in the school criticized these union classrooms as unfocused to the point of anarchy, places where "no teaching was going on" even if some would agree with the union teachers that this might be a more effective way to promote learning.

The non-union group of teachers was more conservative. The Tokyo Board of Education often placed ambitious, middle-aged teachers in the post of principal of these "union castles," with the perceived mandate to quell or at least obscure the most obvious signs of union activity. Many principals saw this posting, even if there were virtually no substantial results, as a stepping stone out of teaching and into the administrative structure of the Board of Education itself. Not knowing much about the school, they took their short rotation (usually just a couple of years), hoping to be able to rally enough of the more conservative teachers around them. According to these teachers, since Musashino students were not "leader" types, it was important for them to learn how to be "useful to society" (*shakai ni yaku ni tatsu*). This usually meant teaching them a somewhat different variant of "group living:" how to mold one's own behavior to the needs of the group. More concretely, this was achieved through instructing them in greetings (*aisatsu*), use of appropriately polite language, and demonstration of an open (*sunao*) character in their willingness to do hard work and obey superiors. As one teacher explained, "Our students at Musashino are going to be doing jobs that anyone could do. They will require virtually no knowledge or skill. So, unless they can be taught to behave, they won't be of use to society, or to themselves." Pedagogically, these teachers were especially strict with students, with classroom conflict ever present, bubbling up into direct confrontation and disciplinary action almost daily. Some teachers within this group exploited the segmentation of the curriculum to codify classroom behavior into similarly discrete and therefore calculable variables. Thus, just as the exam might ask students to recite the five longest rivers in Europe, a teacher would grade each student on proper execution of the five steps for entering a room (call out, wait for acknowledgment, move to one's seat, bow, and sit down). Other teachers who were less meticulous and had more of a stomach for open conflict demonstrated a more explosive classroom culture, where students were frequently and often arbitrarily berated and punished for their ill-defined failings in comportment and attitude.[22] The second approach depended upon the unpredictable and uneven application of rules as weapons in confrontations that were often as personal as they were institutional.

These two approaches are broadly familiar to most public school teachers as addressing the structural and class predicaments of low-level schooling across Tokyo, and probably urban Japan more generally. Despite their diametrically opposed approaches, and the high level of antagonism between the groups, both groups were trying to combat the "drying out" of the moral community that was particularly developed at the working-class school. And, in their own way, they were both trying to restore some aspect of this moral community, of group living (the delegation of responsibility to students by the union teachers and subjugation of personal goals to the needs of the group for the more conservative teachers). The image of this "drying out" was vividly represented by a nearby high school that was organized around a "credit system" (*tan'isei*) where students had no homeroom and no coordinated collective activities. Students showed up to school and took enough credits, mostly in applied subjects, to graduate, as one might in college (or most US high schools). One union teacher complained that "the students might as well take a correspondence course. The Board of Education is just processing students." His conservative adversary said, "Those sorts of places are not schools. They don't teach their students to become anything at all." This school's abandonment of the school as a moral community, as part of the comprehensive education of students for adult society, was virtually unimaginable to these two groups of Musashino teachers, liberal and conservative, both committed, if in their different ways.

It is not surprising that given the choice, students favored the less confrontational union teachers (except for those few who looked forward to a fight, but even this was not an unproblematic format. For Tomo, who had done so badly in the increasingly academic curriculum of middle school, the union teachers' alternative to the regular curriculum was no more successful. He explained why he liked the more conservative teachers' classes better::

It's easier just to study the textbook and fill out worksheets, even if you have to also be disciplined [as in the conservative teachers' way]. Even if I don't understand, it's still better. Sitting there trying to have a discussion about something or other [in the union teachers' class] was meaningless. They should have just prepared a lesson and taught it, but I guess they didn't care enough to do that.[23]

Another student captured one predominant view of the more conservative teachers when she said that "they simply did not like students, and they probably did not like teaching. They were more concerned about catching and punishing us than teaching us anything." Another student countered by suggesting that the union teachers: "didn't even care about us enough to try to catch us."

For almost everyone, especially in their first year, the competing classroom cultures made for contradictory messages about school expectations, and students were often caught in the crossfire. Said Keiko, "At times, it got so bad that every class, every day was so different that you never knew what to expect. All the teachers were pushing you in different directions so that even if you wanted to stay clear [out of trouble], you could not." Keiko, who in her first year prided herself on being able to go toe-to-toe with any teacher in the school, explained that "even though none of those teachers were able to fight me, after a while, you just get worn out. It's not worth fighting anymore. I just moved away." She added, almost puzzled, "And they let me go."[24] You have to have more at stake than most of the Musashino students did to function within, or in opposition to, this sort of school culture. By their last year, most students had learned to hunker down and keep their head out of the line of fire, and most teachers had lost much of the ambition or energy to bring any wet coherence to the moral community of the school. As students got older and increasingly began to see the school as less of a reliable mechanism for their future, they simply did not have that much at stake.

Today, many of the older teachers say the same thing about their schools and even their younger colleagues. The union is largely absent as a political force in the school (or in society as a whole), and unable in most schools to secure numbers sufficient to propose and execute any coherent alternative to the "control education" of the Tokyo Board of Education. The more authoritarian teachers have survived as clusters at some school with reputations for troublesome students, but without the oppositional union teachers to fight against, they seem to be less self-consciously organized at most schools. But today many teachers from both extreme groups lament the current state of education, not as too progressive (although there does seem to be more of a presence of counseling approaches) or too authoritarian (although incidences of some forms of school conflict do seem to be quite high). Instead, both groups report that education has lost its relevance as a shaper of young people's character. The possibility of any moral community, however one sees the politics of group living, is probably most directly challenged by the threat of the dry convenience-store high school. On the other hand, maybe it is particularly well-suited to the needs of today's labor market.

Occupational self-selection

While Sara and her elite classmates were preparing for university exams, Keiko and her Musashino classmates, those who made it to the third year of school (Tomo dropped out) were expected to go through the *shinro shidōbu* (guidance office) to find a job. Each year, fewer of them bothered to do so, except when these sessions were part of their required class time.[25] They knew that finding a good job was difficult, and few of them took seriously the invitations from the guidance office to look through the job files for that one desirable job that might have slipped into their otherwise limited pool. (Most preferred to find jobs through friends or advertisements offering their services.) In one session, where students were supposed to be taught the different skills necessary to pass their interview (entering the room, greeting, seating, self-introduction, explanation of school record, etc.) a quick-witted student had the whole group rolling on the ground by banging on the door, pretending that it was stuck, which prevented him from even entering the interview room. Afterward, in a mixture of exasperation and resignation, the teacher in charge said, "These students really don't know how true to life that was – getting a job these days, at least from Musashino – well, the door is closed to them." Neither demonstrating the drive of their peers at upper-level schools, nor adopting the role of critical consumer of educational opportunities and credentials that these peers assume, Musashino students approached the job search as they approached high school: nothing ventured, nothing lost. Few see it as an opportunity, let alone maximization, but instead as something to go through, to get through, to have done, and be done with. Few imagined that there were good jobs available. After all, their elder brothers and sisters had worked these jobs, and sometimes their moms and dads. Many of them were already working there themselves even before graduating from high school.

On the questionnaire the students filled out at the start of their search, what figured most prominently was the fact that most would like to find a place close to home, with good vacations and not too long working hours. Job title or collective responsibility for work were not often selected (these were options that they could check on the questionnaire). A nice uniform was often mentioned (though it was not on the questionnaire). High salary was also not an option available for students to select on the questionnaire. In interviews with me, the students expressed a somewhat more complex view: they desired a job where the expectations were clearly laid out and where human relations would be more manageable. That is, they wanted to know exactly what sort of commitment was required of them and to be sure that they knew the limits of this commitment. Thus, in many ways, the students were seeking in their jobs a chance to avoid what was so problematic for them in school. The wanted to avoid the messiness of the dysfunctional moral community in which they had failed and that had failed them during middle school, with its diffuse sentiment, vagaries of collective responsibility, yet oppressive and exacting demands for participation. Group living proved mysterious to them during middle school, even as it was evaporating, and in high school, there was no real chance for this sort of community to develop.

In general, students believed that things would be better for them in the world of work. As Tomo explained just before dropping out, "As long as you do what you have to do in your job, you're okay. No one messes with you." No student was seeking a job with as much "freedom" as they found in those years in the union teachers' classrooms. In fact, most seemed to want some structure, at least enough to protect them from the arbitrary authoritarianism they associated with the classrooms of their more conservative teachers. As Keiko explained, "No one treats you like that when you're working. If they do, you can just leave."[26]

By the end of high school, the students were doing more than simply leaving a situation they did not like; they were also narrating a positive move into adult life. They were attracted to the idea of a contract, one which laid out obligations, responsibility, and pay. These were the sorts of agreements that they felt provided them with assurances of stability and predictability. They often mentioned the autonomy and control that they thought would come from earning their own money. Keiko explained it like this: "It's good to have some money, and working gets you money right away. You get paid regularly and for whatever work you do." She explained the criteria by which she selected one job as a telephone operator, a job she stayed with for only a few weeks: "I'm not saying that money is the only thing, and 10 yen more per hour is not very much, but it can add up over time and help you choose the best deal. ... This is especially true when all of the work is pretty much the same." She continued:

> What I like is that I know when I can leave work. I hate staying late because of some sort of business that's not finished, usually because someone else is a slow worker. I like to know exactly what I have to do and then I can just do it. I don't mind working with other people but I don't like to have to do their work, and I don't like to stay late because they have some problem with their personal relations (*ningen kankei*). I like normal work (*futsū no shigoto*).

What they did not quite understand, is that what counted for them as "normal" jobs, jobs with a contract, are in fact distinctive to a particular place in the labor market, one that very rarely leads to sustained let alone permanent work or a stable occupational profile. In effect, students self-select paths that lead them out of group living and thus out of contention for middle-class employment. The jobs that they think that they want do not become permanent (*seishain*) jobs and they do not offer a package of benefits, regular pay raises, and the promise of lifetime employment that most college graduates seek. These are not the sorts of jobs where employers hire for "character" and there is no talk of "destiny sharing" (see Borovoy in this volume) or any sort of real social identity that might be gained. These jobs with a contract are in the low-level service sector: almost always part-time, of undetermined length or short-term, low-paying, or otherwise unstable.[27] Ironically, such jobs appear to many young people as offering control: they can change jobs when they want to move on. They imagine that the contract protects them, and in a way of course it does. But in a society where lifetime employees never have a contract, in part because one does not need something as "dry" as a contact to demonstrate the wet, emotional and moral ties of real and regular employment, a contract becomes a symbol of instability, of the instrumental and tenuous connection between employer and employee. The sort of work that Musashino graduates obtained was something that they could move on from in case things did not work out, but what they did not see then was that most of the time, they simply moved on to other, similarly unstable jobs. They were employed as a particular amount of labor power, for particular tasks, for as long as they were needed and profitable. This is not how group living was supposed to work.

Today, we call those who work these jobs "*freeter*,"[28] but of course, these jobs have always been available because there has always been a need for some segment of the labor market to be flexible and skilled enough to respond to the short-term fluctuations of business cycles. Marx called these workers the great "reserve army," and the Japanese version is probably the most educated and skilled reserve army in the world. But Musashino students' jobs are not very different from those of young people in the lower reaches of the service sector all over the world. These jobs ask them to punch in and out while they work at waitressing, delivery, shelving and clerking, setting up and cleaning up. In the pre-bubble days, these jobs were more plentiful, most often had in local small shops and factories, often family-owned, while today we see a shift into the convenience or chain stores taking up a larger portion of this sector. As one teacher explained, "Often, these are the only jobs available to these kids, but I guess most of them are happier to be working in a clean 7/11 than a dirty old factory. When they look at older workers, they feel lucky."

Recessionary Japan: freeter panic as a class issue

Reduced absolute economic growth can bring into relief otherwise taken-for-granted patterns of inequality and disparity among relative class positions (see Ishida in this volume). While part-time work was increasingly prevalent for the whole period of postwar economic growth, it became more obvious and more obviously problematic after the bubble economy burst in 1991. Many companies increased the use of part-time labor, even promoting it as part of a larger national strategy to climb out of recession. This shift resulted in a percentage of part-time labor that is roughly equal to that in many western capitalist countries. While there was some dismissal of mid-career employees, the most common corporate strategy was to reduce hiring of new recruits, in what some called the "ice age" of employment. A larger number of high school and college graduates were thus unable to find what was once called "regular work" (**seishain**) But these shifts in types of work were not the part of the story that truly captured the imagination of the mass media. The media story focused on the young people who were "opting out" of the constraints of Japan, Inc., supposedly no longer willing to sacrifice for a job that demanded such dedication and emotional participation, that took the toll on body and soul that they had seen in their fathers, who brought Japan out of postwar recovery and into international prominence. The media reported that these young people went to part-time jobs by choice, to be "free" of the onerous expectations of full-time work, and "free" to pursue their own personal (not corporate) dreams. Job creation (Genda 2005), while a priority, was almost always talked about in the same breath as the need to increase young people's "will to work" (Yamada 2004). This was especially ironic given how important this part-time labor was to economic flexibility. A variant of this panic can be seen in the argument that these new jobs were not only chosen by the young out of selfishness or immaturity, but that working the jobs themselves crippled young people in their path to maturity, teaching them none of the important lessons of sacrifice and collective responsibility (group living) necessary to make them responsible members of adult Japanese society. Thus, many worried whether or not a whole generation would ever learn the necessary lessons of dedication and sacrifice, respect and decorum, collective responsibility and social dependence, while doing this increasingly prevalent irregular work. Since the 1980s, with the exception of *enjo kōksei* ("compensated dating"), there has been no other moral panic that has occupied as much newspaper space as the issue of *freeter*.

But looking at this panic from a class perspective, we notice two things. First, while the particular young people who end up as *freeter* might not embrace the ethos of Japan, Inc., nothing they have done has created the need for the progressive increase in the number of part-time jobs. Just as slowed growth in the late bubble years left construction workers homeless, today's *freeter* did not create part-time jobs. The occupational structure shifted during Japan's recession in ways that are common to neo-liberal economies all over the world, and this shift in the labor demand was reinforced by a corporate strategy designed to maintain profit margins in a time of economic hardship. Second, we saw in the media a high rhetoric of distress over the negative moral or social effect of these workers and/or of the work that they are doing, the real moral panic has been largely focused on the middle class, usually without any acknowledgment of this focus.

Working-class young people like those from Musashino have been doing these jobs for many years, decades even, as pointed out above. They took the only jobs available to them, so it is difficult to identify any lack of seriousness or willingness to sacrifice as the reason they are working these jobs today. In fact, probably the more persuasive argument would be that it is the working class, in taking these jobs for generations, who have made the biggest personal and social sacrifices for the sake of maintaining a robust and flexible national economy. But prior to the media panic over *freeter*, little popular or academic attention was devoted to any negative character effects of working in the low-level service sector. When I began fieldwork, it was before the neologism of *freeter* was popular. Instead, many Musashino graduates were often, referred to as *pūtaro*, a term denoting one who does not work regularly even he is able to do so. A *pūtaro* takes a job when necessary but without any ambition or seriousness of purpose. In a society that reads as much into the importance of work, it is not surprising that the term carries moral overtones, connoting laziness, idle or shiftlessness.[29] There was no media outcry when Musashino students worked series of low-level service jobs that working-class youth are supposed to work.

What created the moral panic was not that young people were doing (or even opting to do) this sort of work, or even that they were doing so in large numbers, but that young people from the wrong social class were ending up doing this work. Students educated at schools such as Musashino have always been *expected* to do this sort of work, and when working-class youth end up in working-class jobs (be it primary production or clerking, depending upon the shape of the bottom of the economy), it needs no explanation. The panic began when the Japanese economy needed to expand the "reserve army" beyond its working-class boundaries, when there was more irregular work than the working class (even the "new working class") could supply. And so, when students who had the money to invest in their informal education (cram schools) and who had gained certification from formal education also ended up doing this sort of irregular work, the panic began. The school-to-work mechanism was said to have fallen out of coordination. As one mother of an elite college student explained to me, "I did not spend this sort of money so that my son would end up as a *freeter*." When middle-class youths begin doing working-class work, then youth labor becomes a cause of moral panic.[30]

Thus, while the discourse of *freeter* has drawn attention to the precariousness of part-time work, it has obscured the wide class heterogeneity within this new labor category. The young people who are categorized as *freeter* range from the highly skilled and remunerated freelance graphic designers (for whom *freeter* might be a productive and financially rewarding way of life, even a permanent life strategy); to the elite college graduate earning some pocket money at the convenience store before entering a company (who has the leisure to do this sort of work until a life strategy comes into focus); to the junior college graduate with a technical certificate (who is working the job she has been trained to do, even as she comes to understand its limited potential); to the immigrant working from 10 p.m. until dawn cleaning office buildings (for whom any form of work in Japan is an economic improvement and might even be a way to obtain relative security). For young people such as Tomo, Keiko and other Musashino students, this new classification of *freeter* is both a rhetorical opportunity and a class compromise. Today, few Musashino students would call themselves *pūtaro* unprompted. As Tomo explained, "Who would be a *pūtaro* when you can be a *freeter*." For many, *freeter* is a label that has built into it a narrative of agency, choice, freedom, and individuality. In some more romantic renderings in the popular and academic press, a *freeter* can even be a rebel making a political statement. To the extent that this is a chosen type of work, it is a way to make a claim for social respectability and upward class mobility, something beyond having to take whatever sort of work is available.[31]

But to say that these jobs were "chosen" is misleading, at least for Musashino students. If asked on any survey, Keiko would explain that she has "chosen" all of her part-time jobs since she entered high school, and by her calculation, the 10 yen an hour difference makes one job better and another worse. Indeed, we have heard that she is not looking for the complicated and wet sort of work she associates with "regular" employment, and would rather have a different sort of job. Tomo appreciates the "freedom" he has to ride his bike while working. When they left

Musashino, looking for jobs that were dry and entailed little responsibility, they were well-prepared to "choose" these jobs, but it is important to remember that in most cases, these were the only jobs available. The contradictions inherent in the representation of people "choosing" *freeter* jobs, and eventually, *freeter*-hood, only become evident over time. To these older graduates, who have spent more years in the lower reaches of the service economy, to be reclassified as a *freeter*, as someone who might actually *choose* to do the sorts of work they ended up doing, seems slightly ridiculous. One Musashino graduate, class of 1990, recently commented to me, in trying to make sense of these changes that reclassify him, at least retroactively,

> I guess I must be a *freeta*. That's better than being *pūtaro*, right? But I'm not quite sure what that means. Does it mean that I *want* to do these bad jobs instead of taking good jobs? That I want to pay my own insurance [instead of having my company do it]? If that's what it means, I really am a *pūtaro*. Freeter … *freeter*. What does that really mean? Does that mean my dad is also a *freeter*? What about my mom? She works, when she can.

Just as a sorting mechanism based on academic achievement is able to re-represent social class differences as being the result of exam grades, so does the discourse of *freeter* allow Musashino graduates and the mass media to imagine that working-class youth are working their jobs by choice. This is a complicit fiction that deflects popular and scholarly attention away from the problematic nature of these new categories of work and worker, especially in ways that are complicated by patterns of class formation. The point of this chapter is to recontextualize some of the aspects of school processes within the larger dynamic of class formation; it is to trace some links between family background and school trajectories; from classroom culture, curriculum structure and pedagogical politics; and finally to some of the occupational and discursive effects as they impact on what we can recognize as the younger members of the new working class.

Notes

1   I worked at Musashino from 1991–1993, during which time I was given the slightly ridiculous but affectionate title of *fuku-fuku-tannin,* or assistant to the assistant homeroom teacher. Since that time, I have been following this cohort, and getting to know the more recent graduates (and some dropouts) through the alumni networks and teachers.

2   Tomo's mother told me that due to the lack of manual labor jobs, their "dark and dangerous reputation," she did not enroll him in a vocational school, but instead what is called a "regular course" (*futsūka*), teaching a standard academic curriculum. In fact, although vocational schools have been increasingly more able to place its students in desirable jobs, the negative image is common among those with middle-class aspirations. Keiko's mother advocated clerical high school, but Keiko refused to go to a school that was so overwhelmingly female.

3   While this seems much higher than the national rates, I would suggest the urban rates are somewhat higher than the national, and the national rates often only capture the

legally divorced, and thus miss a whole range of other sorts of family arrangements that are not uncommon, especially among families that are poor and where the mother is forced to work.

4 When one student got what was then considered a job for life in the ship yard of a major trading company, all of the homeroom teachers took out the career counselors for a beer to celebrate the anomalous achievement.

5 This data becomes increasingly unreliable over time, as the career counselor, *shinro shidōbu*, has become less active and less able to place students in desirable jobs (see Brinton in this volume).

6 In societies where formal, institutionalized education is less central than it is in Japan (for example less fully attended; less considered the synecdoche to the society, state and even culture; less a reliable means of social mobility and the production of legitimate credentialization), or where the class differentiation process occurs in other institutional contexts (for example, through regional or neighborhood distribution, through leisure activity or ethnic grouping), comprehensive education plays a less significant role in whole-culture socialization and class sorting. Compare the Japanese case to the work by Paul Willis (1977) or John Ogbu (1992). Both have written about young people entering secondary school from home cultures that put them self-consciously at odds with the official school culture. For them, social difference (class or race) is assumed, and success, even participation, in school is considered a compromise and possibly even a threat to their own social and cultural identity. These students are already aware of their own very different social paths vis-à-vis other students, and take a very jaundiced view of the mainstream culture and the institutionalization of it through education that is being discursively promoted, but differentially made available, by the school. Also, the school has little legitimacy in terms of the content being taught or the credentials that are awarded. In contrast, Japanese schooling is more important and effective in the whole-culture socialization and sorting that is perceived as legitimate. See Okano (1993) for the best discussion of the school-to-work transition in Japan. See Sato (2000) for a more general discussion of Japan as an unequal society.

7 The rich ethnographic literature upon which the present study rests includes Peak (1991), White (1978), Cummings (1980), and Rohlen (1989). I should point out that despite how Rohlen (1983) introduces of five different high schools, which he even acknowledges as clearly class differentiated, his analysis extracts from them the commonality that they share, drawing examples from each to present something that is essentially a Japanese pattern. The results are chapters called "The Japanese Adolescent Patterns" and "Japanese Pedagogy." In this way, it is even more misleading than any initial failure to identify school level at all. The project of class analysis is quite different in this respect.

8 See theorists as varied as Peak (1991) and Koschmann (1978) for discussions of soft authority from two very different perspectives.

9 In fact, this is an overstatement. Social class differences are already shaping the middle school, in at least two ways. First, although not as uniformly or dramatically, neighborhoods do differ in terms of class composition, especially in urban areas. Middle schools in more wealthy areas have more parental participation and support (including financial), which results in better facilities, a wider range of programs, and more parental influence at the school. Based on these differences, some schools are more sought after by parents because they have a better reputation for getting students into better high schools. The difference is that middle schools are nowhere as systematically ranked as any high school. Second, more ambitious and moneyed parents put their children into private schools from kindergarten, removing them from the public school mix altogether. The larger point still stands: middle schools are far more diverse than high schools, but we should not imagine that social class is fully and completely contained within the institutional context of secondary school.

10   Interestingly, I was able to collect narratives from first-year students at Musashino that were full of angst and a burning sense of betrayal at what each student understood as the injustice of his or her abandonment by teachers and peers as the student fell out of the regular academic routines of middle school. And yet, by the student's final year of high school, these same narratives, and even the feelings that had driven the narratives, were almost completely absent. They were no longer interesting to the student; they were so taken-for-granted and so much a part of who he or she had become by the end of high school that they were literally unremarkable – that is, no longer worthy of remark. Such is the effect of high school in naturalizing even the once disturbing effects of class sorting from middle school.

11   Despite the fact that it is high school that is the more self-evidently stratified institution, many richer parents seek to move their children into elite private middle schools that usually serve as "elevator schools," ushering their students into the attached high schools relatively easily. It was at one of these high-level high schools that I did half a year of fieldwork.

12   The other side of this resentment was that most students could identify one or two teachers who spent an inordinate amount of time helping them get out of trouble, informally tutoring them when they fell behind, and sometimes intervening on their behalf in non-school troubles. But this is simply the other side of the same coin: resentment or devotion, where the wet, personal relationships with teachers were in marked contrast to the dryer ones of Sara and her elite classmates. See LeTendre and Fukuzawa (2000) for an overview of student social relations in middle school.

13   One type of data that would be very valuable here is ethnographic analysis of the ways in which middle school teachers recognize and differentially treat those students who are engaged in full-on cram school activities.

14   See Tsukada (1991) for a good overview of cram schools, but note that the image of cram schools as dark and windowless sweatshops of academic production is far out of date. Even by the early 1990s this image had changed, largely due to the professionally managed advertising campaigns that stress the fun and friends you can have in cram school. Most students I talked to reported a bright, fun and relaxed atmosphere, so much so that many elite students saw this as their primary social grouping, their *uchi*, so to speak.

15   See Amano (1992) for the best sociological analysis of the shape and development of the Japanese curriculum.

16   Educational expenditures, expectations, and cram school participation are all clearly linked to class background. See Hida (http://www.childresearch.net/RESOURCE/RESEARCH/2004/HIDA.HTM).

17   An exception might be boarding school, which offers a whole developmental environment.

18   While being at a low-level high school does lead regularly and predictably to low-level jobs, difference in achievement among students at Musashino was not correlated to any different chances of their seeming success in the job market. In fact, the occupational trajectory from any high school is pretty regular, but it is true that the market at the bottom is less finely calibrated. So, for those students competing to get into the best university, a difference of a couple of points on a test score can drop a student down a number of ranks. As one Musashino student explained quite correctly, "I could sit out my whole final year of high school, still graduate and get the same job I would have gotten had I stayed in school."

19   To many Americans, the Japanese convenience store appears to be full of attentive and eager, fully enrolled young people, but to most teachers at Musashino, indeed, most adults in Japan, the service that they receive at convenience stores is often an index of the larger deterioration of service, youth and society.

20   The question of institutional authority is, of course, taken from Marx, but is most clearly developed in the work of Harry Braverman (1974).

21 Besides Rohlen (1977), see Thurston (1973) and Aspinal (2001) for a review of union activity in schools. For more detailed discussion of the workings of the union activity at Musashino, see Slater (2003). For a general discussion of the administrative structure of Japanese high schools, see Slater (2002).

22 See Kondo (1990) for a similar dynamic of border-line abuse as evidence of group cohesion and authority.

23 Of course, many of the union teachers spent a great deal of time structuring their discussion, and their insistence that students come to their own conclusions was as much a reflection of their politics as their pedagogy. They were always discouraged to hear students mistake their methods for indifference, but Tomo's view was far from an isolated case.

24 By her third year, Keiko was going to so few classes she was ironically referred to as "*okyakusama*" (valued customer or guest) by teachers and students alike when she did bother to show up.

25 See Brinton's chapter in this volume. See Honda (2005) for an overview of youth work. It may be that Musashino was a bit ahead of some of the schools in these studies in allowing their connections to local companies to wither. In Musashino's case, many of these connections were based on personal networks, rather than firm institutional ties, and when the head of the guidance office retired, his connections were largely lost to Musashino students.

26 Some years later, I reminded Keiko of her own comment, and she laughed, saying, "I said that? Well, I did leave some jobs earlier on, but after a while, you have to settle somewhere, right?"

27 For example, as a tenured professor at an elite private university, I have no contract with rights or conditions of employment. I did not know what my salary would be before I began. Only part-time teachers have contracts.

28 The term "*freeter*" was created by Recruit Magazine in 1987 as a new type of designation for part-time work by contracting the English "free" and the German "*arbeiter*," meaning worker. The Ministry of Labor has used this term since the early 1990s for irregular, unmarried workers between the ages of 15 and 34. See Kosugi (2003) for a good review.

29 The most well-known *pūtaro* is Tora-san, from the film "Its tough being a man" (*Otoko wa tsuraiyo*).

30 In order to describe the panic around freeter, media reports would almost always focus on the discrepancy between family investment and academic progress, on the one hand, and the failure to find permanent work on the other. For example, we did not hear stories like Keiko's: mother does not graduate from high school, has child, gets divorced, works in a fast food shop; remarries but second husband does not support child, who ends up with irregular school record; but upon graduation, child ends up working in a hostess bar. Working-class trajectories such as this one did not fill the newspaper features. It was almost always the narrative of middle-class descent into labor irregularity.

31 This is, of course, a complex dynamic, especially when one looks at it over time. Musashino students who left school in 1990 saw any sort of non-manual labor, including clerical work, as a step up. Those who graduated 10 years later, when such work became more common, made distinctions between small local stores and the more desirable, brightly lit convenience stores. Today, the image of labor desperation is more often located at these same convenience stores.

References

Amano I. (1992) *Gakureki no Shakaishi* [The History of the Educational Achievement Society], Tokyo: Shinchousha.

Apple, M. and Lois Weiss (1983) *Ideology and Practice in Schooling*, Philadelphia, PA: Temple University Press.

Aspinall, R. (2001) *Teachers' Unions and the Politics of Education in Japan*, Albany, NY: SUNY Press.

Bernstein, B. (1977) *Class Codes and Control*, London: Routledge and Kegan Paul.

Bestor, T. (1990) *Neighborhood Tokyo*, Stanford, CA: Stanford University Press.

Bourdieu, P. (1977) *Outline of a Theory of Practice*, Cambridge, New York: Cambridge University Press.

Bourdieu, P. and Jean Claude Passeron (1977) *Reproduction in Education, Society and Culture,* London: Sage Publications.

Bowles, S. and Herbert Gintis (1976) *Schooling in Capitalist America: educational reform and the contradictions of economic life,* New York: Basic Books.

Braverman, H. (1974) *Labor and Monopoly Capital*, New York: Monthly Review Press.

Cole, R. (1971) *Japanese Blue Collar: the changing tradition*, Berkeley, CA: University of California Press.

Cummings, W. (1980) *Education and Equality in Japan*, Princeton, NJ: Princeton University Press.

Duke, B. (1986) *The Japanese School: lessons for industrial America*, New York: Praeger.

Fujita, H. (1997) *Kyouiku Kaikaku* [Education Reform], Tokyo: Iwanami Shoten.

Genda, Y. (2005) *A Nagging Sense of Job Insecurity: the new reality facing Japanese youth*, trans. Jean Connell Hoff, Tokyo: LTCB International Library Trust, International House of Japan.

Gupta, A. and James Ferguson (1997) *Anthropological Locations: boundaries of a field science*, Berkeley, CA, University of California Press.

Hall, S. and Tony Jefferson (1976) *Resistance through Rituals: youth subcultures in post-war Britain*, London: Hutchinson.

Horio, T. (1988) *Educational Thought and Ideology in Modern Japan: state authority and intellectual freedom*, Tokyo: University of Tokyo Press.

Honda, Y. (2005) *Wakamono to Shigoto: "gakkō keiyu no shūshoku" wo koete* [Young people and Employment in Japan: beyond the "school-mediated job search"], Tokyo: Tokyo Daigaku Shuppankai.

Ishida, H. (1993) *Social Mobility in Contemporary Japan: educational credentials, class and the labour market in cross national perspective*, Stanford, CA: Stanford University Press.

Katznelson, I. (1985) "Working class formation," in I. Katznelson and A.R. Zolberg (ed.) *Working Class Formation*, Princeton, NJ: Princeton University Press.

Kondo, D. (1990) *Crafting Selves: power, gender, and discourses of identity in a Japanese workplace*, Chicago, IL: University of Chicago Press.

Koschmann, V. (1978) *Authority and the Individual in Japan: citizen protest in historical perspective*, Tokyo: University of Tokyo Press.

Kosugi, R. (2003) *Furītā Toiu Ikikata* [Freeter as a Way of Life], Tokyo: Keisō Shobō.

LeTendre, G. and Erwin Fukuzawa (2000) *Early Adolescence in Contemporary Japan: school, family, and friends*, New York, London: Garland.

Murakami, Y. (1977) "Shin chūkan kaisō no genjitsusei [The reality of the new middle class]," *Asahi Shinbun* [Asahi Newspaper], evening edn, 20 May.

Ogbu, J. (1992) *Black Resistance in High School: forging a separatist culture*, Albany, NY: SUNY Press.

Okano, K. (1993) *School to Work Transition in Japan: an ethnographic study*, Clevedon: Multilingual Matters.

Peak, L. (1991) *Learning to Go to School in Japan: the transition from home to preschool Life*, Berkeley, CA: University of California Press.

Roberson, J. (1998) *Japanese Working-Class Lives: an ethnographic study of factory workers*, London; New York: Routledge.

Rohlen, T. (1977) "Is Japanese education becoming less egalitarian? Notes on high school stratification and reform," *Journal of Japanese Studies* 3(1):37–70.

—— (1983) *Japan's High Schools*, Berkeley, CA: University of California Press.

—— (1989) "Order in Japanese society: attachment, authority, and routine," *Journal of Japanese Studies* 15(1).

Rose, N. (1989) *Governing the Soul: the shaping of the private self*, London: Free Association Press.

Sato, T. (2000) *Fubyōdō Shakai Nippon* [Japan as an unequal society], Tokyo: Chūō Kōron Shinsha.

Slater, D. (1998) "Finding class culture in Japan," *Hitotsubashi Journal of Social Sciences,* 30(1).

—— (2002) "Changing formal and informal structure in a working-class high school," in N. Hirochika, ed. *Anthropology of Japanese Organizations*, Osaka: Minpaku Press.

—— (2003) *Class Culture: pedagogy and politics in a Japanese working-class high school in Tokyo*, Ann Arbor, MI: University of Michigan Dissertation Service.

Thurston, D. (1973) *Teachers and Politics in Japan,* Princeton, NJ: Princeton University Press.

Tsukada, M.(1991)*Yobiko Life: a study of the legitimation process of social stratification in Japan*, Berkeley, CA: Institute of East Asian Studies University of California.

Vogel, Ezra. (1971). *Japan's New Middle Class: the salary man and his family in a Tokyo suburb*. Berkeley, CA: University of California Press.

Voloshinov, V. (1973) *Marxism and the Philosophy of Language*, New York: Seminar Press.

White, Merry. (1978). *The Japanese Educational Challenge: a commitment to children*. New York: Free Press.

Willis, P. (1977) *Learning to Labour: how working-class kids get working-class jobs*, Farnborough, UK: Saxon House.

Yamada, M. (2004) *Kibō Kakusa Shakai* [Hope divided society], Tokyo: Chikuma Shobō.

7 What color is your parachute?

The post-degree society

Amy Borovoy

In his 1998 book, *The New Insecurity: The End of the Standard Job and Family,* Jerald Wallulis describes what he perceives as a steady shift in American social life since the 1970s, from the struggle to achieve "employment" to the struggle to achieve "employability;" from the struggle to achieve "marriage" to the struggle to achieve "marriageability." Shifts in capitalist modes of production towards functional flexibility combined with the erosion of social assistance under the Reagan, Bush, and Clinton administrations, have created an environment in which individuals themselves, no longer able to carry out life planning under the guaranteed security of such programs as disability compensation, support for the role of homemaking, or social security, must now become their own individual "planning office," as Wallulis puts it, functioning as the sole manager of his or her own biography (Beck 1995 in Wallulis 1998: 6). The era of long-term career ladders, company loyalty, and the permanent marriage has passed. And, according to Wallulis, along with greater flexibility, individuals now face a considerable degree of anxiety and fear – fear of loneliness, unemployment (owing to corporate reengineering or global competition), inadequacy, and the struggle to maintain employability (8). More than ever, upward mobility is perceived to rest on the individual as a transportable and self-contained package of goods.

Although Wallulis's discussion singles out the United States for its extreme destandardization and "turbo-charged" capitalism, the concept inevitably applies to some extent to all industrialized capitalist nations negotiating the process of globalization, including Japan. A similar set of pressures has accompanied Japan's transition to late capitalism: increasing pressure to compete with low cost labor as well as the demand for "flexible" modes of production and flexibility in labor supply. And yet the situation Wallulis describes is quite antithetical to the system that has characterized large and medium-sized firms in Japan in the postwar period: employees recruited and trained by specific firms, heavy reliance on the company for pension and social security benefits, and the sacrifice of individual autonomy in return for the promise of economic and social stability (Cole 1979; Dore 1973; Dore and Sako 1998; Rohlen 1974).

William Kelly has noted the pervasiveness of what has been called "middle-class consciousness" *(chūryū ishiki)* in postwar social life in Japan. Kelly describes middle-class consciousness as both inclusive and differentiating: able to produce a broadly shared sense of identity (despite material class differences) through a number of enfranchising discourses and institutions, including work, gender, and education (2002: 236–41). Kelly's argument is that a powerful set of shared narratives defined the middle-class identity of a generation of Japanese citizens who entered their productive (and reproductive) years in the immediate postwar decades. This narrative, what Kelly calls "cohort talk," was shaped by a set of institutions designed to rehabilitate the Japanese economy, including the "dual economy" of large, stable industries, sustained by the fluid labor pools of smaller firms. Kelly writes, "As this generation begins to die off and the demographic profile ages, we can expect serious repercussions" (242). As the Japanese economy is changing, new demands are being made on employees that shape education, the transition to work, and the definition of valuable human capital itself. This is the process that I begin to explore in this chapter.

Employment and promotional practices of the large-scale company have been central to maintaining the postwar social fabric. While such companies employ roughly only a third of the male working population, they have expanded the sphere of middle-class identity by offering long-term blue-collar employees employment stability, benefits, and a measure of upward mobility – what is often described as of "white-collarization" of male blue-collar workers (Kelly 2002: 240; Brinton this volume). However the notion of "success" and upward mobility has been defined in a way that differs from what Americans might associate with "meritocracy." Although the United States and Japan share a notion of upward mobility through a level playing field, with emphasis on equal opportunity offered through education rather than through social assistance provided by the state (Lash and Urry 1987: 80–1), the notions of "opportunity" and upward mobility what it takes to succeed differ greatly.

In American meritocracy, there is a strong belief in the importance of individual ability and effort to upward mobility – the notion of success as dependent upon one's own wits, cultivated skills, and resourcefulness, the promise of being "self-made."[1] A different story is told about the implicit assumptions concerning the middle class which grew dramatically in the postwar years of the 1950s, 1960s and early 1970s, and although this story is now familiar, it bears recounting in the effort to understand how a younger generation must negotiate the current changes.

Postwar Japanese enterprise drew in large numbers of rural farm workers as well as workers in small family-owned business, who came to identify themselves with the middle class, in part based on their relative prosperity compared with one previous generation prior (Ishida this volume: 00–00; Vogel 1963). During the high-growth decades of the 1960s and 1970s, many of these workers experienced upward mobility as hitching one's fate to the fate of the company and proceeding up the ranks, under the premise of guaranteed job stability, life security, and a family wage. Large- and mid-size Japanese firms acceded to the demands for job stability among postwar unions in return for commitment to the company, flexibility on the part of workers, and extraordinary extractions of labor (such as unpaid overtime) (see Gordon 1993: 385–7). Although smaller firms faced savvy, skilled, urban workers who resisted the fate-sharing ideology and often took advantage of opportunities for job mobility, workers at mid- to large-size firms (both white and blue-collar) were promoted rank by rank, with the largest portion of their pay based largely (though not exclusively) on seniority (Cole 1971: 62–4; Rohlen 1974: 161–2).

A key feature of this style of human capital development has been an emphasis on "character" or human potential over transferable skills. Companies hire employees "fresh" from high school or college based largely on school status (Kariya 1991: 17–19; see also Ishida 1998: 288). Employability in this context refers to trainability and flexibility as well as character and family background considerations (Dore 1973: 48; Dore and Sako 1998: 16; Lee-Cunin 2004: 37).[2] The status of a school is seen as a measure of human character and potential, in part because of the exam system that sorts students is thought to measure in large part tenacity, effort, self-discipline, and the ability "to endure under difficult circumstances for a fairly long period of time" (Lee-Cunin 2004: 37; see also Rohlen 1983: 93–100). Companies train, shape, and mold their human capital in the assumption that workers will stay and ply their skills as proud and loyal members of a particular company as a "Hitachi man" in Dore's well-known example (see Dore 1973). Historically, this training, pronounced in large companies, involved not merely skill-transferal, but a process of socialization, which included company dormitories, uniforms, a "company slogan," "company song" and attention to what most Americans would consider the "private" world of the employee – family life, "character," "attitudes," and "conduct" (Dore 1973: 62–3; Rohlen 1974, 1988).

It is this system that has prompted the problematic claim that social class functions fundamentally differently in Japan, since workers identify not primarily with their "horizontal" class status or lifestyle but rather with their "vertical" strata of institutional affiliation. (Ishida this volume: Kariya 1998; see Nakane 1970). While the category of "social class" has not been prominent in postwar American Japan studies, Japan is a fascinating case, precisely for the ways in which the realities of structured class differences have been obscured and effaced in everyday consciousness. While anthropologists' historic commitment to studying the subjective experience of entrenched social structures may have deflected their attention from (or perhaps allowed them to underestimate) the systematic effects of education and labor markets on social inequality (Ishida and Slater this volume), this ethnographic analysis of lived experience is one way – and perhaps the only way – to understand how the empirical reality of inherited differences in profession and wages is made to appear acceptable, legitimate, natural, and even "fair."

Ishida (this volume) points out that the coexistence of persisting social status differences with broad-based self-identification as "middle-class" is not unique to postwar Japan. And yet the discourse and rationale that underpin this middle-class identity is historically and culturally shaped. The notion of upward mobility through "fate-sharing" has a different logic of fairness, which promises that each individual will be rewarded for his/her hard work, devotion, and loyalty. These assumptions are embedded in the educational system and exam system, and crystallize in the context of the school-to-work transition. As David Slater argues, the work of socialization is crucial here, as students are groomed to equate success with one set of qualities (good character, tenacity, motivation, and sociability) and failure with another. Among those who attend the lower-level schools, failure is typically individualized, Slater writes, despite the structured inequalities that go into its making (see Slater, this volume).

However, as the Japanese economy adjusts to the demands of global competition and the effects of the bursting of the economic bubble, it appears increasingly difficult to maintain the premise of shared background, the fruits of effort, and the premise of a level playing field. In contemporary Japan, the qualities of pedigree, good character, and future success and upward mobility increasingly appear to untwine, leaving place for new ideals of what it takes to succeed to emerge. The following section explores these growing fissures.

Shifting notions of human capital

In the wake of the bursting of the economic bubble and heightened global competition, Japanese enterprise has reached a point where increasingly fewer companies can afford to treat human capital as something to be molded from scratch. The hollowing out of the manufacturing industry since the 1970s, the trimming of the workforce to include fewer low-skilled highly-compensated workers, and the outsourcing of low-skilled work to part-time or temporary workers who do not receive similar benefits has seemingly ushered in an era in which fewer workers are eligible for the trajectory of upward mobility through fate-sharing. While Japanese firms in more prosperous times integrated diverse class segments into a seemingly coherent institutional frame, and college (or high school) graduation served as a baseline credential for upward mobility, this broader shift has presented new challenges and new opportunities for some, and foreclosed opportunities for others. One way to understand the class effects of this wider transformation of the practices and ideology of neoliberal shifts is to examine the process of school to work: in particular, the ways in which differently ranked tertiary schools socialize their students to embrace quite different views of success, mobility, and skill.

This chapter considers the transition from school to work in three settings: an elite private university, a third-tier small college, and a vocational school. A brief look at students' approaches to job hunting *(shūshoku katsudō)* in the three contrasting institutions reveals that students are very much grappling with what they perceive as the new importance of "merit" and "individual ability" *(jitsuryoku)*, a rhetoric which has emerged in direct contrast with the familiar forms of lifetime employment *(shūshin koyō)* and seniority-based promotion *(nenkō joretsu)*. One of the most significant fault lines that that is already appearing within this market shift is the breakdown according to class, or more specifically, according to the ways in which different class segments of young people are entering the market.

Crucial to this story is the fact that once success based on gradual promotion, job stability, company benefits, and socialization and training was not particular to the white-collar salaried or managerial track classes. Brinton (this volume) points out that mid- to large- size firms have historically hired large numbers of high school graduates each year, training them to work in manufacturing and other skilled blue-collar sectors. Brinton reminds us that while crossing the "collar line" has been historically difficult in Japan (more difficult than, for example, Britain or the U.S.), more than education or social background, labor force experience is the most striking variable affecting eventual earning capacity (Brinton this volume:). Because this experience tends to be firm-specific in Japan, blue-collar workers (typically high school graduates) are not penalized as significantly in terms of earnings capacity; furthermore, they receive the training, socialization, and gradual upward mobility that have characterized white-collar workers in postwar Japan.[3] Brinton's analysis allows us to see how notions of upward mobility through labor force participation (working one's way up) as well as exposure to forms of corporate socialization once cut across different levels of educational attainment. Hence as seniority-based positions become increasingly scarce, a fissure is likely to occur. This divide would most likely hinge not on college vs. high-school education but on those who are able to obtain full-time, relatively permanent positions and those who are not.

What color is your parachute? The new "ability-ism"

A brief look at students' approaches to *shūshoku katsudō* in the three contrasting institutions reveals that students are very much grappling with what they perceive as the new importance of "merit" and "individual ability" *(jitsuryoku)*, a rhetoric which has emerged in direct contrast with the familiar forms of "lifetime employment" *(shūshin koyō)* and seniority-based promotion *(nenkō joretsu)*. As companies, particularly smaller firms, increasingly value skills over pedigree, students are forced to rethink their strategies for employment, their views of human capital, and the notion of middle-class citizenship itself. Smaller numbers of students who cannot make the established system work for them, join the ranks of students who study for various certificates of qualification *(shikaku)* while simultaneously attending college, an increasingly common phenomenon known as "double-schooling" *(daburu sukūru)*. *While* attending college, students increasingly study to receive a variety of "licenses" and "certificates" in various trades including cooking, paramedics, accounting, and preparing legal documents; some study to pass civil service examinations. Many enterprising universities are offering their own certificate training programs, including some of the largest private universities in Japan. In fact it has been reported that some universities appear to be diminishing their humanities offerings and instead establishing programs that cater to growing demand, such as in psychology or pharmaceuticals (Muraki 2005).[4]

The notion of Japan as a society increasingly oriented towards individual opportunity, "ability-ism" *(jitsuryokushugi)* or "merit," and risk-taking is very much in evidence in public discourse. Japanese bookstores prominently display books (often Japanese translations of American popular books) on efficiency, time-management, and entrepreneurship, such as *One-Minute Problem Solving (Ippunkan no Mondai Kaiketsu)*, *The Way Successful People Think (Umaku Itte Iru Hito no Kangaekata)*, and *Okuman Chōja ni Naru Tame no 21 Hōsoku* (Brian Tracy's *The 21 Secrets of Self-Made Millionares)*. Interestingly, the American college student classic, *What Color is Your Parachute*, has recently been translated into Japanese and appears to be selling briskly. *What Color is Your Parachute* is a guide to job-searching targeted, also, to those making mid-life career changes. It sends particularly American messages about the meaning of employment, self, and "growing up." In sections such as "geographies of the heart," and "how to find your mission in life," it urges readers to find that job which is most suited to their unique and inhering interests and abilities, sending the message that work is about capitalizing on and cultivating one's inner talents, rather than about paying one's dues, learning on the job, or simply paying the bills. These ideas run in contrast with the notion of labor that crystallized in postwar Japan, which conceptualized "merit" as effort and commitment to the corporate entity (Gordon 1993) and which maintained social and economic stability through making one's way up the ladder.

Although "ability-ism" is central to the way in which Japanese youths across a spectrum of tertiary institutions imagine the opportunities available and groom themselves to achieve, the rhetoric of ability-ism surpasses its reality. The effects of the new economy appear to vary depending on the nature of the industry and size of the enterprise. Based on the presentations made by the "blue-chip" companies who appeared to recruit at a top-level university, many continue to tout the importance of "Japanese-style management" *(Nihon-shugi keiei)* and (including Cannon and Hitachi) have made explicit their commitment to the postwar employment practices of lifetime employment *(shūshin koyō)* and seniority promotion *(nenkō joretsu)*.

Yet even at these traditional companies marginal yet culturally significant changes appear to be underway. The companies are shortening general training (during which new employees learn to bow, exchange business cards, and sing the company song), allowing employees greater freedom in choosing their jobs and departments (a process known as "job matching" *[jobu macchingu]*), and promoting talented young employees more rapidly[5] – all of which subtly challenge the mindset of employees as corporate "members" rather than as free agents in possession of transferable skills and talents.[6] A Matsushita Electronics spokeswoman told the students, "We don't want someone who just wants to work at Matsushita. We want someone who knows what they want to do and can do it at Matsushita." Sony, known to be a maverick company that has been proactive in moving towards American-style "meritocracy,"[7] declined to send along an "OB" (old boy) of the university as its representative and instead sent along a young member of the personnel department, who berated the students attendees for showing up in their uniform, black recruit suits. "Why are you wearing that suit?!" he demanded of one student. "I thought it was the correct thing to do," the student responded meekly." "Well, to the interviews, please wear your ordinary clothes *(shifuku)*," the Sony representative replied. (Later, one student who seemed to have missed the point inquired, "What kind of regular clothes should we wear to the interview?")

The trend towards individual initiative, the cultivation of inhering skills, efficiency, and originality is closely connected to the phenomenon of the "learning society," astutely observed by Takehiko Kariya (this volume). Kariya documents trends in education and the workplace which are critical of the instrumentalism of the old credential society (in his terms, the "J-mode" society) in which learning is extrinsically motivated and success is awarded to those who are good test-takers. Entrepreneurship, "trainability," flexibility in human capital formation, "self-learning," and the capacity to exploit a range of situations to develop newly relevant knowledge and skills are what is meant by the "learning society," a society better adapted to the knowledge economy than the credential society. Students of all demographic sectors are now being exposed to these demands, and some are better poised to take advantage of them than others. Yet, as Kariya reminds us, while the "life-long learning society" model is at first glance a more meritocratic model that takes advantage of individual initiative, it carries the great capacity for inequality, since students are differentially poised to take advantage of it. If the credential society erred on the side of limiting the effects of merit, ambition, and individual initiative by measuring potential in terms of fixed, codified credentials, the learning society has the great potential to exacerbate them.

The three institutions examined in this chapter reveal the ways in which the shifts in the organization of labor, skill, and human capital are affecting students with very different credentials. It also explores how the new society is calling into question many premises of the credential society itself – in particular the centrality of good character and firm-specific skills as the key assets of the productive worker.

The elite school is still able to place the majority of its students into prestigious, full-time jobs that are competitive and desirable, the sorts of jobs that still demonstrate the ideal of occupational stability and security often associated with the Japanese firm. However, the low-level 4-year college faces a difficult situation in the changing economy. The 4-year colleges once capitalized on the credential-based system which rewarded students with a college degree (regardless of their skills or performance) with stable jobs and a heavy investment in training. Yet even mid-to large-size firms increasingly face a shortage of resources for training students and they increasingly rely on temporary and part-time labor for unskilled work. These institutions are struggling with their *raison d'être,* and students themselves look to new rhetorics of "skill" and "choice" but without the training to truly capitalize on the opportunities the new economy affords. This is in contrast to the vocational school (*senmon gakkō*), which, more than the others, is a by-product of the more flexible, service-oriented economy. It prepares its students with transportable skills which they then can carry with them in the endeavor to bid up their offer and maximize their compensation – the very antithesis of the postwar ideal of stability and mobility through commitment. At the same time, such schools are unequal in their quality of education and, depending on the profession, expose students to a considerable degree of risk in the absence of a well-developed welfare state. The great trade-offs of such a life-style remain to be examined, but I offer a few thoughts on how we might understand this rapidly-growing alternative to the postwar credential society.

Traditional paths to upward mobility: the virtues of hierarchy, endurance, and commitment

At the elite university, the divisions of humanities, foreign languages, comparative culture, and science and technology placed top numbers of students at large, prestigious, and highly popular companies in 2004 – including JTB, Fuji Television, Sony, and JR (Ōda 2004).[8] (Out-of-college employment rates [*shūshoku ritsu*] vary greatly across departments.) The university is a well-established, private university in central Tokyo that has a strong focus on the humanities and foreign languages and literatures; it is counted in the top ten in almost all rankings of universities in Japan.

During February and March, the height of the job-hunting season, three companies a day come to recruit at the university's job fair – all top-level companies registered on the Tokyo stock exchange. Each offers a PowerPoint presentation outlining the company's products, business plan, job opportunities, and corporate culture *(shafū)*. Companies include brand makers (for example, Suntory, Toyota), financial institutions (banks, insurance companies), trading companies (Mitsubishi, Sumitomo), retail (Isetan), electronics/technology (Cannon, Matsushita, Hitachi, IBM), and service (Hotel Okura).

The traditional pattern of job-searching at the elite universities, featured a fixed season of recruitment, in which Japanese firms work through closely established university networks of faculty and alumni in order to advertise themselves, interview students, and make a fixed numbers of informal offers *(naitei)*. Job offers were based largely on the recommendations of faculty from designated institutions *(shiteikō)* (Kariya 1988: 323–5). Facilitating these connections were institutionalized networks of alumni who formed the bridge between employer and school, notifying the school of job openings and networking with potential candidates.[9] Because an offer was based largely on the student's pedigree and recommendations, college became a time for students to enjoy themselves, to cultivate their connections to senior students *(senpai)* through club activities, and the early years of employment represented a stark shift, in which students focused all their attention on their new job, gradually making their way up the ladder.[10]

Koyama Kenji's story epitomizes this ladder of success. He was a business major at a top private university and had entered the university by gaining admission as an elementary school student to one of the expensive feeder schools. Koyama never entered a seminar in the major,[11] owing to his intense focus on rugby. In his senior year, he secured a job in one of the top trading companies, Mitsubishi Corp. *(Mitsubishi Shōji),* by relying heavily on the alumni connections available to him through the feeder school and through the university's rugby club. He told me that his job search began and ended with alumni interviews or "old-boy visits" *(OB hōmon).* He started with informational interviews of several recent graduates of the rugby team (some of whom he knew as a freshman), asking them about the company's business, and then gradually worked his way up the hierarchy of the rugby alumni *(tate no tsunagari de)* currently employed at Mitsubishi. He applied mainly to places where there were university rugby connections. By the time of his first formal interview at Mitsubishi, Koyama had already met with ten or more rugby OBs who had given him various advice on his job search.

While school clubs have often been treated as little more than evidence of the intellectual bankruptcy of Japanese college education, more recently, scholars have shown how these activities are central to understanding students' socialization (Cave 2004: 383). Club activities at this university are known to be particularly lively. Students often spend the better part of their college days devoted to the club, particularly in the case of sports clubs, and the friendships forged there endure, often providing key alumni connections for future employment.[12] Yet beyond these connections, it is fair to say that club participation, along with the entrance exam system (and perhaps the *shūshoku* process itself), are the central spheres for forging the kinds of subjectivities that are required in the corporate world, specifically the rewards of effort and endurance, the virtues of hierarchy, and the beneficence of paternalism. While clubs may play a declining role in job-seeking as students grow more independent and atomistic (Koyama's rugby team was an exception – a notably old-fashioned club with strong connections) (Chiavacci 2005: 33–7), the socializing effects of these clubs on students' construction of work and maturity are still very much in evidence.

In particular, the hierarchical models of friendship and camaraderie *(jōge kankei)* which undergird club sociality groom students for traditional paths to upward mobility. The "senior-junior" *(senpai-kōhai)* relationships establish older members *(senpai)* as leaders and teachers to younger members of the groups. *Senpai* train and guide younger members, and in return, juniors *(kōhai)* defer to their seniors, often doing menial labor such as carrying or cleaning equipment, and, in some clubs, treating their seniors with a great deal of deference (formal language, bowing, deferential greetings). Through this system, obedience and authority are legitimated.[13] A "good" superior, like a good manager, is strict and domineering, but has his junior's best interests at heart (a *senpai* who is "kind enough to scold" [Cave 2004: 40]). (Needless to say, this logic has commonly legitimated acts of abuse and exploitation of juniors by seniors, and such phenomena are well-known in the history of clubs from as early as junior high school.) Through the rounds of training and competition, the clubs socialize the students into values that have sustained Japanese organizations: the merit of submitting to an authority that is deemed worthy, susceptibility to being molded and shaped, the value of endurance and hardship as a means of self-cultivation, and the importance of cooperation, teamwork, and self-sacrifice (Cave 385, 390; see also Rohlen 1974, 1988).

Ehara Motoki

Ehara Motoki received an offer from Sumitomo Warehouse. When he emailed me to report on the outcome of his job hunt, he wrote that although he had made it to the final round of interviews with Nippon Express *(Nippon Tsūun)*, he had withdrawn and selected Sumitomo because of its amicable corporate culture *(odayaka na shafū)* and good human relationships. He told me, "I feel that my job-search process *(shūshoku)* has been the culmination of my all my experiences up to this point." Chief among these experiences were the process of studying for college entrance examinations and his participation in the lacrosse club at university.

Ehara took pride in his struggle to gain admission to a top university. "Passing the entrance exams is not just a matter of brain power *(nōryoku)* by learning math or English, it is a matter of character *(jinkaku)*". He is proud of his exam successes and has appropriated them as manifestations of his own drive and determination (not the result of external pressure). As a result, he has fond memories of the process, and sees the outcome as valid.

Ehara regrets that studying has been a low priority for him in college. Instead of studying regularly, he relied on nights of cramming *(ichiyazuke)*,[14] often with notes borrowed from a friend in return for another set of notes or a dinner out. His central preoccupation in college has been membership in the lacrosse club. The big event in the club is the summer tournament in August; the students spent the entire year preparing for that one event. When asked how his life will change when he begins work, he replied,

> I'll enter a much more demanding world with a lot of responsibility. But those demands are what make me push myself *(kibishii jōkyo denai to ganbarenai)*. Being in the lacrosse club has taught me the value of sustained effort over time *(nagai kikan no doryoku)*, keeping one's eyes on fixed target and planning *(mokuhyō o motte, keikaku o tatete)*, and reflecting on one's losses *(nayande)*. … When we win, there's nothing better. When we lose, it's so painful we cry.

He expects to keep in touch with his lacrosse friends after graduation. With respect to *"jitsuryoku shugi"* versus *"shūshin koyō,"* he largely supports the system that has dominated large Japanese enterprise in the postwar period. Ebara comments, "To preserve a company's bottom line, some restructuring may be necessary. But more and more companies treat their employees like property *(zaisan)*, and I don't want to enter a company that treats its employees that way."

Of all Japanese youth, students at this top-level university are perhaps the most shielded from the shifts taking place in conceptions of labor and human capital. Through their clubs they enjoy a network of connections at elite companies and are socialized to believe in the legitimacy of hierarchy and authority and the rewards of effort and commitment. The exam system in particular appears to legitimize the entitlement of those who do well (they are seen as having succeeded through their own efforts) and is seen nostalgically as a character-forming experience (see also Rohlen 1988). Those who succeed in exam and club contexts have proven their character and commitment – essential criteria for firms in selecting new employees. In addition, both candidates share quite traditional views of their life outside work, conforming to enterprise society notions of the home as a supplement to work. These dispositions clearly benefit and anticipate the expectations that they will encounter in the elite managerial jobs for which they are being groomed.

All students must evaluate the trade-offs of this new economy and the definition of upward mobility as the maximization of individual potential. But for elite students, the balance appears to lie in favor of supporting the traditional ideals. "Ability-ism" offers to these students the attraction of out-competing their peers based on a direct evaluation of talents and ambition; and yet it exposes them to greater risks: the possibility of failure, of loss of dignity, of being treated "as property," and perhaps (though not likely) the possibility of losing one's job. It is interesting that on the balance, many elite students still seem to favor the old system ("with some modifications") and support its virtues. Interestingly, "ability-ism" appears to not have entirely seduced the graduates of elite colleges – the same constituents who most stand to gain from its implementation. These are the same students who gained most from prior notions of human capital, and many seem reluctant to forfeit those benefits.[15] Interestingly, and perhaps tragically, it is those who perhaps stand to gain less from a new economy based on skill and competition who more enthusiastically seem to embrace it. In the following section I explore the repercussions of the new flexibility for those who are farther down the chain of valued credentials and tertiary education.

The declining importance of pedigree

The second institution, the lower-level four-year college, is a key window into remarkable changes in the labor market and emerging fissures in social class. Since the 1960s, the number of students who attend college has increased dramatically under the assumption that a college credential is the single most important credential to stable, upwardly mobile employment. There were 132, 296 new entrants to universities and colleges in 1955 (including national, local, and private universities and junior colleges) and 603,760 entrants in 2005 (Monbukagakushō Statistics 2008). In particular, the number of private universities and colleges grew rapidly. (Private universities and colleges constituted 53.5 percent of all universities and colleges in 1955 and 74.9 percent of all in 2003.) The 1990s was a particularly rapid time of growth (Currently, almost half of Japanese students attend college, including junior college).[16]

Yet, while a college degree in itself (no matter from where) may have conferred some benefits in the go-go era of the 1970s and 1980s, when companies had the resources to hire and train young men and women they perceived to be of good character and pedigree, this is less true today. The many private colleges and junior colleges which rose up at the height of Japan's economic growth to meet the demands of the pedigree society now face a significant challenge.

At a small 4-year college located in Chiba Prefecture, outside Tokyo, the socialization of students through the job-search process, through classes, and activity-based clubs is a peripheral and remote part of everyday college life. The college was originally founded in 1926 as a women's dental school. In 1992 it opened as a women's junior college under the banner of "internationalism," focusing heavily on English language training and exclusively in the humanities. It became one of the top women's junior colleges *(joshi tanki daigaku)* which aspired to train women to become successful clerical workers and, ultimately, housewives.[17] Its rankings declined significantly after its recent transformation to a co-ed college. A survey conducted of 360 universities and colleges ranks the college number 343 in the percentage of students who have found a work destination by first term senior year. The percentage of students who continue on to full-time jobs after graduation is estimated at 51 percent *(Ekonomisuto* 2004: 43). A significant portion of the remaining 50 percent (students who do not advance to graduate school) become what are known as "permanent part-time workers" or *furiitaa*.[18] The *furiitaa* rate is calculated as the number of students in the class *minus* those who go on to graduate school *minus* those who receive a full time contract, divided by the number of students in the class. Almost 100 percent of the students gain entrance through high school transcripts and recommendations of teachers at specified high schools *(shiteikō)* rather than through the more competitive entrance exam process.[19] Most students come in the pursuit of the college credential only, often at the suggestion of their parents, and many work while they are there, often during class hours. (The night shift is also desirable since it is the most lucrative.)

In contrast with the elite university, the school does little to foster the same forms of socialization into hierarchy, in which students are taught to believe in the rewards of effort and endurance – and in the notion that trust in one's superiors and sacrifice for the collectivity will ultimately benefit oneself. At this college, only 30 percent of students participate in club activities. Club activities are a significantly smaller element of the college experience, since 50–60 percent of the students live at home in neighboring prefectures and commute to school, and thus do not hang around for long hours after classes. A more casual alternative to the clubs, known as *"dōkōkai"* (groups for shared interests), has become popular – a trend which one professor cynically characterized as "easy come easy go." The college festival *(daigakusai)* is, by report, similarly lackluster.

The students at this lower-tier private college face a lack of opportunity, boasting neither elite pedigrees nor marketable skills. In many ways, these colleges, though numerous, are the remaining vestiges of a system which began to fray over ten years ago. Students themselves have veered away from the academic credential *(gakureki)* mentality, placing more emphasis on individual autonomy and personal preferences.

In the heyday of the junior college, large holding companies such as Mitsui & Co. Ltd. (Mitsui Bussan) and top Japanese companies such as Toyota used to come and recruit for their manufacturing and clerical divisions. Yet these companies are an increasingly thinner presence, as manufacturing and clerical sectors are downsized. In recent years the job-search process has become a source of concern, particularly among parents of students. In the informational gathering for families that follows the school's yearly entrance ceremony *(nyūgakushiki),* the head of the career placement center has joined the list of officials who lead the presentation – and the audience's questions focus increasingly intensively on the students' future job prospects (Hirose 2004: 1).

The director of the *shūshoku* division, Hirose-sensei (pseudonym), arrived at the college in 2001 to teach courses in business studies. He founded a job fair for the college, which was attended by ten companies, including the sales division of Toyota, several mid-level Tokyo hotels, and the multi-national Japanese cosmetics company, where Hirose sensei had formerly been a manager. Few OBs or OGs joined the fair, as they had changed jobs enough times that they were difficult to track down. Or, they had not kept the *shūshoku* office informed of their whereabouts. Many students work in part-time jobs as waiters and waitresses, and cooks at family restaurants. For such jobs, no expertise is required and students undergo only a two or three-week training.

Through his courses Hirose attempts to fill in for the forms of socialization missing in this environment – at times in ways that would appear almost remedial in higher level colleges. The students in his business culture seminar have titles, such as "division chief," "director," and "communications manager." He told me that if he did not install some discipline in the students they would gradually become "less and less presentable" *(dan dan darashinakunaru)*. In a course focused solely on job-hunting *(shūshoku)*, Hirose teaches the basic skills of how to fill out an entry sheet, checking to make sure everyone has an email address, and running practice tests of the ubiquitous "common knowledge" *(ippan jōshiki)* exam. He urges the students to have pride in their small college and not to be scared when facing interviewers. The issue of the low ranking of the university is ever-present, indelible in the students identities, and when students answer questions successfully, he often makes remarks such as, "See what talent we have here at our college!" (On the importance of school status for students' identities from an early age, see Slater, this volume).[20]

Hirose has also made use of his contacts to develop a number of "internships." Such internships are currently fashionable and endorsed by the Ministry of Education, which has promoted them in a world in which students are increasingly interested in finding work which develops their talents and interests. A two-week internship for seniors at the city government office *(shinyakushō)* is one of the most prominent. Students get experience writing reports, preparing graphs, attending meetings, writing memos, and working with *senpai*. Ultimately, the seniors have the possibility of entering the office upon graduation if things go smoothly. One student, who reported on her experience at the office during class, had the responsibilities of sorting out which confiscated bicycles should be thrown away, putting plastic bottles into plastic bags for recycling, and attending weekly office meetings. During the presentation, which came at the close of her two-week internship, the student began crying has she greeted the city official *(yakunin)* who had come to attend the class presentation: "I'd like to thank you for this experience. It has been for my benefit."

However despite the earnest efforts on the part of the students during their two-week stint, the internship has had limited success in connecting students to the local prefectural offices upon graduation. While the students enjoy the two-week internships, the ward office at the city or prefectural-level holds little attraction in an era when many students are disenchanted with traditional paths towards upward mobility. Although the job is stable and the hours reasonable (features which would have made it attractive in a former era), it is notoriously boring, and promotion, while steady, is slow. While such a stable, upwardly mobile profession was once desirable, and for these students it is perhaps one the best outcomes they could hope for by prior standards, the students have become enchanted with notions of choice, work as self-cultivation, and quick success, and hold out for something they see as more attractive.

During a class I attended at the end of May (2003), seniors in Hirose's business seminar reported on their *shūshoku* progress. Of eight students, two had received offers. Imai-san would go to work for a supermarket with stores all over Japan. Fumi-san would be working as a cook at a food preparation company selling food to supermarkets.

The others were still struggling to pull things together. In the absence of a structured recruitment process, students used whatever resources they had to gain more knowledge about job opportunities and the content of the jobs – including the internet, word-of-mouth, and even job interviews themselves. They were interviewed for jobs for which they had few qualifications (computer programming, business consulting), failing the various written tests, simply to learn more about what was available. Others contemplated entering private vocational schools upon graduation in order to receive training in the area of their interest. Some students idealistically applied only to one kind of business, such as companies that make slot machines or music companies.

Some sought to find full-time work through the part-time job *(arubaito)* they had been doing – a marked departure from the elite experience of college as a largely recreational endeavor, leading to employment at a large firm where one would then be trained from scratch. Part-time work is an important part of college life for students at lower-ranked colleges and universities; and, in the context of the depleted meaning of the college credential and declining need for full-time, permanent manual and clerical workers, these *arubaito* formed the most viable launching pad the students had for hooking up to stable, full-time employment. Katsutoshi-san had been working at Eneos (a gas station) for four years. Eneos agreed to hire him full-time with the possibility of promotion. He must work for one to three more years as a gas station attendant, and then pass a basic level test. Within three years, he could be transferred to the *honsha* (headquarters), where he would work in sales. Another student had decided that if he was unable to obtain a full-time contract he would continue on at the sports shop where he had been working part-time. In nine months' time he would be eligible to take an employment test which, if passed, would allow him to move up the ranks.

In a personal essay reflecting on the growing rate of *furiitaa* (those who move from temporary to temporary position, without becoming a regular employees or *seishain*), Hirose reflects on the cultural rifts between his own generation and the students whom he educates. In the context of the harsh economic climate that greets students from non-elite colleges and the promise of fulfilling one's passions promoted in the mass media, students see little attraction to the life of slow but steady upward mobility (and fewer such positions are available to them). They decline to participate in *shūshoku* activites, claiming that they "need to take two or three years to find their calling *(yaritai koto)*," or that they "cannot forsake their hobbies for daily overtime and working on Saturdays," or sometimes that they "cannot forget the wonderful time they had in the United States during their high school homestay" (Hirose 2004: 3). Those who take Hirose's business seminars are, in his eyes, naive and skeptical about the world of business, peppering him with questions such as "Is unpaid overtime a crime?" and "Why do even top-tier companies have so many unnecessary meetings?" One student's question gave Hirose cause for reflection: "Sensei, will your eventual pension have to be taken out of our meager salaries?" *(Sensei no nenkin wa watashitachi no sukunai gekkyū kara harau koto ni naru no?)* To this he reflects, "What I'd like to answer is, 'In fact I will receive the money that I earned and put away slowly but surely *(kotsu kotsu)*, month after month – and that the company matched – during my days as a salaryman. It's my own money that I will be receiving. *(Dakara jibun no tsunde oita okane o morau no da yo.)*'" Yet Hirose pauses to note the fact that the next generation may not have this same luxury, and that the young are after all adept at seeing the injustices of a system that adults have become accustomed to. In the end, however, he concludes his thoughts by describing the final lesson that he offers his students, asking them to carefully write it down: "First, find gainful employment as a full-time company member *(seishain to shite shūshoku shiyō)*. Grow through your work *(shigoto o tōshite seichō shiyō)*. The life of a salaryman surely also has good things to offer. *(Sarariiman raifu ni mo kitto yoi koto ga aru kara.)* Through your work, you will discover your passions and your own path. *(Hatarakinagara yaritai koto ya jibun no michi ga mitsukaru koto ga ooi no da yo)*" (Hirose 2004: 4–5).

The numerous, private low-level four-year colleges and universities stand in-between the pedigree-society notions of human capital as "character" (companies hiring well-groomed students from elite schools regardless of their skills) and the new notions of skills and self-making. Graduation from such schools is in itself, no longer a meaningful pedigree, and yet the colleges do not offer the kinds of training that would equip the students with transportable skills. The section above reveals how Hirose and faculty members like him must seek to reconcile shifting notions of human capital with traditional notions of loyalty, commitment, self-deprivation, and the rewards of the protection of the company. For the students, the older social compact (protection in return for commitment) has lost both its persuasiveness and attraction, and yet the new system is, in many ways, out of reach for them.

Credentials vs. qualifications: the vocational school

The number of private "vocational schools" *(senmon gakkō)* has been growing since the 1980s, yet little is known about the vastly expanding sector of private vocational schools overseen by the Ministry of Education, Culture, Sports, Science, and Technology (Monbukagakushō) in Japan today, the schools are an obvious response to the perceived demand for "skills" rather than "credentials."[21] Vocational schools *(senmon gakkō)*, which used to be stigmatized as schools for those who did not perform well enough to be college-bound, have taken on new cache, as a counter-alternative to old-fashioned views of human capital as pedigree (a degree from a lesser-known four-year college or junior college, which affords a college pedigree but little else). By the 1990s, in the context of ever-increasing demand for technological skills, some schools, in the fields of software design and computer studies have established a reputation for imparting important new skills which are not easily obtained elsewhere (Dore and Sako 1998: 89).[22] *Senmon gakkō* specialize in a range of skills, from accounting, preparing legal documents, copyrighting, data-processing, and other clerical skills, to more glamorous skills such as hairstyling and Englisht eaching. Many schools claim higher rates of job placement than many four-year universities.[23]

One of the students who attended the school, who, according to his teacher, was slated to become the next trend-setting hair designer *(karisuma byōshi)*, later told me that his family had at first opposed his decision to attend the school. His father was a civil servant in the local prefectural government, a stable, yet tedious position, which guarantees lifetime stability and gradual upward mobility – precisely the opposite of the beauty vocation. Ultimately, his brother, also a civil servant at the postal branch of the town government, convinced his parents that it was a waste to attend college merely for the sake of the credential, and that Japan was moving away from the era of educational pedigree *(gakureki no jidai)* and entering the "era of qualifications" *(shikaku no jidai)*. Eventually his parents consented.

Ebara Riyō Biyō Senmon Gakkō (pseudonym) is located in a hip, young area of western Tokyo, just west of Shinjuku. It is one of the oldest beauty vocational schools in Japan (opened in 1958). The school accepts less than half of its applicants, and has become extraordinarily profitable in the wake of the professionalization of the beauty industry in the past 20 years. Currently they are adding an extension to their main building, which they plan to use for fashion shows. The school trains students in a two-year program to pass the national qualification exam to become stylists and beauticians. The test includes both a written portion *(hikki shiken)* and a technical portion *(jitsugi shiken)*, which includes a hair cut and "finger wave" (clearly an anachronism from the early days of the profession). Their success rate at passing students is 93 percent.

The school's grandiose entrance ceremony *(nyūgakushiki)* conveys the way in which the school positions itself as a significant moment of socialization and learning in students' lives – akin to high school or college. On a bright Saturday morning, a flood of trendy young women (mixed with a far smaller number of trendily-dressed young men) stride down the wide sidewalk towards Nakano Sun Plaza, one of the biggest performance arenas in central Tokyo. All the students are dressed in black, their bleached hair, earrings, and hair extensions standing out all the more. A few parents are also in attendance.

The young women are obviously attracted to the glamour and perceived freedom of self-expression of the profession. Yet it is also known that one quarter of the students who enter *Ebara Riyō Biyō Senmon Gakkō* are from families who run hairstyling or barber shops *(shinzoku keiei),* following in the tradition of inheriting the family business.

The tone of the ceremony is somber, with all the pomp and somberness of *nyūgakushiki* conducted all over the nation at more prestigious schools. At 10 a.m. promptly the curtain opens to reveal two groups of figures, sitting on the stage, including officials and teachers of the school, selected alumni, salon owners closely linked to the school, representatives from the trade press, and one member of the Diet. From the two large speakers on the stage, a somber voice-over begins, "Our apologies for having kept you waiting!" A welcoming speech begins beginning with a number of images that connote Japanese pride and nationhood: "The rain has at last stopped ... the falling cherries enters our Japanese hearts." The *hinomaru,* the Japanese national flag, hangs at center stage.

The Dean of the school addresses the students soberly. He begins by chastising them for not reflecting on their lives more thoughtfully – they go through their daily lives routinely, "with eyes clouded." He tells them that the lesson in life is not to be able to do what you most love but to learn to love what it is that you must do *(Yaritai koto o suru janakute, surubeki koto o suki ni naru yōni).*

Later, the current owner of the school, Ebara Michiko, dressed in an elaborate kimono, addresses the audience. She comments on the tight economy and the fierce competitiveness in Japanese industry, including the beauty industry. But the beauty school has many contacts in the field who know the reputation of the school. Ninety percent of its graduates are able to find secure employment immediately upon graduating. "Don't be ashamed of yourselves as specialized/ skilled students *(senmonsei),*" she urged. "Stability is assured to you in your future *(Hazukashikunai senmonsei de ganbatte kudasai. Shōrai ni anteisei ga arimasu.)*"

The nature of the *senmon gakkō* trajectory is difficult to paint in broad strokes. On the one hand, schools that offer certificates in accounting, preparing legal documents, writing advertising copy, software development and so forth, offer an alternative path to stable employment as the value of the college credential per se is called into question. Many of the private vocational schools boast rates of employment after graduation which well exceed the rates posted by colleges and universities on average, and the schools are closely networked with the growing market in temporary employment.[24]

At the same time, the market for skills comes with discernable risks for students – the same students who in a prior era would likely have followed the path from high school graduation to stable employment in larger firms. These stark trade-offs are especially clear in the context of the beauty industry, which may not be representative of many of the trades for which *senmon gakkō* training their students. The school's desirability hinges on the chance for students to cultivate their passions, and yet the career paths offer few guarantees of stability or even a modicum of social security.[25]

A typical hair-stylist working at a small shop works from 9:30 a.m. (for a 10:00 opening) to 8:00 p.m. and takes a total of six vacation days a month, mostly on weekdays when the shop is closed, with the longest consecutive holiday being three days for *o bon* (the New Year). Graduates often shop for jobs individually through classified ads *(kyūjinshi)*. The profession typically offers none of the stability, guarantees of gradual promotion, or safety nets offered by larger firms. The time required to establish oneself in the profession inevitably puts these employees on a substantially different life course from previous generations of skilled working class employees who followed a path of graduation from high school (or junior high school), immediate employment followed by marriage and (for women) child-birth. Marriage and families are unthinkable at least until after the age of 30; and the idiosyncratic holiday schedule makes it difficult to lead a normal social life. The profession is notably harsh for women, offering few opportunities for leave or guarantees of returning to work after child-birth. (It is noteworthy that the admired figures of the *karisuma biyōshi* era were exclusively male.)

The beauty school may not be typical in the alternative path that it offers to traditional blue-collar upward mobility. While it holds the promise of glamour and self-cultivation, precisely what is not available in the context of traditional paths to success, the path is considerably riskier, and few succeed in realizing their dreams of becoming the next *karisuma biyōshi*.[26] The trend towards vocational schools more broadly may very well be indicative of a successful means of circumventing the arduous exam system and pedigree path to upward mobility. Such schools may offer skills which lead to greater stability – accountants who are hired by larger firms, or those who prepare legal documents – without the hours of studying for ultimately meaningless exams and the practice of attending an expensive four-year university that offers little more than a degree. But it seems likely that the era of "skills" will bring complex consequences, with some able to seize the opportunity to fill a valued niche or realize long-held ambitions and others left to scramble for any job at all. In some cases the *senmon gakkō* certificate may simply be a more pragmatic credential than the college degree. In other cases it holds a promise of opportunity that is elusive at best and deceptive at worst.

Conclusion

The students' approaches to the *shūshoku* process in the three schools reveal the over-simplification of many accounts of the values of Japan's youth today. At times the voice of Japanese conservative social commentators (who see Japan's youth as the "moratorium" generation, failing to assume their responsibilities as adults) seems to join in chorus with the voice of the American mass media (which is always eager to see in Japanese society the embracing of American values) to proclaim that Japanese youth are simply waking up to individualism. Certainly *jitsuryoku* is more explicitly recognized as valuable and rewardable in Japanese enterprise, and many students, particularly those without elite pedigrees, search for ways to explore their interests and gain autonomy in the work place. Yet the embrace of *jitsuryoku shugi* seems much more complicated and qualified, even among those posed to gain from its changes.

In the case of students at the smaller college, their protest against the sacrifice of past generations for Japan's productivity appears different from a protest against hard work. They search for ways to match their interests to their future jobs in a market which is little equipped to help them do this. A number of students told me that they had their parents' support in hoping to become a professional skateboarder (for example) or equestrian jockey, as long as their parents could see that they were giving it their all. *"Bari bari hatarakitai"* (I would like to work hard) was a phrase I heard from these students.

The myth of the typical *furiitaa* as lazy or engaging in a form of social protest has already been dispelled by a number of scholars, including Genda Yūji and Kosugi Reiko. Kosugi's studies of *furiitaa* have shown the stunning rate of both failure to obtain success in the sought-after dream profession and also the desire on the part of *furiitaa* to find employment as a full-time committed employee *(seishain)* (Kosugi 2000a, 2000b).

There is little question that increasing global competition and shifting employment practices will have important effects on middle-class identity and notions of upward mobility. These will call for new constructions of self and subjectivity among young Japanese.

Kelly (2002) has described the postwar system as structured differentiation. We now see new fissures emerging between temporary and fully-employed workers – fissures which are no longer held together by the shared experience of socialization through companies and the shared belief in upward mobility through commitment and diligence. Temporary workers do not receive the same induction into particular sets of values that was central to postwar social cohesion – the importance of trying hard, "fate-sharing," merit based on loyalty, paternalism (trust in leaders), and knowledge of the full company. Nor do they receive the same benefits – which allow them to believe in the social contract – job stability, pensions, health care, and family support/need-based support.

The middle-class identity which encompassed a broad swath of Japanese society in the high-growth era seems in jeopardy as the socializing and wage mechanisms which preserved it are increasingly bankrupt. Emerging divisions have become the object of social commentary (Ishida this volume: 00–00; Sato 2000; Tachibanaki 2006), and, more importantly, have increasingly emerged as categories that shape subjective perceptions of identity (Ishida this volume: 00). As the editors of this volume remind us in their introduction, "where individuals grow emotionally, symbolically, and economically distant from the once-stable firm, the primary ways in which individuals are locating themselves within society is by virtue of their position on the class map, class-specific goals and strategies, and lifestyles" (Ishida and Slater, this volume).

The new system will offer more opportunities to the truly talented – what both critics of Japan and many talented and ambitious workers within Japan have been waiting for – and more rewards for risk-taking. Yet it is worth noting that something will be lost in this system. In the past, at least college offered Japanese students a chance to cultivate their outside interests and to learn the value of cooperation. Increasingly the road is paved with risks and liabilities that the neoliberal rhetoric of ability, choice, and opportunity does not account for (Borovoy, forthcoming). The *senmon gakkō* offers new ways to exploit these opportunities – though these paths are somewhat riskier. The elite colleges seem to continue to exploit the old model of "merit" as effort, grooming students to view human capital as "potential," good character, and malleability. The smaller colleges, large in number, seem to be grappling for some *raison d'être,* increasingly relinquishing claims to offering a broad, liberal arts education and scrambling to offer more pragmatic lessons.

Acknowledgments

I would like to thank a number of scholars for valuable comments and conversations: Mary Brinton, Ehara Yumiko, Hiroshi Ishida, William Kelly, Gerald LeTendre, Hiroshi Hirai, Brian McVeigh, Sonia Ryang, and Ayumi Takenaka. My conversations with David Slater during my year on leave at Sophia University in 2003–2004 were particularly informative. I would also like to thank the students who took time to talk with me. The research was made possible by an Abe Fellowship, 2002–2003, awarded by the Japan Foundation, Center for Global Partnership, and jointly sponsored with the Social Science Research Council and the American Council of Learned Societies.

Notes

1 Wallulis's "turbo-charged capitalism" has roots in early American capitalism and the association between the working wage and "independence" (Fraser and Gordon 1994). In Mary P. Ryan's ground-breaking analysis of the birth of middle-class consciousness in Oneida County, New York (1790–1865), *Cradle of the Middle Class* (1983), she highlights the increasingly privatized and individualized nature of middle-class life for American families in the early nineteenth century, owing to the nature of middle-class occupations themselves, the declining frequency of following in the family business, and the increasing emphasis on the home as a site of private sentiment and domesticity rather than productivity. In this context, Ryan notes the apotheosis of the "self-made man," – the middle-class businessman or entrepreneur who must rely increasingly on his own skills and resources in order to succeed. Corresponding to these demands, Ryan describes a pervading careerism present in boys' education, in which boys were encouraged to "calculate their interest in the world." Job ads targeting youth "who want to stand on their own two feet" and accompanying tales of rags to riches became some of Oneida County's "most cherished clichés" (166).

2 As Dore (1973) and others have shown, since the 1920s, Japanese employers have relied on a system in which vocational education occupies the lower level of the educational hierarchy (see also Honda 2004). Employers choose their candidates for their "non-cognitive" abilities, including "punctuality, diligence and trainability" (Takeuchi; 1995; Ishida 1993: 150–151).

3 This boost is particularly pronounced at large firms of over 1,000 employees.

4 The psychology certificate has been particularly popular since the Ministry of Education decided that the every Japanese junior high and high school should have a school counselor.

5 As recently as within the past five years, the average age of those attaining the level of the director of a department (*buchō*) at Hitachi has dropped to 47–8, an idea unheard of 20 years ago (Hitachi promotional literature).

6 New employees are still expected to become generalists to some extent. Top college graduates who join Toyota spend at least three months on the assembly line, working 6 a.m. to 3 p.m., and then two months selling cars door-to-door. Those who go to Hotel Okura to work in service management make beds for two weeks. Two Hitachi managers, one engineer and one personnel manager, shared their laments over the

current changes. While it was clear that no one could explicitly denounce the new ethic of *jitsuryoku-shugi* for fear of appearing complacent, they had plenty of hesitations with it.

7 Sony was one of the first companies to conduct "blind" written tests where students did not write the name of their university on the written exams that were part of their application.

8 *Shūshoku ritsu* are typically measured by dividing the number of students who receive naitei by the number of graduates minus those heading to graduate schools. Some measures (typically those provided internally by the schools themselves) subtract the number of students who decline to participate in *shūshoku* activities, thereby elevating the percentage for external appearances. The numbers vary significantly by department within any school, with engineering departments doing well overall (Ōda 2004: 16–23). According to the 2004 Aera survey, many departments at even top universities, hover at the 50 percent mark for students who receive offers. It is difficult to know how to interpret this, and I am not sure how students who will continue to work part time are counted.

9 Although this "closed-door policy" (as Kariya and others have referred to it) has been democratized and most employers now accept applications from students of any school who chooses to apply, these networks persist informally (as I shall show), a reminder of a system which prioritizes human capital as generalized quality rather than skills and experience.

10 Students (particularly women) at top universities who have become cynical with this established system, increasingly seek positions at foreign affiliate firms See Karen Kelsky's *Women on the Verge: Japanese Women, Western Dreams* (2001) for an analysis of the significance of these firms to women in particular who wish to transcend Japanese gender divisions.

11 Japanese college students often enroll in a seminar with one of the senior faculty members in their department: it is typically a two-year seminar, student-led, in which students grow close to a particular faculty member and a specialized body of literature. Often this faculty member serves as a primary reference for students on the job market. The fact that Koyama never enrolled suggests first his lack of seriousness as a student and also his need to rely more heavily on his rugby connections as an alternative source of connections.

12 Brinton and Kariya (2001) talk about social embeddedness (how institutional and inter-personal environments affect job outcomes) as central in contexts where (1) employers seek high-quality labor and invest in it over the long term through training, benefits, and so forth and (2) where school's reputations are based on their ability to place their seniors in top positions. These qualities capture the college-to-work transition in Japan, and Brinton and Kariya show that such embeddedness (particularly through alumni networks) is still important in the Japanese market (2001: 184).

13 One recent alumnus of the elite university I studied, currently working at Daiwa Think Tank (Daiwa Sōken), an innovative division of Daiwa Securities, reminisced, "I obeyed my senpai in college not just because he was my senior (*senpai to iu koto dake janakute*) but because he was good at golf and I genuinely admired him as a person."

14 Ichiyazuke is literally "soaked" or "pickled" overnight.

15 Those who are attracted to this system typically seek work at foreign affiliate companies in Japan where promotion is based on more European or American-style practices.

16 While there were 132,296 new entrants in 1955 (including national, local, and private universities and junior colleges), there were 604,785 new entrants in 2004 (*Monbukagakushō* Statistics, http://www.mext.go.jp/english/statist/06060808/pdf/100.pdf, accessed June 2004, June 2008).

17 The recent closing of many *joshi tanki daigaku* is powerful evidence of the dramatic shift in the employment landscape that is occurring. The colleges were the training ground for future "office ladies," women who aspired to stable employment at a large

company after graduation with the ultimate objective of making a good marriage (McVeigh 1997). Yet the OLs were an expensive form of clerical labor, often enjoying similar starting salaries to men on the managerial track as well as a host of benefits. As companies are gradually pruning back this expensive sector of the labor force and men themselves are taking longer after college to find solid work, the path from junior college, to work, to marriage is less reliable, and the clientele for the junior colleges (which specialize more in self-presentation than skill-training) has dramatically waned. See Matsui 1997 for a provocative analysis of this trend and Muraki 2005 for a glimpse into changing subjectivities of these middle-class women.

18 The word comes from a mix of English and German foreign loan words, "free arbeiter," in Japanse, *furii arubaitaa*, or, someone who free-lances and works part-time or temporary jobs.

19 The college used to be a well-known and respected women's junior college, founded some thirty years ago. However as the demand for a junior-college education has waned, the college board decided to make the college co-educational, with the effect of losing any particular niche for the college and making it simply a place where students can obtain a college degree.

20 On one of the days that I visited, Hirose began the class by taking attendance. When he found that several students were missing, he ordered the "division chief" to get on his cell phone to call the missing members on their cell phones. Tonight was the class party (*konpa*) – a tradition in many college-level seminars, where students and teacher gather and get to know one another in a more relaxed environment – and Hirose had determined that any student who missed the party would fail the class. The division chief told Hirose that Ota was not answering. "Leave a message!" Hirose barked. "He has to let us know clearly, will he come or not? If not, he's axed [Konai to kubi!]" Another student who was paged answered his phone. The student passed the phone to Hirose. "Fuse! What the heck are you doing! You're in the train? You idiot! (Bamo! [*Baka yarō!*]) Get over here now! (*Hakkoi!* [*Hayaku koi!*])

21 Until this time, many specialist schools, formerly known as "miscellaneous schools," functioned largely as finishing schools for women, teaching cooking, sewing, and other domestic skills (Dore and Sako 1998: 81).

22 Dore notes that the most likely students to enter a senmon gakkō in the mid-1980s were students referred to as the "might as well" tribe: students not from the lowest level high schools but the mediocre ones – students who were not confident in gaining admission to universities but not wholly resigned to going straight to work (84–5). Employers reported varying rates of satisfaction with these students, including some complaints that they were not as intelligent or trainable as graduates from liberal arts colleges (87–8). The scene appears to be changing, however, with greater numbers being hired specifically for their specialist knowledge or skills.

23 Dore cites an average of 80 percent placement rate throughout 1990–1996, in contrast with the rates of male university graduates, which were 80 percent in 1990 and below 70 percent in 1996 (Dore and Sako 1998: 88).

24 The small amount of evidence I was able to collect suggests that the best temp agencies attempt to mimic some of the "care" offered historically by large Japanese enterprises, including paying into pension plans and dispatching representatives to check in on workplace relations.

25 Indeed by all evidence hair-styling is an extraordinarily demanding and hierarchical profession in Japan. A student who graduates from *senmon gakkō* and passes the national exam must work as an apprentice for three years, enduring the eccentricities of their employers with little compensation or recourse for complaint. Hierarchy reigns, and the attrition rate of new graduates entering the profession is said to be quite high during this time.

26 According to one teacher, at the time of 10 years after graduation, only 10 percent of students are still working. I was not able to verify that statistic, but it is likely not representative of graduates of *senmon gakkō* on the whole.

References

Beck, U. (1995) *Ecological Enlightenment: essays on the politics of risk society*, trans. M.A. Ritter, Atlantic Highlands, NJ: Humanities Press.

Borovoy, A (forthcoming) "Japan as mirror: the limits of neoliberalism," in C.J. Greenhouse (ed.) *Politics, Publics, Personhood: ethnography at the limits of neoliberalism*, Philadelphia, PA: University of Pennsylvania Press.

Brinton, M.C. (this volume) "Social class and economic life chances in post industrial Japan: the 'lost generation'," in H. Ishida and D. Slater (eds.) *Social Class in Contemporary Japan*, London: Routledge.

Brinton, M.C. and Kariya, T. (2001) "Institutional embeddedness in Japanese labor markets," in M.C. Brinton (ed.) *New Institutionalism in Sociology*, Stanford, CA: Stanford University Press.

Cave, P. (2004) "*Bukatsudō*: the educational role of Japanese school clubs," *Journal of Japanese Studies*, 30(2): 383–415.

Chiavacci, D. (2005) "Transition from university to work under transformation: the changing role of institutional and alumni networks in contemporary Japan," *Social Science Japan Journal*, 8(1): 19–41.

Cole, R.E. (1971) *Japanese Blue Collar: the changing tradition*, Berkeley, CA: University of California Press.

—— (1979) *Work, Mobility and Participation: a comparative study of American and Japanese industry*, Berkeley, CA: University of California Press.

Dore, R. (1973) *British Factory-Japanese Factory: the origins of national diversity in industrial relations*, Berkeley, CA: University of California Press.

Dore, R. and Sako, M. (1998) *How the Japanese Learn to Work*, London: Routledge.

Ekonomisuto (2004) "Shuyō 360 daigaku no 'shūshokuritsu'" ["The successful employment rate of 360 leading Universities"], *Ekonomisuto* [Economist], 28 Sep: 8–41.

Fraser, N. and Gordon, L. (1994) "A genealogy of dependency: tracing a keyword of the US Welfare State", *Signs*, 19(2), 309–336.

Gordon, A. (1993) "Contests for the workplace," in A. Gordon (ed.) *Postwar Japan as History*, Berkeley, CA: University of California Press.

—— (2000) "Society and politics from transwar through postwar Japan," in M. Goldman and A. Gordon (eds.) *Historical Perspectives on Contemporary East Asia*, Cambridge, MA: Harvard University Press.

Hirose, H. (2004) *Furītā Ritsu to Shūshoku Ritsu* [Freeter Rate and Employment Rate], Unpublished.

Honda, Y. (2004) "The formation and transformation of the Japanese system of transition from school to work," *Social Science Japan Journal*, 7(1): 103–15.

Ishida, H. (1993) *Social Mobility in Contemporary Japan: educational credentials, class and the labour market in cross national perspective*, Stanford, CA: Stanford University Press.

—— (this volume) "Does class matter in Japan? Demographics of class structure and class mobility in comparative perspective," in H. Ishida and D. Slater (eds.) *Social Class in Contemporary Japan*, London, Routledge.

Iwauchi, R, Kariya, T. and Hirasawa, K. (eds.) (1998) *Daigaku Kara Shokugyō e II: Shūshoku kyōtei haishi chokugo no daisotsu rōdō shijō* [From University to Work: the labor market after the abolishment of university-enterprise agreements], Hiroshima: Hiroshima Daigaku, Daigaku Kyōiku Kenkyū Sentā.

Kariya, T. (this volume) "From credential-society to 'learning capitalist' society" in H. Ishida and D. Slater (eds.) *Social Class in Contemporary Japan*, London: Routledge.

—— (2001) '*Gakureki Shakai*' *to Iu Shinwa* [The Myth of the Credential Society], Tokyo: Nihon Hōsō Shuppan Kyōkai.

—— (1991) *Gakkō, Shokugyō, Senbatsu no Shakaigaku*. [School, Work, and the Sociology of Selection]. Tokyo: Tokyo Daigaku Shuppan.

—— (1988) "Shūshoku Katsudō to Daigaku Kyōiku" in R. Ishiuchi, T. Kariya, and K. Hirasawa, (eds) *Daigaku Kara Shokugyō e II: shūshoku kyōtei haishi chokugo no daisotsu rōdō shiba* [From University to Work: the labor market after the abolishment of university-enterprise agreements]. Hiroshima Daigaku: Daigaku Kyōiku Kenkyū Centā.

Kelly, W.W. (2002) "At the limits of the new middle-class Japan: beyond 'mainstream consciousness'," in O. Zunz, L. Schoppa, and N. Hiwatari (eds.) *Social Contracts Under Stress: the middle classes of America, Europe, and Japan at the turn of the century*, New York: Russell Sage Foundation.

Kelsky, K. (2001) *Women on the Verge: Japanese women, Western dreams*, Durham, NC: Duke University Press.

Kosugi, R. (2000a) *Furiitaa no Ishiki to Jittai. 97 Nin e no Hearingu Kekka Yori* [The Consciousness and Actual Conditions of "Freeters": the results of ninety-seven ethnographic interviews]. JIL Chōsa Kenkyū Hōkokusho no. 136, Tokyo: Nihon Rōdō Kenkyū Kikō.

—— (2000b) *Shinro Kettei o Meguru Kōkōsei no Ishiki to Kōdō: Kōsotsu 'Furiitaa' Zokka no jittai to haikei* [The Mentality and Behavior of High Schools Students Facing Life Decisions: the conditions and context of the growing "freeter" phenomenon]. Japan Institute of Labor Chōsa Kenkyū Hōkokusho no. 138, Tokyo: Nihon Rōdō Kenkyū Kikō.

Lash, S. and Urry, J. (1987) *The End of Organized Capitalism*, Cambridge: Polity Press.

Lee-Cunin, M. (2004) *Student Views in Japan: a study of Japanese students' perceptions of their first years at university*, Rochdale: Fieldwork Publications.

Lo, J. (1990) *Office Ladies, Factory Women: life and work at a japanese company*, Armonk, NY: M.E. Sharpe.

McVeigh, B. (1997) *Life in a Japanese Women's Junior College: learning to be ladylike*, London: Routledge.

Matsui, M. (1997) *Tandai wa Doko ni Iku? Jendā to Kyōiku* [What Happened to the Junior College? Gender and Education], Tokyo: Keisō Shobō.

Ministry of Education, Culture, Sports, Science and Technology (MEXT) (2006) *Japan's Education at a Glance*, Tokyo: Ministry of Education, Culture, Sports, Science and Technology. Online. Available http://www.mext.go.jp/english/statist/07070310.htm (accessed 04 June 2008).

Monbukagakushō Statistics. http://www.mext.go.jp/english/statist/index11.htm. Accessed June 2004, June 2008.

Muraki, N. (2005) "The making of service professionals at women's colleges: the transformation of middle class citizenship in Japan's new economy," presentation at the Annual Meetings for the American Anthropological Association, Washington D.C. December.

Nakane, C. (1967) *Kinship and Economic Organization in Rural Japan*, London: Athlone Press.

Nakane, C. (1970) *Japanese Society*, Berkeley, CA: University of California Press.

Nihon Rōdō Kenkyū Kikō [The Japan Institute for Labour (JIL)]. (2000a) *Furītā no ishiki to jittai: 97 nin e no hiyaringu kekka yori* [The Consciousness and Actual Conditions of Freeters: the results of ninety-seven ethnographic interviews], JIL Chōsa Kenkyū Hōkokusho no. 136, Tokyo: Nihon Rōdō Kenkyū Kikō.

—— (2000) *Shinro Kettei o Meguru Kōkōsei no Ishiki to Kōdō: kōsotsu 'Furiitā' zōka no jittai to haikei* [The Mentality and Behavior of High Schools Students Facing Life Decisions: the conditions and context of the growing "freeter" phenomenon]," JIL Chōsa Kenkyū Hōkokusho no. 138, Tokyo: Nihon Rōdō Kenkyū Kikō.

Ōda, M. (2004) "67 daigaku 370 gakubu shūshoku rankingu" ["Employment ranking among 67 universities and 370 academic departments"], *AERA*, 23 Aug: 30–34.

Rohlen, T.P. (1974) *For Harmony and Strength: Japanese white-collar organization in anthropological perspective*, Berkeley, CA: University of California Press.

—— (1977) "Is Japanese education becoming less egalitarian? Notes on high school stratification and reform," *Journal of Japanese Studies*, 3(1): 37–70.

—— (1983) *Japan's High Schools*, Berkeley, CA: University of California Press.

—— (1988) "'Spiritual education' in a Japanese bank," in T.S. Lebra and W.P. Lebra (eds.) *Japanese Culture and Behavior*, Honolulu, HI: University of Hawaii Press.

Ryan, M.P. (1981) *Cradle of the Middle Class: the family in Oneida county, New York, 1790–1865,* New York: Cambridge University Press.

Sato, T. (2000) *Fubyōdō Shakai Nippon* [Japan as an Unequal Society], Tokyo: Chūō Kōron Shinsha.

Schlosser, E. (2001) *Fast Food Nation: the dark side of the all-American meal,* Boston, MA: Houghton Mifflin.

Schneider, B. and Stevenson, D. (1999) *The Ambitious Generation: America's teenagers, motivated but directionless,* New York: R.R. Donnelley & Sons.

Slater, D. (this volume) "The 'new working class' of urban Japan," in H. Ishida and D. Slater (eds.) *Social Class in Contemporary Japan*, London: Routledge.

Takeuchi, Y. (1995) *Nihon no Meritocracy* [Meritocracy in Japan], Tokyo: University of Tokyo Press.

Tachibanaki, Toshiaki (2006) *Kakusa Shakai: nani ga mondai na no ka?*, [What is the Matter with the New Class Disparity?], Tokyo: Iwanami Shoten.

Vogel, E.F. (1963) *Japan's New Middle Class: the salary man and his family in a Tokyo suburb*, 2nd edn, Berkeley, CA: University of California Press.

Wallulis, J. (1998) *The New Insecurity: the end of the standard job and family,* Albany, NY: State University of New York Press.

Part IV

Class strategies

8 Motherhood and class

Gender, class, and reproductive practices among Japanese single mothers

Aya Ezawa

Introduction

The full-time or "professional" housewife (*sengyō shufu*) is central to many discussions of postwar Japanese society.[1] First introduced by Ezra Vogel's study on *Japan's New Middle Class* (1963) as the counterpart of the *salarīman*, the housewife has become a symbol of postwar middle-class family life. Dedicated to the well-being of her family and devoted to the educational success of her children, the role of the housewife has been considered as a profession, lifelong career, and a sign of status matching that of her white-collar husband (Hendry 1993; Imamura 1987; Vogel 1978). Although studies of the housewife phenomenon have generated a greater understanding of gender aspects of family life and women's life courses in postwar Japan, relatively little attention has been paid to class aspects of the role of the housewife. As research on working class and blue-collar women has shown (Fuse 1984; Kondo 1990; Roberts 1994), the role of the housewife and emphasis on stay-home motherhood is largely limited to the middle-class. Working class women often need to work in order to add to the family income, and tend to reject the lifestyle and ideal of the full-time housewife. Viewed from this perspective, the full-time housewife is a class-specific phenomenon, and rather than representing women in general, sheds light on gender aspects of social class in contemporary Japanese society. As housewives not only gain their status through marriage, but socialize children, they provide insight into existing class differences between women as well as the socialization and reproduction of class in contemporary Japan.

In this chapter, I explore the relationship between women's class location in terms of resources and education, and practices and dispositions toward motherhood. Research on mothering and reproduction has come to increasingly emphasize how practices and attitudes toward mothering are stratified and vary by race, class and social standing (Collins 1994; Ginsburg and Rapp 1995). Class, viewed from this perspective, cannot be separated from our understanding of motherhood and reproduction. Just as there are class differences in terms of resources, occupations, prestige and status among men, so are there class differences in the living conditions, practices and prestige associated with mothers. Differences in reproductive practices thus do not merely constitute different styles of parenting, but are also related to the socioeconomic status of women and families. Moreover, since socialization is an important element of ensuring children's cultural capital, motherhood is not just an additional aspect of class, but, as I will argue in this chapter, needs to be considered as central to class-specific practices, class culture, and the reproduction of class.

To explore the class dimensions of motherhood in Japan, I rely on Pierre Bourdieu's conceptualization of class (1984; 1987), which broadens its definition from material conditions to a wider constellation of social, cultural, and symbolic aspects. Class, according to this view, consists not only of differences in material wealth but also generates a situation with similar conditions, which lead to similar dispositions and cultural practices. Class positions and boundaries are not only derived from material conditions and relations of production, but are also created through struggles to define class identity and its representation in everyday practice. Class is thus not merely an objective position, but consists of subjective perceptions and representations of identity and difference. Lifestyle choices – such as the role of the full-time housewife – in this sense serve as symbolic representations of class as well as sites where class positions and distinctions are contested and transformed.

Placed in the context of Japan, it can be argued that the role of the full-time housewife is facilitated by the high income and status of husbands; indeed, spouses of full-time housewives tend to work in large companies and in management positions (Osawa 2002: 264). The role of the housewife also comes with a specific culture of mothering, heavily invested in facilitating an offspring's upbringing and future career. Full-time motherhood, in this case, is not merely a cultural value, but also a symbol of a middle class status. Mothers' reproductive practices may thus reflect on mothers' class position and resources, as well as class-specific dispositions and strategies for asserting and maintaining that status. Reproductive practices, in this context, do not merely constitute ways of ensuring a healthy upbringing for children, but also represent expressions of class, and a means for its reproduction.

To shed light on the relationship between social class and reproductive practices, I examine a group of women facing serious challenges toward their class status and practices of mothering: divorced single mothers. Single mothers come from a variety of social and class backgrounds, and do not constitute a unified group that shares particular attitudes or lifestyles. Instead, they share constraints, which differentiate their lifestyles as single mothers from that of the normative middle-class family in important ways. Whereas the married wife of a *salariman* can usually rely on the stability and benefits attached to her husband's employment in a large company, a single mother's income does not amount to much more than one third of the average family income and is often close to the poverty line (Ezawa and Fujiwara 2005; Abe 2005). In addition, the ideal of the housewife places great emphasis on maternal care for children under three, and mothers' presence and support for their children's educational success and future career (Imamura 1987: 9; Vogel 1978: 24ff; Ehara 2000). Yet, even though employment remains uncommon among married mothers, the dominant majority of single mothers in

Japan work even when their children are young (Ezawa 2006). As a recent study by the Japan Institute of Labor (2003) has shown, whereas only 37 percent of married mothers work when their children are ages two or three, 83.5 percent of single mothers do so. As even a relatively high income of a working single mother tends to be lower than the average family income, divorce and single motherhood can mean downward mobility and comparatively constrained living standards, particularly for middle-class women. In addition, working single mothers have little time to devote to childcare and children's education as compared to full-time housewives, making it difficult to not only finance but also to be involved with the upbringing of children to the same degree as a full-time housewife.

Single mothers' strategies in coming to terms with this situation, I argue, shed light on class-specific dispositions toward motherhood. Single mothers experience major shifts in their material and social conditions in becoming a single mother, from changes in their financial resources to new constraints on their lifestyle and practices of mothering. They also face contradictory demands in ensuring children's material well-being as breadwinners, and providing care for their children. A middle-class mother, for instance, may feel challenged to take up a full-time job to provide an income that supports a middle-class living standard, but may also want to stay home to ensure appropriate care and socialization of her children, consistent with the full-time housewife ideal. In a situation, where reclaiming all aspects of a class identity may be impossible, mothers are forced to renegotiate economic, social, and cultural aspects of their identity, and invest in those aspects that they consider as most central to their understanding of their identity as mothers. Their practices and interpretations in coming to terms with their situation, thus reveal both, dispositions and understandings of motherhood and class, as well as struggles to assert or maintain their class identity.

In what follows, I examine single mothers' everyday strategies between children's needs and the demands of work and income, focusing in particular on class-related concerns and practices. I begin with an overview of the characteristics and practices of motherhood in contemporary Japan and class differences in resources, attitudes and practices of motherhood. I then introduce the general situation of single mothers and how it affects single mothers' socioeconomic status, followed by an analysis of individual life histories and everyday strategies of single mothers in Tokyo.

Motherhood, class and women's life course in contemporary Japan

To be able to grasp the significance of single mothers' reproductive practices, we first need to examine general trends in practices of mothering and women's work patterns in Japan, as well as their variation by class. Among the best-known aspects of motherhood and women's life course in Japan is a tendency for women to interrupt work with marriage and childbirth, and return to work in middle-age leading to an M-shaped pattern of work participation. As compared to other advanced industrialized countries, a sharp decline in women's work participation rate between ages 25 and 34 remains remarkably persistent (Iwai and Manabe

2000). Whereas 70.5 percent of women between ages 20 and 24 worked in 2000, only 57.0 percent did so between ages 30–34, indicating a high work participation rate of unmarried women and a pattern of retirement from work with marriage and childbirth in the late twenties and early thirties. As many women return to the workforce (mostly as part-time workers) after children have entered school, women's work participation rate rises again in middle age, reaching a peak of 70.3 percent for ages 45–49 (Sōmushō 2000). In short, interruption of work during childbearing years remains a common pattern of women's life course in Japan.

The decline of women's employment during childrearing years is often attributed to a persistent emphasis and high value associated with the activities of full-time housewives and mothers, particularly among middle and upper class families (cf. White 2002). Joy Hendry, in her study of "professional" housewives asserts: "Housework and the care of children has undoubtedly always been a part of the working life of Japanese women, as it is part of the lives of most women, but in few parts of the world have these roles been granted the importance and status they have acquired in Japan" (Hendry 1993: 224). The role of the mother entails not merely "quality time" with children, but requires mothers' full-time presence in the home, which is considered as crucial for children's development and education (White 1987:155; Ehara 2000). Until age three, an old saying asserts, it is best for children to be raised by their mothers' hands. Mothers also play an important role in supporting their children during high school and university exams by cooking nutritious meals, preparing late night snacks, and ensuring that children do not forget any important school items. Also called "education mothers," dedicated mothers have made ensuring their children's educational success and future career into their full-time job (Imamura 1987; see also Allison 2000). Even if housewives are working, they do so under the precondition that these activities do not interfere with their role as housewives and mothers (Leblanc 1999). Motherhood, in this context, does not merely constitute a practice of nurturing and child rearing, but also comes with a specific lifestyle and status, associated with the postwar *salarīman* family. In dedicating themselves to their children full-time, mothers have made motherhood into a full-time job and career, which allows them not only to contribute to their children's upbringing but also assert their identity and status as middle-class mothers.

Although often thought of as a remainder of family traditions, the role of the full-time housewife is actually a modern phenomenon, which has been reinforced by a range of policies and institutions aimed at the promotion of national and economic progress. As Kathleen Uno (1993) has shown, the idea of the "good wife, wise mother" (*ryōsai kenbo*) evolved in the early twentieth century as a result of state policies and campaigns. Schools for middle-class girls as well as educational campaigns emphasized women's contribution to the nation as loyal wives and dedicated mothers, raising future citizens of the nation (Koyama 1991; 1999; see also Smith 1983). In other words, rather than a traditional gender role, the role of the dedicated housewife and mother has been shaped by broader political objectives, which see women has playing an important role in the reproduction of strength and prosperity of the nation.

The term *ryōsai kenbo* is no longer used in postwar Japan, yet government policies have continued to promote the full-time housewife and mother as a model of the postwar middle-class family (Yokoyama 2002). The tendency for women to retire from work during their childrearing years actually became stronger among early postwar cohorts as compared to prewar cohorts, indicating a process of "housewife-ization" of women in postwar Japan (Ochiai 1994: 18ff). Tax incentives, which make it more advantageous for women not to work or to work at most part-time, have been widely criticized for discouraging women from pursing careers (Osawa 1993; Osawa 2002). In addition, company hiring practices have made it difficult for women to pursue careers despite higher educational attainment (Brinton 1993). Such practices have allowed companies to place high demands on their male employees' work and time (Gordon 1997; Meguro and Shibata 1999) and rely on women as an expendable workforce, necessary to uphold the system of lifetime employment of salaried men (Ogasawara 1998; Osawa 1999). The role of the full-time housewife, viewed from this perspective, supports the lifestyle and employment patterns of *salarīmen* working in large companies. Rather than a traditional gender role confined to the private home, the role of the housewife is integral to the organization of the Japanese economy and society.

To be sure, the role of the full-time housewife does not capture the experience and lifestyles of all Japanese women, but has been largely limited to parts of the middle class. In the 1950s, when the role of the housewife began to enter public discourse, full-time housewives constituted only a minority among married women (Partner 1999: 152). Although their number increased during the years of high economic growth and peaked in the late 1960s and 1970s, full-time housewives have never accounted for more than 38 percent of married couples, and can be estimated to be largely accounted for by families of salaried husbands in management positions in large companies (Osawa 2002: 260–4). The widespread availability of public day care centers, which, unlike kindergartens, provide full-day care for children of working mothers, instead indicates that full-time work among married mothers is not uncommon in Japan. In 2000, 35.7 percent of four and five-year olds were attending day care centers; that is, institutions which provide full-day care for working parents (this excludes children attending kindergartens which do not provide full-day care, MHLW 2003a). As Uno's study (1999) of the evolution of day care centers in the early twentieth century has shown, the ideal of the *ryōsai kenbo* was promoted among middle-class girls at a time when the state actively engaged in the building of full-time day care centers for poor working families indicating that a recognition and reinforcement of class differences in practices of mothering has been part of government policy since the early twentieth century.

Research on working class families in Japan further underlines existing class differences in practices and attitudes toward motherhood. Glenda S. Roberts notes that most of the blue-collar women she interviewed worked for economic reasons, that is, to keep up with rising living standards and pay for consumer goods associated with the lifestyle of the new middle-class: refrigerators, cars and cram school (Roberts 1994: 27–9). While aspiring to a middle-class living standard, the women in Roberts' as well as Kondo's study also tried to assert themselves against the (middle-class) housewife ideal by rejecting the role of the full-time housewife as an "easy lifestyle" which comes with "three meals and a nap" (Roberts 1994: 30–1) and as boring, snobbish, and narrowly focused on household matters and TV watching (Kondo 1990: 282–3). Some women also consciously rejected the idea of "pushing children to study" and instead expressed their dedication to their families and children's welfare through their commitment to work (Kondo 1990: 285). That is, working class women in these studies considered work *outside* the home as a sign of their dedication to their children.

Such class differences in practices and meanings of mothering are also apparent in recent data on women's work and childcare patterns. Among university educated couples with white collar husbands, women have a stronger tendency to stay home and tend to emphasize the importance of parenting over work, and parents tend to make significantly larger financial investments in their children's education (Kanbara 2000). Married women are more likely to work if the family has loans, and husbands have a lower educational attainment and income (Ushijima 1995). Women in blue collar marriages, meanwhile, rarely become full-time housewives and tend not to be as concerned with children's schoolwork (Kanbara 2000).

The above studies confirm significant class differences in parental resources and attitudes toward childcare and children's education. Highly educated couples tend to make significant financial and time investments in their children's education, and stress the importance of mothers' presence in the home. Although blue collar families recognize the importance of education, they usually have fewer resources to draw from, as women often need to work to add to the family income and have less time and money to invest in their children's education. The full-time housewife and "education mother" ideal is thus not merely a social ideal, but rather a lifestyle that has been reinforced by government policies and company practices, which is affordable only to a few. Such class-based variation in motherhood and childcare practices suggests a strong relationship between class location (in terms of education and occupation), resources and mothers' reproductive practices.

Single motherhood in contemporary Japan

The experiences of single mothers in Japan add a further angle to this setting as they highlight the social and economic consequences of living outside the married mother and nuclear family norm. Whereas marriage, motherhood and full-time home-making remains a dominant norm and aspiration, single mothers remain a very small minority, often pitied as well as criticized for living outside the married mother and nuclear family norm. The description of one interviewee captured this image:

> How shall I say, poor and wretched, a mother and her children; the family is huddling together because there is no father – what a misfortune! It is a type of misfortune, but to think this way is also a kind of prejudice. ... To have

become like that means that you are "missing" something, that is the view held by society.

Single mothers, according to this image, are in dire straits because of the absence of a breadwinning husband and women's presumed inability to be emotionally and materially self-sufficient.

Since the 1980s, movements of divorced and unmarried single mothers have consciously tried to resist this image by asserting their independence and happiness, and criticizing the male breadwinner model of family. In a bold move, a group based in Tokyo published pamphlets entitled "what's fun about being a single mother today" and "cheers to the single mothers" (Jidō Fuyō Teate no Kirisute o Yurusanai Renrakukai 1986; Single Mothers' Forum 1993; 2001). Becoming a single mother, they asserted, allowed them to become an "independent person" for the first time, and enjoy living by their own efforts, despite a low income and a stressful everyday life. They criticized the subservient role women were expected to play as wives, and showed how many of the problems facing single mothers derived from the institutionalization of the full-time housewife ideal and women's dependence on breadwinning husbands in the economy and society (Nonaka 1987; Renrakukai 1986). Although support for the role of the housewife provides women with protection within marriage, it also makes it difficult for women to pursue a lifestyle outside the married mother norm (Fujiwara 1997). Single mothers' experiences, viewed from this perspective, shed light on gendered aspects of the economy and society, which, in building on a male breadwinner and full-time housewife ideal of family, reinforce a gender division of labor and create difficulties for those outside the middle-class family norm. Besides asserting a two-parent middle class norm of family, the *salarīman* family ideal also reinforces women's dependence on husbands and disadvantage in the economy.

The social and material repercussions of single motherhood are reflected in the limited presence as well as difficult living conditions facing single mothers in contemporary Japan. Only 6.4 percent of families in Japan are headed by single mothers, a ratio which is strikingly low as compared to other industrialized countries, where, with the exception of Ireland and Southern Europe, single mothers constitute between 10 and 25 percent of families (JIL 2003; Uzuhashi 1997: 127). Moreover, although the composition of single mothers has shifted significantly from a dominant majority of widows in the early postwar years (85.1 percent in 1952) to 79.7 percent divorcees in 2006, only very few single mothers (6.7 percent) today are unmarried (MHLW 2007). Unplanned pregnancies are not uncommon, yet often lead to abortion (Coleman 1983; Kanbara 1991) or marriage. In 2000, 26.3 percent of first born children were conceived before marriage, which indicates that marriage remains a crucial precondition for parenthood in Japan (IPSS in Inoue and Ehara 2005: 11). As a consequence, as few as 1.9 percent of children in Japan are born outside marriage (MHLW 2004). Even though women's lifestyles have become more diverse in the past decades, these figures underline the continuing difficulties associated with becoming a single mother in contemporary Japan.

Single mothers' material circumstances also differ from those of middle-class housewives in important ways. Single mothers come from a variety of social backgrounds and work in a range of occupations, yet their average annual income remains very low as compared to that of other households. Single mothers' average annual income in 2003 was ¥2.3 million, less than half of that of the average annuall income of Japanese households (¥7.0 million), a disparity which has been increasing in the past decades (MHLW 2003b).This increasing disparity can be related to an overall increase in the income of other households and an increasing number of dual-earner families. Single mothers' low income also illustrates persisting differences in women's and men's average income: as of the year 2002, women's average wage remained at 64.9 percent of that of men (MHLW 2003c). Typical female jobs also tend to be located in small companies, have lower salaries, and lack age-related promotion (Brinton 1993). In short, it remains very difficult for single mothers to maintain the living standards of the average family in Japan.

Moreover, in contrast to the emphasis on maternal care for small children in public discourse, governmental and company policies, almost all single mothers in Japan are engaged in paid employment (84.5 percent in 2006), and most work even if their children are below school age (MHLW 2007; JIL 2003: 56). Single mothers' high work participation rate is in part facilitated by the widespread availability of day care centers, which subsidize fees for low-income single mothers and give them preferential treatment in obtaining a place for their children. Single mothers have however also few other sources of support outside income from work. Although public assistance (*seikatsu hogo*) is available to single mothers without other sources of income, it requires the depletion of all assets and involves a complex process of application, which has made it an uncommon source of support. Child support payments from fathers, although required, are only poorly enforced to the extent that only 19.0 percent of single mothers in 2006 reported receiving child support payments (MHLW 2007; Shimoebisu 1989). Instead, the majority of single mothers (60.8 percent in 2001) are relying on the dependent children's allowance (*jidō fuyō teate*), a cash grant which supports single mothers with a low or no income (JIL 2003). As the amount of the allowance is not sufficient to make ends meet, it in most cases adds to rather than substitutes income from work. Thus, although government policies in general are known to emphasize women's domestic role as mothers, single parent policies are primarily treating them as workers rather than mothers (Ezawa and Fujiwara 2005; Peng 1997).

Becoming a single mother, therefore, often means significant adjustments to a woman's living standard and lifestyle. Being a single rather than a married mother has significant implications for a woman's resources and practices of mothering. As single earners and women of middle-age, single mothers' incomes are often significantly lower than those of the average family, making it difficult to uphold a middle-class lifestyle without additional support. Moreover, whereas discourse and policies have emphasized the importance of maternal care particularly for small children, single mothers rarely have the opportunity to devote themselves to their children full-time.

Negotiating motherhood and work in everyday life

Between 1998 and 2000, I conducted 39 interviews with divorced, unmarried, widowed, and otherwise separated mothers in Tokyo. Of these, 24 were divorced, five unmarried, four widowed, and six otherwise separated mothers.[2] While this group of women cannot accurately represent a larger population of single mothers, their experience allows insight into the challenges of taking care of small children as a single parent. The dominant majority of the mothers I interviewed were young mothers with small children or mothers who had become single mothers when their children were below school age. Twenty-nine of the mothers were between ages 30 and 49, four in their twenties and six over 50. The youngest child of 21 of the mothers was under six, in the case of seven between 6–11, and another 11 had children aged 12 or older.

Single mothers in this study managed the balance between work and childcare in different ways, revealing important differences in their social background, attitudes and material resources. Whereas some had grown up in affluent families of professionals and attended private school, others came from families that ran an independent business and yet others grew up with mothers on welfare, unable to afford the attendance of senior high school. In terms of education, three had not completed senior high school, 17 had graduated from senior high school, three had attended junior college, and 16 had a university degree or higher. Similar to the general experience of single mothers, the dominant majority of women in this study was engaged in full-time employment. Thirty-one of the 39 single mothers were working full-time: as clerical workers in small companies or institutions (11), as public employees in school kitchens (4), as employees in office jobs in large corporations (4), while others were self-employed or working freelance (9), or as teachers or professionals (3). Those who were not engaged in full-time work were stay-home mothers (3), were attending school (1), were unemployed (1) or worked part-time (3).

In managing their everyday life, a general problem for many of the mothers was to find a job that accommodates their needs as mothers of small children. Public day care centers are an important source of support, as they provide subsidized care at low or no cost to single mothers. Even though public day care centers usually have opening hours from 8:00 am to 6:00 pm, and increasingly to 7:00 pm or even later, however, working single mothers often have difficulties in accommodating long commutes and overtime work with day care hours. In addition, since public day care centers do not provide care for sick children, parents often have to take off from work to take care of their children when they develop a fever. The possibility of lateness and frequent absences, as well as the inability to work overtime for many became a "bottleneck" when searching for a job as a single mother. Even if employers are lenient, lateness and absences can affect work performance, and lead to reduced salaries and limited access to promotion, as has been shown in the case of single fathers (Kasuga 1989). While this is a problem faced by working parents in general, single mothers face the additional difficulty of earning a family wage as single and middle-aged mothers with generally lower earning potential than two-parent families. As Sakamoto Mitsue,[3] who separated from her husband when her son was an infant, explained, the difference in being a single mother is that:

> [As a single mother] one has a different sense of stability. For example, when the child gets sick, there is the possibility that one's income decreases. If there is a husband, there is his income, and one can feel reassured. In this case of single mothers, such things [as children's illnesses] soon influence everyday life conditions.

In other words, as a single mother, women felt more vulnerable to fluctuations in income and employment, and the potentially negative impact of children's needs on their performance at work. Reproductive practices and children's needs, in this case, are more closely intertwined with women's material welfare: maximizing work performance meant limited attention to children's needs, while an emphasis on children's needs could lead to a reduced income and material welfare.

For the majority of mothers in this study, working motherhood was a delicate balancing act between providing appropriate care for their children and ensuring an adequate income. To minimize the impact of absences on their salaries, many saved their paid holidays and used them when their children fell ill, as private services were unaffordable, and few could rely on family for child care. Others, pressed to stay at work, had to leave toddlers in the care of older children who skipped school for this purpose, or by themselves until they got better. Their low income and limited resources often left mothers with few options, and a daily struggle between children's needs and the demands of work.

Yet, although mothers shared similar problems, the strategies of two groups of women at the opposite extremes of educational attainment stood out. Contrary to the observation that working-class women have a stronger tendency to work as mothers, it was women with junior or senior high school qualifications and a low-income family background, who were among the few who worked at most part-time and consciously prioritized time with their children, as opposed to a full-time job. Conversely, it was women with bachelor's and masters degree's and the largest amount of resources at their disposal, who had the stronger tendency to invest most time and resources in their work performance, contradicting the idea that stay-home motherhood is a high priority among middle-class mothers.

Chisa Fujiwara's (2005) recent findings based on a survey of the Japan Institute of Labor confirm this pattern. Single mothers' work participation rate of 87.3 percent, she shows, varies significantly by educational attainment. Whereas single mothers who are university graduates have a work participation rate as high as 94.4 percent, single mothers with a junior or senior high school qualification have a significantly lower work participation rate (76.5 percent and 87.1 percent respectively). Moreover, single mothers with a junior or high school qualification are less likely to work in a permanent job (as opposed to part-time work, contractual employment, self-employment, other types of employment, or no work). Whereas 57.6 percent of university graduates held permanent jobs as single mothers, only 28.3 percent of junior high school graduates and 40.0 percent of senior high school graduates did so. Similarly, junior high school graduates more often held part-time positions (42.8 percent) than university graduates (10.2 percent). Notably, this higher engagement in full-time work among university graduates only emerged after becoming a single mother. Before becoming a single mother, more university graduates (37.6 percent) than junior high school graduates (31.0 percent) were full-time housewives. As Fujiwara's analysis shows, single mothers with lower educational attainment do not lack work experience, but may have greater difficulties in obtaining a permanent job. These disparities indicate significant differences in women's opportunities in work and income depending on their educational and class background.

To explore the meanings of such seemingly contradictory tendencies in single mothers' work patterns and practices of mothering, in what follows, I examine three accounts of single mothers from different class backgrounds. I define single mothers' class background here based on their educational attainment, as it reflects on the resources and class standing of single mothers' parents and hence their socialization, as well as mothers' own resources and opportunities as working women and mothers. The first case, Tanaka-san, reflects the experience of an upper-middle class woman with an exclusive private school education. The second case, Yamamoto-san, who grew up with parents running a business, also went to university, but not to one of the top four schools and paid for tuition with her own salary. She might be best considered as a middle-class woman of petit bourgeois origins, who has made her way into the urban middle class. Finally, Kimura-san is of working class origins. She grew up with two working parents in blue-collar jobs, and completed a high school education. Although three cases pose limits to generalization, they are typical cases whose work patterns and reproductive practices are consistent with tendencies within my sample as well as tendencies reflected in larger investigations (Fujiwara 2005; JIL 2003). Each of the accounts examines the family background of each case, changes the mothers experienced in becoming a single mother, attitudes and dispositions toward work and motherhood, as well as their own reasoning behind their reproductive practices.

Tanaka Miyuki (40)

Tanaka Miyuki grew up in a well-to-do family in Tokyo with a professional father and part-time working mother, and attended a prestigious private high school and university. Although she was interested in becoming a teacher, she also aspired to marriage. She says:

> Personally, marriage was a dream for me. When I was younger, there was still the idea of Christmas cake: until 24, it sells, 25 sells OK, 26 does not sell. That was the silent assumption. My parents and I thought I should marry early; those days, many thought that to marry and become a good wife meant happiness. I wanted to become a good wife and have children, and have a happy family.

Discouraged by her father, she dropped the idea of a master's degree and married someone working in a large corporation. As her husband's company disapproved of employment among wives of employees, she became a full-time housewife.

Her lifestyle as a married housewife radically changed when she decided to divorce after several years of an unhappy and childless marriage. Pursuing her long-term aspiration, she obtained a masters degree with the support of her parents and began to work as a teacher. Moreover, fulfilling her dream of family and motherhood, she became pregnant and gave birth outside marriage. As a mother of a small child, she shared many of the problems facing other single mothers. When I first met her, she was juggling two high school teaching jobs with one-year contracts, and everyday life with a child under six. Unlike other mothers, however, she had contacts and qualifications, which helped her find employment. She also received considerable support from her parents, which made it possible for her to manage her everyday life with a toddler and a low income. In addition to financial support and help in obtaining a loan for a modern two-bedroom apartment in central Tokyo, her mother took care of her child when needed: if her child had become ill in the morning, she would call her mother, who would travel for one hour by train to arrive at her apartment shortly before her departure for work. Without such arrangements, she explained, she would have difficulties keeping her jobs as absences and lateness would make it difficult to get her contracts renewed.

Although Tanaka's everyday life was a delicate balancing act between work and her child's needs, her family's support, cultural capital and connections allowed her to manage, and afford living with a low income and contractual employment. She knew that obtaining a long-term job after age 40 would be difficult, yet she decided that it would be better to have more time with her daughter while she was small, even if it meant a lower personal income. As she states:

> My relatives tell me that I should better get a stable job, given my age. …
> But I think I want to get a stable job only once [my child] is a little older.
> In many schools, the working hours [for full-time teachers] are really long,
> even though the pay is good and there is security. … Right now, I have more
> time [for my child] and although I only have a low income, I would like to
> continue like this for a couple of years.

Although she was eager to work and pursue a career as a teacher, she could not quite divorce herself from the idea that it is best to spend more time with her daughter when she was below school age. As a teacher, she had more flexible work hours, but with two part-time jobs, actually had as little leisure time as full-time working mothers.

Tanaka-san had much greater resources to draw from than most other mothers, yet she also felt more strongly the implications of single motherhood for her social identity as a woman from an upper-middle class family. Fearing discrimination, she hid her identity as a single mother at work, claiming that her partner was working in another city (*tan'shin funin*). Employees of large companies in Japan are quite regularly placed in branch offices in other cities and even foreign countries, to the extent that a father's absence arouses little suspicion. She further reported that among her peers – former classmates from high school – divorce and single motherhood was associated with a decline of status and constraints on children's education. At an alumni meeting of former classmates of her high school, she overheard her classmates, many of them housewives married to well-to-do business men, making disapproving comments about the upbringing of children who attend day care centers. She says:

> Many still believe that it is best for children to be raised by their mothers until age three, and say such things as "because they are raised in a day care center" [they don't have manners], but when learning that my child goes there they quickly add "oh, she is very well behaved!"

In addition, many seemed to fear that single motherhood would obstruct the ability to maintain children's class status. "Since I graduated from a school where a lot of children of good families go," Tanaka-san explains, "I heard that many worry that children of one-parent families cannot get into certain schools or get certain jobs, because of prejudice. I am not sure whether that is true, but that is an incentive for them not to divorce until their children are in those schools. There are a lot of families like that." What is at stake here, then, is not merely norms of motherhood, but rather the ability to maintain the identity of a middle-class mother by ensuring children's educational success and a stereotypical career in a large corporation.

Tanaka-san herself did not elaborate on her feelings about her own daughter's future but in making these observations, underlined the challenges she and her daughter faced. When I met her again five years later, her daughter was attending a public elementary school as well as cram school, and approached an age when many middle-class parents begin to think about high school entry exams and their children's educational future. Tanaka-san was evasive about possible financial and social constraints to her daughter's education and instead stressed that she should pursue her "own interests" rather than a prescribed career. Even though attending the same private school and university as she herself did was common among children of her classmates, she argued that attending the same school as she did was not as important to her, as other schools are able to provide an education of "similar standards." Her approach to her daughter's education, while sounding progressive and open-minded, masked the constraints she began to feel about her daughter's education. Not being able to send her to the same private school was a major sign of financial and social constraints, which she displaced by stressing the importance of respecting her daughter's individuality. Rather than conceding to limited opportunities, she stressed the importance of allowing for individual interests and an alternative approach to a "good" education.

Tanaka-san's life trajectory visualizes the classic aspirations of the middle class. As a full-time housewife, she lived the lifestyle of a typical upper-middle class woman. Becoming a single mother radically changed her everyday life, and made her conscious about the implications of becoming a single mother for her identity as a middle-class woman as well as her daughter's education. Whereas she had previously been able to take her status and access to an exclusive education for her daughter for granted, as a single mother, she had to recognize constraints in resources and educational opportunities as a consequence of her low salary and identity as a single mother.

Yamamoto Akiko (33)

Where Tanaka-san was concerned about spending time with her daughter as well as schooling, Yamamoto Akiko worried most about her employment and income, and financing of her son's education as a single mother. Raised in a family running a small but quite successful business, she attended an academically ambitious high school. After several years of working in a large company, she decided to obtain a bachelor's and master's degree, which she financed from her savings, to be able to further her career. Her lifestyle after marriage had the features of the life of a well-to-do dual-earner middle-class couple. Together with her husband, she bought a three-bedroom apartment (*mansion*) in a high rise building in central Tokyo, located close to the train station and work. During her marriage, she outsourced many household and childcare tasks. Most often, she reported, it was her husband who brought her son to the day care center and took time off from work whenever her son caught a fever. "If I do the housework," she argued, "that means that my time is being sacrificed [for household chores]. To take advantage of my time this way also means taking advantage of me economically [in form of unpaid labor]." To ease the tensions surrounding housework, she hired help for household chores and paid a tailor to make many of the hand-made items required by day care centers (such as a bag for pajamas or aprons made of towels, which have to be handmade by mothers). Rejecting housework and childcare as a woman's task, she was more eager to obtain and maintain a well-paying career-track job.

Whereas Tanaka-san had been able to take her education and living standard for granted, for Yamamoto-san, her lifestyle as a middle-class professional was an achievement based on her own efforts. Her life trajectory was built on the ideal of meritocracy and upward mobility promised by the postwar educational system. Proud of her achievements, she was conscious and concerned about the material repercussions of becoming a single mother. When asked about material changes after divorce, she responded: "In financial terms," she notes, "I don't feel all that impoverished, but I try not to buy luxurious items, and although I was traveling quite frequently in the past, I don't do so now. … I do worry more about money now though. I try to be more frugal, and I do not go to the hairdresser as often." Although her adjustments were minor, her immediate association of single motherhood with "impoverishment" indicated a stronger recognition that her living standard, unlike in Tanaka-san's case, could not be taken for granted.

Her primary concern in becoming a single mother moreover, was not the time she could spend with her son but the quality and costs of his education.

In addition to swimming lessons and drawing classes, she proudly told me, he soon would also take up piano lessons. In negotiating child support payments during her judicial divorce, she also made sure that her former husband would make payments until their son's graduation from university. Underlining her goal to provide her son with the best possible education, she had already begun to look into the admissions process for exclusive private elementary schools, which would guarantee attainment of a prestigious university degree. "If it's a matter of ¥400,000-¥500,000 a year," she self-confidently told me, "[financing a private school education] won't be a big problem."

Although Yamamoto-san was comparatively well off in financial terms, combining work with her son's needs was a major challenge. She explains:

> I usually do not come back [from work] when my child suddenly gets ill, I just can't take off from work. I think that the underlying assumption [in getting this job] was that I was not going to take off from work because of the child. I think I have to respond to this to a certain degree.

She answered to these expectations by paying for expensive babysitting services during child care emergencies, unable to rely on family or friends. Whenever her son had become ill in the morning, she called the babysitting service, waited for the babysitter to arrive and went to work late, explaining: "Sorry I am late, I fainted." Moreover, she felt pressed not to publicize her divorce at work. She confided in me: "Actually, I have only told some people at work. It will eventually spread over time, but as far as possible, I would like to keep a lid on it." To minimize negative effects, she changed her name back to her maiden name only two years after her divorce.

Tanaka-san and Yamamoto-san experienced similar pressures in balancing their careers and children's needs. Yet, their priorities in managing this balance differed. Whereas Tanaka paid relatively little attention to her finances, Yamamoto-san was conscious of the importance of income for maintaining her own and her son's class status. Having worked hard to attain her own education and middle-class life style, she was well aware of the fragility of her status and potential risk of downward mobility as a single mother. Less bound to the ideal of a full-time housewife, Yamamoto-san invested herself fully in work, as a means to ensure a good education for her son and maintain her status as a middle-class mother. Contrary to the emphasis on maternal care for young children among the middle classes, Yamamoto-san thus expressed her dedication to her son through her commitment to work – leaving her with little control over her role as a mother.

Kimura Eiko (mid-thirties)

In contrast to Tanaka-san and Yamamoto-san, Kimura Eiko was among the few mothers who emphasized the importance of spending most of her time with her children and worked only part-time when becoming a single mother. Kimura grew up with two working parents in blue-collar jobs in an industrial district, attending a day care center from a young age. As a child she felt lonely and deprived of the attention of her mother. She recounts:

> When I was little, I always came back [from school] to an empty home. I really hated that. And if I went to a friend's house, if the mother stayed home ... you would sometimes get home-made chou-crème or waffles. I always aspired to that.

These childhood experiences left a mark on how she thought about family and motherhood as an adult. In speaking about her relationship with her children, she emphasized the importance of mothers' presence and psychological support for their children. Yet, she was also aware of the economic realities she and her parents had faced. She adds: "Although I hated [being alone at home] as a child, I now understand that they worked because they had no money. ... So now, I feel grateful."

As a teenager, she quit senior high school and worked part-time for a while, but then came to realize that she needed at least a high school qualification to find a decent job. With the goal to attend a professional school to obtain skills that would ensure better employment, she decided to finish her high school qualification by attending an evening (*teijisei*) high school. Yet, a few months before graduation, she became pregnant, and barely out of school, she married and moved out of her parents' home.

Kimura-san imagined marriage as a lively family gathering, where "spouses and children sit in a sunlit room, watching TV together, having fun." She and her spouse thought she should be a full-time housewife, taking care of her two small children. But soon, also here, the economic realities set in. Her husband was in his early twenties and earned barely enough for them to make ends meet. As she says "we always had debts. But if there is no money, that's alright. ... I am used to not having money, since I have always lived without it. I can have bean sprouts (*moyashi* – the cheapest source of protein) for breakfast, lunch, and dinner, if necessary. I really have no problem with that." Eventually, they were able to move into a subsidized public housing unit for low-income families, an apartment with two large rooms and a kitchen diner, which significantly improved the family finances.

When her children were in elementary school, her marital relationship deteriorated and she filed for divorce. Having no income of her own, she began working part-time in the evenings, a few nights a week. As a single mother, she was able to keep the public housing unit, which, as a single mother with a low or no income, she could rent for as little as ¥2,000 a month (approximately $20). She made ends meet with the dependent children's allowance for single mothers, child support payments and occasional part-time work.

Her choice to work part-time at first, and to stop working altogether later, she explains, was guided by her concerns for her children. She stressed that working in an evening job in a bar enabled her to participate more easily in the PTA of her children's school. PTA meetings are often, and notoriously, scheduled during the week and in the mornings, making it very difficult for working mothers to participate in the required tasks. Yet, responsibilities for organizing school events and activities rotate, and are thus inevitable. Working at night, she points out, enabled her to make time for these duties. Quitting her job as a hostess, moreover, allowed her to dedicate herself to her children more fully. She explains:

> That I stopped working in *mizushōbai* (nighttime entertainment) was in my view good for the children. Maybe it's just me thinking this way. They come home and say "tadaima" (I'm home), and they probably walked home thinking [about their day and such things as] 'that teacher really sucks' or that she argued with another girl. If you can talk to someone [about your day] you can feel relieved. ... Once they have told me, they relax and say – "let's have some snacks (*oyatsu*)!" ... In this sense, it is great that I can now be there for them.

Initially, she notes, she was not sure about her future after divorce and thus decided to take up work. She recounts: "I wasn't sure whether I could make ends meet. In any case, 'I have to earn money!' I thought." But her friends explained to her that to get the full amount of the dependent children's allowance, she should try not to have too much income. "If you work too much you get less, it's a delicate balance," she explains. "It's best if you live in a public housing unit, work part-time, and you will be better off than working full-time. I love to go to the ward office and ask [about policies and programs]. I always go and ask a lot of questions." Although she had much less money to work with than Tanaka-san or Yamamoto-san, Kimura-san was satisfied with her lifestyle since she had, in her own words, always lived without money. She was also familiar with the welfare system, and had few qualms in making use of public services. In other words, her disposition toward income and public welfare differed markedly from those of mothers with university degrees. It was also this more laid-back attitude toward income and living standards, as well as her feelings of deprivation as a child, that allowed her to stress the importance of staying home, evoking the stereotypical image of a middle-class mother.

Similarly, she dealt with her divorce with much greater ease. She initially felt ashamed and her mother worried about what relatives would think. "The relatives all insisted that I should bear with it a little more. Or they said I should let the children go and remarry. But I convinced them." Among her friends and neighbors, she confidently spoke about her divorce. She explains: "I told my friends that I divorced and also the other mothers at my children's school. People here are really easygoing and say 'Oh, really?' They do not say 'oh, it must be hard,' they rather say [something unrelated such as], 'it's nice weather today.'" Where Tanaka-san and Yamamoto-san felt the pressures of social norms in their social environment and at work, Kimura-san confidently spread the news of her divorce, and changed her name (but not her children's) back to her maiden name, making her divorce noticeable in public and in her immediate environment. Rather than feeling threatened by downward mobility, she was happy to learn that as a single mother she was entitled to receive the dependent children's allowance and could get reduced rates for her water bills. Instead of a source of instability, she saw single motherhood as coming with a number of benefits.

Discussion

Single mothers' reproductive practices, in the context of these three narratives, stand in a complex relationship with their class origins, resources, and attitudes toward motherhood. They shed light not only on differences in resources and attitudes toward motherhood, but also mothers' active engagement with the maintenance and reproduction of their class status. In this section, I re-examine single mothers' reproductive practices in relation to class differences in resources and dispositions toward motherhood.

The family background of the three women visualizes important class differences in their family life and upbringing as well as their resources in becoming single mothers. Tanaka-san came from an upper-middle class family, and had considerably more economic, social, and cultural capital at her disposal than Yamamoto-san and Kimura-san. As a graduate from a prestigious university, she had social connections and an upper class demeanor, which helped her find a job. She also received significant financial support from her parents, as well as help with emergency childcare, which allowed her to work part-time, as she did not need to worry about her income. As a recent study has found, her experience is not unique: single mothers with a university education receive substantially more support from their parents, from assistance in obtaining housing to financial help and support with childcare, than single mothers from less affluent households (Iwata 2001).

Kimura-san, by contrast, had no economic, social or cultural capital of significance. She barely completed high school and faced financial hardship during her marriage. Even though her parents lived nearby, she received no support from them after becoming a single mother. Her only asset was a subsidized public housing unit for low-income families, which significantly reduced her housing costs, and allowed her to make ends meet on allowances and occasional part-time work. Also here, the pattern is typical: according to Iwata's study, single mothers with junior or senior high school qualifications are more likely to have experienced financial instabilities before and during marriage, an experience that is absent from the life trajectories of university graduates (Iwata 2001).

Yamamoto-san's experience, in turn, illustrates a case of social mobility of a woman who achieved a college degree and an affluent urban lifestyle despite her petit bourgeois origins. But even though her income was high, unlike Tanaka-san, she had no social connections and received no financial or other help from her family, and as consequence, felt heavily dependent on her income from work. She was well aware of the possibility of downward mobility, and therefore gave high priority to her performance at work. Different class backgrounds thus provided each of these mothers with different educational opportunities and very different resources to draw from as single mothers – parental support and assets, public support, and income from work.

Also their strategies in managing work and childcare differed quite significantly. While Tanaka worked in two part-time jobs rather than a full-time job to be able to spend more time with her children, Yamamoto was working full-time in a career-track job with long working hours. Kimura first worked part-time and then stopped working altogether to be able to stay home with her children. Differences in their resources of course played an important role in determining whether they stayed home or pursued a career-track job. Had it not been for the ample financial support from her parents, Tanaka-san would have had difficulties in managing everyday life with two part-time teaching jobs and a toddler. Yamamoto-san could only invest herself into her job because she could afford expensive baby-sitting services. Kimura-san, in turn, could make ends meet with a part-time job and government allowances because she had access to subsidized public housing. But their resources alone cannot fully explain their strategic choices between motherhood and work. If being able to stay home is a luxury and norm among the middle-class, why would Kimura-san, who had very little income and who was from a working class background, and not Tanaka-san, be the one to stay home? And if working motherhood is a common element of working class motherhood, why would Yamamoto-san, who was of petit bourgeois origins and had the highest income, and not Kimura-san be the one who was invested most in earning an income?

Although neither Tanaka-san nor Yamamoto-san pursued the role of a stay-home mother, upon closer examination, their strategies reveal a shared disposition toward their children's upbringing and education, which matches key elements of the role of the middle-class housewife and "education" mother. Tanaka-san knew that children attending day care centers not only faced prejudice among middle-class mothers, but might also have difficulties in entering an exclusive private school. In other words, she was well aware that her status as a working single mother could affect her daughter's socialization, cultural capital and educational future. Consequently, it was important for Tanaka-san to grant at least a little more time to her daughter to be able to ensure an upbringing appropriate for a middle-class child.

Yamamoto-san, in turn, saw her son's ability to attend university as her major concern. Yet, if the primary responsibility of a middle-class mother is to ensure her children's educational success, in the case of Yamamoto-san, this also meant that she had to earn an income that could pay for a middle-class education from cram school to private school and university. Earning such an income as a woman and single parent is of course no minor matter, which meant that Yamamoto-san had to give high priority to her work performance and income. Her concern about financing a middle-class lifestyle and education was not unusual. In fact, a higher proportion of single mothers over 40 with a university degree than single mothers with a lower educational attainment work in more than one job (such as a daytime and nighttime job), even though university graduates tend to earn significantly more than single mothers with high school qualifications (JIL 2003). Although single parents may have similar educational aspirations for their children as other parents, their actual attainment tends to be lower, often ending with junior or senior high school (Kudomi 1993; Okano and Tsuchiya 1999). Financing a university education thus remains a major challenge for a single mother.

If higher educational attainment is a central middle-class aspiration and necessary condition for the reproduction of a middle-class status, it also requires mothers with middle-class ambitions to make income from work a high priority unless they have ample family support. Thus, whereas commitment to work has been identified as a way in which working class mothers show their dedication to their children (Kondo 1990; Roberts 1994), in the case of single mothers, such a strategy can become an expression of middle-class ambitions. Being a middle-class mother is therefore not really about staying home. As the examples of Tanaka-san and Yamamoto-san show, being a middle-class mother means taking responsibility for children's educational and cultural capital, be it through a particular type of socialization, or by earning an income that can pay for piano lessons, private school, and university.

Kimura-san's story adds a further twist to this discussion. Even though she had little income, she consciously prioritized time with her children, and mostly stayed home after becoming a single mother. Also here, class-specific dispositions toward motherhood played an important role. Kimura-san's ability to stay at home was of course in part facilitated by the resources she had at hand, particularly residence in a very cheap, subsidized public housing unit. But it was also a different disposition toward motherhood, children's education and living standards that made this a possible option. Because of her low-income family background, Kimura-san was able to associate single motherhood with stability rather than decline. Although she had very little income, she was not worried about finances because she had always managed with very little money. Kimura-san was also not particularly concerned about her children's educational attainment, since a college education had also for her been out of reach. Instead, having felt deprived of her mother's attention as a child, she dreamed of a carefree family life devoid of the economic hardships of her childhood and marriage, and wished to devote herself more fully to her children. Her ability to stay home was therefore not only made possible by cheap housing, but also her limited concern with her living standard and income, as well as her children's educational attainment.

Yet, although Kimura-san was able to emulate the middle-class ideal of a stay-home mother and housewife, she did, from the perspective of the other mothers, actually not achieve a middle-class status. Being a middle-class mother, they might say, is not just about home-made chou crème and waffles, but about putting your children through college. Although Kimura-san was able to stay home, she lacked the cultural capital to actually advance her children's education and class status. A middle-class mother, by contrast, may have seen a cheap apartment as a unique means to make the most of her low salary and afford a better education for her children.

Together, the reproductive strategies of these three single mothers show not only how class is expressed through different attitudes and practices of motherhood. These cultural dimensions of class also play an important role in the reproduction of social class. Tanaka-san and Yamamoto-san were not just concerned about their children's socialization and education. They were also aware of the possibility of downward mobility and thus consciously worked on the maintenance of their children's cultural capital and class status as single mothers. Kimura-san, by contrast, was not concerned about downward mobility or her children's cultural capital, since she was already from a low-income family background. Yet, while she was able to manipulate representations of middle-class motherhood, she lacked the economic and cultural capital to actually change her own or her children's class position. As a consequence, she not only set different priorities in being a mother, but also unwittingly contributed to the reproduction of her class status among her children. Recognizing the class dimensions of motherhood in Japan, therefore, is not just a question of identifying class differences in attitudes and practices of motherhood. Motherhood, in this context, is not merely a lifestyle or gender aspect of class, but also plays an important role in forging children's economic, social, and cultural capital. In examining single mothers' strategies in balancing work and child care, we can thus identify some of the mechanisms which contribute to the reproduction of social class in contemporary Japan.

Notes

1 The research for this chapter was made possible with the support from the Itoh Scholarship Foundation, the Matsushita International Foundation, and a University of Illinois Dissertation Grant. I would like to thank David Slater and participants of the "Researching Social Class in Japan" conference for their helpful comments on an earlier version of this chapter.
2 This includes mothers who have separated from their partners but have not completed divorce papers, mothers who separated after living in a common-law marriage, as well as mothers who are divorced but also gave birth to children outside of marriage.
3 All names and minor details have been changed to ensure the anonymity of the interviewees.

References

Abe, A. (2005) "Kodomo no hinkon [Children in poverty]," in Kokuritsu shakai hoshō jinkō mondai kenkyūjo [National Institute of Population and Social Security Research] (ed.) *Kosodate Setai no Shakai Hoshō* [Social Security for the Families with Small Children], Tokyo: Tokyo Daigaku Shuppankai.

Allison, A. (2000) *Permitted and Prohibited Desires: mothers, comics, and censorship in Japan,* Berkeley, CA: University of California Press.

Bourdieu, P. (1984) *Distinction: a social critique of the judgment of taste,* trans. R. Nice, Cambridge, MA: Harvard University Press.

—— (1987) "What makes a social class? On the theoretical and practical existence of groups," *Berkeley Journal of Sociology,* 32:1–17.

Brinton, M.C. (1993) *Women and the Economic Miracle: gender and work in postwar Japan,* Berkeley, CA: University of California Press.

Coleman, S. (1983) *Family Planning in Japanese Society: traditional birth control in a modern urban culture*, Princeton, NJ: Princeton University Press.

Collins, P.H. (1994) "Shifting the center; race, class, and feminist theorizing about motherhood," in E.N. Glenn, G. Chang and L.R. Forcey (eds) *Mothering: ideology, experience, and agency*, New York: Routledge.

Ehara, Y. (2000) "Hahaoyatachi no daburu baindo [The double bind of mothers]," in Y. Meguro and S. Yazawa (eds) *Shōshika jidai no Jendā to Hahaoya Ishiki* [Gender and Maternal Identity in the Context of the Falling Birthrate], Tokyo: Shinyōsha.

Ezawa, A. (2006) "How Japanese single mothers work," *Japanstudien*, 18: 57–82.

Ezawa, A. and Fujiwara, C. (2005) "Lone mothers and welfare-to-work policies in Japan and the United States: toward an alternative perspective," *Journal of Sociology and Social Welfare*, 32: 41–63.

Fujiwara, C. (1997) "Boshisetai no shotokuhoshō to jidō fuyō teate [Single mothers' income security and the dependent children's allowance]," *Josei to rōdō 21* [Women and Labor 21], 6: 6–28.

—— (2005) "Hitorioya no shūgyō to kaissei [Class aspects of single mothers' work patterns]," *Shakai Seisaku Gakkai Shi* [The Journal of Social Policy and Labor Studies], 13: 161–75.

Fuse, A. (1984) *Atarashii kazoku no sōzō* [Imagining the new family], Tokyo: Aoki shoten.

Ginsburg, F. and Rapp, R. (1995) "Introduction," in F. Ginsburg and R. Rapp (eds) *Conceiving the New World Order*, Berkeley, CA: University of California Press.

Gordon, A. (1997) "Managing the Japanese household: the new life movement in postwar Japan," *Social Politics*, 4(2): 245–83.

Hendry, J. (1993) "The role of the professional housewife," in J. Hunter (ed.) *Japanese Women Working*, London: Routledge.

Imamura, A.E. (1987) *Urban Japanese Housewives: at home and in the community*, Honolulu, HI: University of Hawaii Press.

Inoue, T. and Y. Ehara (eds) (2005) *Josei no Dēta Bukku: Dai 4 han* [Women's Data Book: The 4th edition], Tokyo: Yūhikaku.

Iwai, H. and R. Manabe (2000) "M-jigata shūgyō patān no teichaku to sono imi [The stabilization of the M-shaped work participation rate and its meaning]," in K. Seiyama (ed.) *Nihon no Kaisō Shisutemu 4: jendā/shijō/kazoku* [Class Stratification System of Japan 4: gender, market, family], Tokyo: Tokyo Daigaku Shuppankai.

Iwao, S. (1993) *The Japanese Woman: traditional image and changing reality*, New York: The Free Press.

Iwata, M. (2001) "Ribetsu boshikazoku to shinzoku no shien: hahaoya no gakureki kara mita kaisōsei [Parental support among divorced single mother families: examining class based on the mothers' educational attainment]," *Kyōiku Fukushi Kenkyū* [Journal of Education and Social Work], 7: 57–72.

Jidō Fuyō Teate no Kirisute o Yurusanai Renrakukai (1986) *Ima Boshikatei ga Omoshiroi* [What's Interesting about Being a Single Mother Today], Tokyo: Jidō Fuyō Teate no Kirisute o Yurusanai Renrakukai [Network against Cuts in the Dependent Children's Allowance].

JIL (Japan Institute of Labor) [Nihon Rōdō Kenkyū Kikō] (2003) *Boshisetai no Haha eno Shūrōshien ni Kansuru Kenkyū* [Research on the work support for the mothers of single mother households], Nihon Rōdō Kenkyū Kikō Chōsa Kenkyū Hōkokusho [Japan Institute of Labor Research Report], (156).

Kanbara, F. (1991) *Gendai no Kekkon to Fūfu Kankei* [Marriage and Marital Relations in Contemporary Japan], Tokyo: Baifūkan.

—— (2000) "Kazoku kaisō to kosodate [Social class and child rearing]," in F. Kanbara and Y. Takada (eds) *Kyōikuki no Kosodate to Oyakokankei* [Child Rearing and Parent-Child Relationship during the Period of Education], Kyoto: Minerva Shobō.

Kasuga, K. (1989) *Fushikatei wo Ikiru: otoko to oya no aida* [Living in a Single-Father Family: between a man and a parent], Tokyo: Keisō shobō.

Kondo, D.K. (1990) *Crafting Selves: power, gender, and discourses of identity in a Japanese workplace*, Chicago, IL: University of Chicago Press.

Koyama, S. (1991) *Ryōsai Kenbo no Kihan* [The Model for the Good Wife, Wise Mother], Tokyo: Keisō shobō.

—— (1999) *Katei no Seisei to Josei no Kokuminka* [The Creation of the Family and the Making of Women's Citizenship], Tokyo: Keisō shobō.

Kudomi, Y. (1993) *Yutakasa no Teihen ni Ikiru: gakkō shisutemu to jakusha no saiseisan* [Living on the Edge of Affluence: educational system and reproduction of the weak], Tokyo: Aoki Shoten.

Leblanc, R.M. (1999) *Bicycle Citizens: the political world of the Japanese housewife*, Berkeley, CA: University of California Press.

Meguro, Y. and Shibata, H. (1999) "Kigyōshugi to kazoku [Corporatism and the family]," in Y. Meguro and H. Watanabe (eds) *Kōza Shakaigaku 2: Kazoku* [Lecture on Sociology 2: Family], Tokyo: Tokyo Daigaku Shuppan.

MHLW (Ministry of Health, Labor and Welfare) [Kōsei Rōdōshō] (2003a) *Shakai Fukushi Gyōsei Gyōmu Hōkoku* [Report on Social Welfare Administration and Services], Tokyo: Kōsei Tōkei Kyōkai.

—— (2003b) *Kokumin Seikatsu Kiso Chōsa* [Comprehensive Survey of Living Conditions of the People on Health and Welfare], Tokyo: Kōsei Tōkei Kyōkai.

—— (2003c) *Josei Rōdō Hakusho: hataraku josei no jitsujō* [White Paper on Women's Labour: the actual condition of working women], Tokyo: 21 Seiki Shokugyō Zaidan.

—— (2004) *Jinkō Dōtai Tōkei* [Vital Statistics of Japan], Tokyo: Kōsei Tōkei Kyōkai.

—— (2007) *Zenkoku boshisetai to chōsa kekka no gaiyō* [Summary of national survey on lone mother and other households], Tokyo: Kōsei Rōdōshō.

Nonaka, I. (1987) "Rikon, soshite henshin [Divorce and transformation]," *Boshi Fukushi* [Mother and Children Welfare], 37:4–5.

Ochiai, E. (1994) *21 Seiki no Kazoku e* [The Japanese Family System in Transition], Tokyo: Yūhikaku.

Ogasawara, Y. (1998) *Office Ladies and Salaried Men: power, gender, and work in Japanese companies*, Berkeley, CA: University of California Press.

Okano, K. and Tsuchiya, M. (1999) *Education in Contemporary Japan*, Cambridge: Cambridge University Press.

Osawa, M. (1993) *Kigyōchūshin Shakai wo Koete* [Beyond a Corporate-Centered Society], Tokyo: Jiji Tsūshinsha.

—— (1999) "Shigoto to katei no chōwa no tame no shūgyō shien [Career support to achieve balance between work and family]," *Kikan shakai hoshō kenkyū* [The Quarterly of Social Security Research], 34(4): 385–91.

—— (2002) "Twelve million full-time housewives: the gender consequences of Japan's postwar social contract," in O. Zunz, L. Schoppa and N. Hiwatari (eds) *Social Contracts Under Stress: the middle classes of America, Europe, and Japan at the turn of the century*, New York: Russell Sage Foundation.

Partner, S. (1999) *Assembled in Japan: electrical goods and the making of the Japanese consumer*, Berkeley, CA: University of California Press.

Peng, I. (1997) "Single mothers in Japan: unsupported mothers who work," in S. Duncan and R. Edwards (eds) *Single Mothers in an International Context: mothers or workers?*, London: University College London Press.

Roberts, G.S. (1994), *Staying on the Line: blue collar women in contemporary Japan*, Honolulu, HI: University of Hawaii Press.

Shimoebisu, M. (1989) "Rikon to kodomo no yōikuhi [Divorce and child support payments]," *Kikan shakaihoshō kenkyū* [The Quarterly of Social Security Research], 25: 156–65.

Single Mothers' Forum (1993) *Boshikatei ni Kanpai!* [Cheers to the Single Mothers!], Tokyo: Gendai shokan.

—— (2001) *Shinguru Mazā ni Kanpai!* [Cheers to Single Mothers!], Tokyo: Gendai Shokan.

Smith, R.J. (1983) "Making Village Women into 'Good Wives and Wise Mothers' in Prewar Japan," *Journal of Family History*, 8(1): 70–84.

Sōmushō [Ministry of Internal Affairs and Communications]. (2000), *Heisei 12 nen Kokusei Chōsa Hōkoku* [Population Census of Japan 2000], Tokyo: Sōmushō Tōkeikyoku [Statistics Bureau, Ministry of Internal Affairs and Communications].

Uno, K.S. (1993) "The death of the 'good wife, wise mother'?," in A. Gordon (ed.) *Postwar Japan as History*, Berkeley, CA: University of California Press.

—— (1999) *Passages to Modernity: motherhood, childhood, and social reform in the early twentieth century Japan*, Honolulu, HI: University of Hawaii Press.

Ushijima, C. (1995) *Jendā to Shakai Kaikyū* [Gender and Social Class], Tokyo: Kōseisha Kōseikaku.

Uzuhashi, T. (1997) *Gendai Fukushikokka no Kokusai Hikaku: nihon moderu no ichizuke to tenbō* [Comparison of Contemporary Welfare States: the positioning of the Japanese model and its prospects], Tokyo: Nihon hyōronsha.

Vogel, E.F. (1963) *Japan's New Middle Class: the salary man and his family in a Tokyo suburb*, 2nd edn, Berkeley, CA: University of California Press.

Vogel, S.H. (1978) "Professional housewife: the career of urban middle-class Japanese women," *Japan Interpreter*, 12:16–43.

White, M. (1987) "The virtue of Japanese mothers: cultural definitions of women's lives," *Daedalus*, 116: 149–63.

—— (2002) *Perfectly Japanese: making families in an era of upheaval*, Berkeley, CA: University of California Press.

Yokoyama, F. (2002) *Sengo Nihon no Josei Seisaku* [Women and Social Policy in Postwar Japan], Tokyo: Keisō shobō.

Yuzawa, N. (1993) "Josei to hinkon [Women and poverty]," in C. Hayashi and Fujin Fukushi Kenkyūkai [Research Group on Women's Welfare] (eds) *Gendai no Baibaishun to Josei: Jinken toshite no fujin hogo jigyō wo motomete* [Contemporary Prostitution and Women: calling for public protection of women's human rights], Tokyo: Domesu Shuppan.

9 How ethnic minorities experience social mobility in Japan

An ethnographic study of Peruvian migrants

Ayumi Takenaka

Introduction

Studies on social class in Japan have paid little attention to foreign migrants' mobility patterns. Whether this is due to lack of data or to the small, and thus negligible, number of foreign residents (estimated at 1.5 percent of Japan's total population[1]), it has reinforced the tendency to focus exclusively on individuals' achieved status (e.g. education and skill levels) rather than ascribed status, such as ethnic and national origins. This lack of attention may have reinforced the widespread notion that Japan is a credential-oriented society, at least in comparison to other industrial – above all, more ethnically heterogeneous and stratified – societies.

An examination of foreign migrants' mobility patterns, though rarely brought up in a society regarded as homogenous, is nonetheless critical. It is critical, not simply because the number of foreign residents has steadily increased over the last decades, and is expected to increase further in the near future (Kim and Inazuki 2000). More importantly, the extent to which foreign migrants achieve upward socio-economic mobility, as well as who does and how they do it, poses a critical question of how ethnic, in addition to class, backgrounds matter in mobility patterns. Ultimately, this question is a test to assess the degree of Japan's openness: where the boundary lies between those who have and do not have access to upward mobility, and how fluid class boundaries are in Japan.

Numerous studies have documented the marginal status of recent foreign migrants (e.g. Kajita 1998; Komai 1997) and point out various discriminatory forces that persistently exclude ethnic minorities from the mainstream labor market (e.g. Kim 2003; Okano 1997). Yet none of them addressed whether minorities' mobility chances were limited due to their ethnicity or if their chances hinged upon other factors such as class. How does ethnicity matter to the mobility patterns of migrants from different class backgrounds? Do ethnic minorities of different class origins have different chances of, and strategies for, climbing up the socio-economic ladder? This chapter examines how foreign migrants achieve, and do not achieve, upward social mobility, who does, and why, by looking at the interplay between ethnicity and class. By so doing, this study draws some implications about Japan's class structure and boundaries.

Here I focus on Peruvian migrants because of their diverse ethnic and class backgrounds. Peruvians began to migrate to Japan in large numbers in response to the revised immigration law of 1990 that allowed Japanese descendants (*Nikkeijin*) to enter and work in Japan. The policy was justified on the premise that Japanese descendants would assimilate more smoothly than other foreigners due to their "shared blood and culture" (Ministry of Justice 1990).

This ethnic focus was also motivated by class. Because of the predominantly middle-class backgrounds of *Nikkeijin*, Japanese officials hoped that their stay in Japan would be temporary. Due to their relatively high educational credentials, officials believed, they were more likely to return than low-skilled laborers with lower levels of human capital. Warned by the seemingly incessant flows of migrants coming in from poorer and larger neighboring countries (such as China), an official of the Ministry of Foreign Affairs expressed, "Asians might end up staying in Japan, but *Nikkeijin* will return to their home countries when their economic situations improve. Most *Nikkeijin* lead good lives there anyway" (Ministry of Justice 1990: 13). While lower-skilled laborers might cause social disorder by committing crimes and causing friction, *Nikkeijin*'s high educational attainment, together with their shared descent, was believed to facilitate their smooth adaptation in Japan.

Thus, Peruvian migrants were officially brought in as "ethnic kin" together with other South Americans. Unlike other South American migrants, however, Peruvians were more ethnically mixed. According to a 1992 JICA study, 30 percent of Japanese-Peruvian respondents reported to be of "mixed descent" as opposed to only 10 percent of their Brazilian counterparts. This was not necessarily due to their higher intermarriage rate in Peru (about 60 percent of Japanese-Peruvians in Lima were estimated to be endogamous (see Morimoto 1991)). Racially-mixed Japanese-Peruvians simply migrated to Japan in greater proportion than other South Americans;[2] and so did other Peruvians of non-Japanese descent. Some of those non-descendants entered the country as spouses of *Nikkeijin* or on fraudulent documents, while others entered as tourists (and overstayed) before Japan abolished the visa waiver program with Peru in 1994. Today, close to half of all Peruvians residing in Japan, officially at 55,000 in 2004, are estimated to be of non-Japanese descent (according to remittance companies). Many of these non-Japanese Peruvians, as described later, hailed from lower socio-economic backgrounds than Japanese descendants (of racially "unmixed" backgrounds). In sum, the variance in Peruvian migrants' ethnic and class backgrounds allows us to examine their effects on social mobility.

Once in Japan, the majority of Peruvians, along with other South Americans, were incorporated into the marginal sector of the Japanese labor market. Thus, regardless of their descent and class origins, they took up manual factory construction work, at least initially. Little has changed since then, although some have achieved upward mobility.[3] Curiously, the successful were mostly Peruvians of non-Japanese descent from more modest economic backgrounds. Why so, and how did they achieve it?

Generally, there are two ways for immigrants to "make it" in the host society (Portes and Rumbaut 1996). One is by way of educational attainment. The other is through independent entrepreneurship, for which an ethnic community is often a prerequisite. Ethnic communities provide information, credit, and clientele for businesses. This is how early Japanese immigrants in Lima, or the ancestors of Japanese-Peruvian migrants in Japan today, succeeded by amassing capital through rotating credit associations. And so too did Korean residents in Japan who relied on independent businesses in attaining socio-economic success (Kim 2003).

For the majority of Peruvians, as well as other recent migrants, however, neither human capital nor ethnic networks have enabled them to achieve the same degree of upward mobility. Even though many arrived in Japan with relatively high levels of education (according to various surveys, 30–40 percent of Peruvians in Japan received some type of higher education in Peru), they have been unable to utilize their skills as a means to move up the occupational ladder. Some acquired white-collar and professional jobs after completing their graduate training in Japan, but the number of Peruvians who do so is so miniscule that "you can count them with your fingers" (Peruvian Consulate official in Tokyo); according to the consulate official, only three Peruvians came to Japan in 2004 to pursue a graduate education with scholarships from the Japanese Ministry of Education, Culture, Sports, Science and Technology and during the year before, only 103 Peruvians, in total, were in Japan under student visas (Ministry of Justice 2004). At the same time, ethnic communities have not readily been available, either, because of their relatively small population and short immigration history in Japan.

Thus, those who have achieved social mobility have done so via another alternative, namely, by utilizing ethnic resources. Ethnic resources, or cultural resources associated with Peru and Latin America (e.g. the Spanish language, Latin dance and music), I argue, are a critical strategy for foreign migrants' upward social mobility. I elaborate below on how some Peruvian migrants used ethnic resources, paying attention to their ethnic and class backgrounds.[4]

Peruvian migrants' class position In Japan

Officially incorporated as "ethnic kin," Peruvian migrants were, in reality, laborers, filling in labor shortages as "temporary" contract workers often mediated through brokers. In 2003, the majority (over 90 percent) of Peruvian workers I surveyed (see note 5) were still doing similar type of work. According to the 2000 Japanese census, 88 percent of Peruvians surveyed (19,771 in total) reported that they engaged in manual labor, whereas only 1 percent held professional, technical, and managerial jobs. Their lack of mobility was primarily attributable to the nature of their work – dead-end jobs that were unstable, vulnerable, hard, and replaceable.

Their jobs were unstable, first and foremost, because they worked under contracts of usually three or six months. Contract workers were susceptible to economic cycles; in times of recession, bonuses were cut, as were hours of overtime work. They were also vulnerable to government policies. The increase in the Japanese consumption tax from 3 percent to 5 percent in April 1997, for instance, affected many Peruvian workers. Before April, Fernando Guibu, an auto manufacturing worker, worked "like mad": "Now our production level is high because people (consumers) are buying a lot before the tax goes up." After April, his work was significantly reduced as predicted. Since the availability of overtime work was unpredictable, migrants felt compelled to work whenever work was available: "If I said no (to overtime work)," Fernando feared, "no more extra work would be offered or my contract would not be renewed." Workers lived day by day without knowing what would happen next.

Migrants often worked long hours fundamentally because of the payment method. According to my survey conducted in 2003, about 90 percent of Peruvian workers reported that they were paid by the hour. That was why extra hours of work (*zangyō*) were so important to them. Extra hours not only paid more; they also mattered as a status symbol. Luis Kuwata explained: "If you have more *zangyō*, your status goes up, because that means that you earn more." The hourly payment method also compelled migrants to work even when they were sick. Carlos Shimoda, 40, the father of a daughter, said his greatest concern was his health. "Honestly, my work is hard. I have to carry heavy truck parts all day long. I wonder how long my body will last. And if I get sick, what will happen to my family?" Indeed, the number of hours put in, or their mere physical presence in the factory, was the primary determinant of their wages.

Gender also mattered, as women ubiquitously earned less than men. In the factory where I worked in 1997, men were paid 1,300 yen per hour compared to only 900 yen for women. Although employers justified the gap through job differentiation, in reality, men and women often engaged in the same work, as I observed in several factories. As Tsuda *et al.* (2003) demonstrated, achieved status, such as levels of education and skill, language proficiency, and legal status and length of stay in the host society, mattered little in determining foreign migrants' wages in Japan. Consequently, Peruvian migrants often put up with long hours of work.

Their work was hard. In a way, hard work meant physical pain. Some jobs were dangerous involving poisonous chemicals, while others required precision, such as checking computer chips. Carrying 23-kg computer monitors, for instance, Carlos Motobu hurt his fingers. His fingers shook so much during the first week of work that he could not even hold a pen. Overall, the work was hard, fundamentally and ironically because it was simple.

> My job on an assembly line was so simple as to cut scotch tape and put it around computer monitors, but the line moved so fast that the task had to be completed in 15 seconds and the procedure was repeated 240 times in 60 minutes. By 5pm, I normally would have repeated the task 1,920 times. After a week, my fingers indeed began to shake, to the extent that I could not hold a cup.

Carlos consoled me: "Once you become *roboticized* (become a robot), you'll get used to the work and even to the pain itself," he laughed. "Robotization" was the term Peruvians frequently used to describe their work, as were expressions, such as "working as if we had never worked in our entire lives" and "working like donkeys." Middle-class Peruvians of Japanese descent also used an expression, "working like *cholos* or *indios*," referring to Peruvians of Indian descent who tend to occupy lower rungs in the Peruvian class hierarchy.

Being simple and mechanical, their jobs were also impersonal and replaceable; such simplicity made absentees easily replaceable. What counted was the quantity of labor (the number of hours worked or the number of products completed), rather than the quality of workers. Unlike native workers, Peruvians got paid the same amount regardless of their skills, education, and age. And they knew their jobs were dead-ends with little prospect for promotion. Nora Uchida observed the difference between Japanese and foreign workers in her TV assembly factory; while Japanese got promoted and earned more as they stayed longer in the factory, foreigners' pay stayed the same. Consequently, Peruvian workers had little attachment to their work and workplace.

Being locked in such jobs, Peruvians, together with other South American *Nikkeijin*, have become labeled as casual and marginal laborers as "*dekasegui*" workers (temporary workers) in Japan. The government-run NIKKEIS employment agency, established to support their ethnic kin (and officially ceasing to exist in 2004), treated *Nikkeijin* as blue-collar manual workers. The agency's numerous multilingual pamphlets, published for the purpose of "promoting *Nikkeijin*'s smooth adaptation in Japan," automatically labeled *Nikkeijin* as "*dekasegui*," constantly depicting them as blue-collar workers wearing uniforms, helmets, and boots. These publications explained in detail how to deal with heavy machines and how to cope with work in "dangerous" places. In the process of their incorporation into Japanese society, South Americans became synonymous with "*Dekasegui* workers." Such typification helps confine groups to low-wage menial labor ("foreigners' work," "Mexicans' work") (Portes and Rumbaut 1996). And so, it reinforced Peruvian migrants' class position in Japan, making it difficult for them to climb up the socio-economic ladder.

Reasons for immobility

Most Peruvian migrants have continued to withstand such work conditions partly because of lack of alternatives. While employers commonly attributed Peruvian migrants' occupational immobility to their lack of Japanese language proficiency, there were, in reality, few skilled or white-collar jobs available. Jobs advertised for *Nikkeijin*, either at the government-run job recruitment agency NIKKEIS or in the Spanish weekly newspaper *International Press* were almost always blue-collar menial jobs; though they were often gender-specific, these jobs did not require skills, education, or knowledge of the Japanese language. Out of 2,415 jobs advertised during 1993 at NIKKEIS, virtually all were unskilled jobs in manufacturing (52.9 percent) or in construction (27.2 percent). More recently in 2004, the only jobs that "welcomed" or "permitted" foreigners at the public employment office in municipalities with high concentrations of *Nikkeijin* (e.g. Hamamatsu) were still confined to construction and manufacturing.

Peruvian migrants' occupational immobility also stemmed from their own motives. Most of them, regardless of their ethnic and class origins, migrated to Japan for economic reasons; factory jobs in Japan simply paid more than white-collar jobs in Peru. With the money earned in Japan, migrants aspired to start a business in Peru (23 percent), support their family (21 percent), save money in general (18 percent), or build a house in their country (17 percent) (survey conducted by NIKKEIS 1994). Ethnic or cultural reasons were secondary. So, Japanese-Peruvians, many of whom traced their origins to Okinawa, did not settle there; instead, they went to mainland Japan where wages were higher. Ishi (1997) pointed out that Japan might have been a convenient destination for Japanese descendants who were able to use cultural reasons to justify, or hide, their true (economic) motives for migration. While their migration was officially induced by ethnic ties, migrants themselves saw this as an opportunity to make extra money.

So long as their moves were driven by economic motives, they found it convenient to work through labor brokers. This was because indirect employment yielded higher real wages. *Nikkeijin*'s overall average earnings of 336,600 yen were significantly higher than the average monthly wages of direct employment, 200,000–240,000 yen after benefits were deducted (NIKKEIS 1994; Koyo Kaihatsu Sentā 1991). Thus, they continued to work in unstable and vulnerable conditions, because these jobs paid well. *Nikkeijin* workers, on average, earned more than native workers of comparable ages. In 1990, South American males earned 336,000 yen per month (and 204,400 yen for women), compared to the average monthly wage of 179,000 yen for Japanese male university graduates (typically 22–23 years old) in white-collar positions in 1991. It was almost comparable to the overall average monthly wage of all Japanese workers: 345,000 yen.

Peruvians earned relatively high wages, partly because they did not, or opted not to, pay for benefits. According to my survey in 2003, only 25 percent of Peruvian households surveyed reported that their social security payments were deducted from their salaries; none of them were provided health insurance by their employers (67 percent subscribed to the national health insurance plan on their own). They earned well, also because they tended to work long hours and night shifts. "Foreigners work harder," said many Peruvian as well as Japanese employers. Surely, they wanted to earn as much and as quickly as possible before returning home. But they also had to work hard because of vulnerable status. Every day they punched a time card in and out, and after all, their pay was based on each and every hour of actual work. The type of work Peruvian migrants engage in – manufacturing, construction, and heavy industry – also paid more than white-collar (e.g. secretarial, administrative) jobs, as the former were harder to attract workers. Ironically, therefore, there was little incentive to move out of unstable work conditions.

High turnover, another consequence of engaging in vulnerable jobs, also made it hard to move up the socio-economic ladder. According to a 1991 study, almost half (49 percent) of *Nikkeijin* workers surveyed had changed jobs once, while 25 percent had changed twice, and 21 percent, three times (Koyo Kaihatsu Center 1991). The 40 Peruvian household heads I surveyed in 2003 had held 4.5 jobs, on average, with most staying with a job for 2–3 years. In most cases (68 percent), workers changed jobs on their own initiative rather than by an act of their employers (26 percent) (JICA 1992). They often did so in search of better-paying jobs or jobs with more hours of extra hours of work (i.e. better pay). In a way, slim prospects for promotion led to high turn-over. Another factor was Peruvian migrants' motive, or what the Spanish weekly *International Press* called "*dekasegui* mentality," to earn, save, and go home. Since they wanted to earn the maximum amount of money before returning home, they frequently changed jobs, constantly switching for better-paying ones. Meanwhile, employers regarded their high turn-over as lack of loyalty to the workplace or lack of "proper" work ethnic (cultural deficiency), thereby justifying their continuous status as temporary dispensable workers.

"*Dekasegui* mentality," indeed, remained strong among Peruvian migrants. After 15 years of staying in the country, many had no clear future plans and, despite their prolonged stay, continued to talk about "going back to Peru one day." According to a survey conducted by Kajita and his colleagues (1998), only 2 percent of *Nikkeijin* responded that they intended to stay in Japan, while 37 percent were indecisive about their future plans. The same survey also showed that very few had career ambitions or objectives other than "to save money" (38 percent) and "to enjoy life" (17 percent) (Kajita 1998). Luis Kuwata, a Peruvian migrant, said his primary objective was "to live well (*vivir bien*)" which he meant as "life without work." Jorge García also aspired to "make as much money as possible now so that I can relax in Peru later." Others justified their hard work by seeing it as a sheer means to "have fun on weekends" (i.e. going to Latin discos and partying, etc.) (Ishi 1997). Migrants originally migrated to Japan with various dreams and aspirations. As they prolonged their stay in Japan (and away from Peru), however, they increasingly found it difficult to realize these objectives. Over time, then, their "objectives" became more general and ambiguous with fewer concrete plans. These dispositions, themselves a result of their newly placed class position in Japan, reinforced and self-justified migrants' class immobility.

Due to the nature of their work and persistent sojourning mentality, the migrants' Japanese language command has not significantly improved over time. According to the 2004 survey conducted by the *International Press* (1/1/05), only 10 percent respondents claimed to "understand and speak Japanese well enough" and 40 percent "did not understand or speak it." Moreover, the smattering of Japanese acquired were often limited to a work vocabulary (e.g. *zangyō* for overtime work, *hanchō* for group leaders, and *yakin* for night work) and a few words used daily (e.g. *densha* for trains, *apāto* for apartments).

Most Peruvians were not so keen to learn the language, because they perceived no incentives at work and had no intention of staying in Japan for long. Some said they were simply too busy with work to dedicate themselves to language learning. Although free language courses were widely available at local municipalities (in addition, some language courses were subsidized by the government through the Japan International Cooperation Agency (JICA) for *Nikkeijin*), most Peruvians did not bother to attend them (Kajita 1998). Kazu Yamashiro, a Peruvian migrant, explained, "You can live in Japan (without learning the language), because all the signs are written in roman characters. Prices are clearly shown and tagged and restaurants have visual displays of menus, so it's not like Peru where you have to negotiate the price, from taxi fares to apples in the street market." Negative experiences in Japan were another disincentive for learning Japanese. Isabel Kanai expressed it most directly, "The Japanese treat us horribly. So why should I study their language and even try to make friends with such people?" Lack of prospects for job mobility also deprived them of a motive to learn the language. Some also perceived it more convenient not to speak, or to pretend that they do not speak the language so long as they remained vulnerable, dispensable workers. According to Yoshi Shiroma, "Because (Japanese) factory people are hard-headed and their way of doing work it not always efficient, it's better if you pretend that you don't understand them and work your own way."

As reflected in their lack of Japanese language command, Peruvians' social interactions with Japanese remained limited. The language barrier was a cause, as well as consequence, of limited interactions with the Japanese. According to a 1992 study by JICA, half of Peruvian *Nikkeijin* surveyed reported to have few Japanese friends. Their interactions, moreover, were mostly limited to the workplace. As I observed in several factories, conversations at work rarely exceeded the minimum level of job instructions and daily greetings. During lunch hours and breaks, Peruvians (and other South Americans) almost always ate separately and sat apart from the Japanese. Since Peruvians were employed through a distinct system apart from native workers, job segregation contributed to isolation. Also, the impersonal and mechanical nature of work required no communication; highly segregated jobs, such as fast-moving assembly line work, limited interaction with other workers.

While the nature of their work perpetuated their sojourning orientation, this tendency, in turn, reinforced their marginal status as "temporary" contract workers. Due to their high turn-over, employers preferred to continue hiring Peruvians as temporary workers. So long as they remained "temporary," there was little incentive to learn the language. And even if they mastered the language, migrants reasoned, there was little prospect for upward mobility as contract labor migrants. In sum, their vulnerable class position deprived them of a sense of motivation and career aspirations. And this made it more difficult for migrants to move up the socio-economic ladder.

Lack of entrepreneurship opportunities

Another obstacle to social mobility was limited entrepreneurship opportunities. While the number of Peruvian businesses (grocery stores, video rentals, newspapers, restaurants) has increased over time, there were only about 80 Peruvian-owned businesses as of 2005 (according to the *International Press* and the Peruvian Consulate). According to the 2000 Japanese census, the rate of self-employment among Peruvians was less than 1 percent. Catering to a small clientele of fellow Peruvians, many of these businesses have had difficulty sustaining themselves. Moreover, running such (small-scale) businesses did not always yield as high and stable wages as factory work, according to many Peruvians interviewed. Due to their limited Japanese language command and social interaction with the Japanese, Peruvian migrants generally found it difficult to penetrate the mainstream labor market.

Lack of cohesive ethnic community was a cause (and consequence) of limited entrepreneurship opportunities. Although a number of Peruvian associations have emerged over time, most of them have failed due to lack of unity or financial difficulties. (A major association failed in the early 1990s, because its leader reportedly took the money and fled to Okinawa. Another one failed, according to some witnesses, after members, being drunk at a party, ended up destroying the furniture and carpet in a public place.) Moreover, Kajita (1998) documented relatively little reliance on community resources among *Nikkeijin* workers, other than occasional visits to ethnic grocery stores and video rental stores; most of those he surveyed reported that they seldom went to ethnic restaurants on a regular basis and did not attend religious services (in Spanish or Portuguese) at all.

One reason for this lack of community was Peruvian migrants' "temporary" status reinforced by their sojourning mentality. Their high rotation and geographical mobility in search of better-paying jobs was also attributable to this, as was their heavy reliance on brokers. Relying on brokers meant that places of work and residence were determined by brokers rather than by personal networks; this implied discontinuity of ties cultivated in Peru, such as village and regional ties that often served as an important basis for building immigrant communities (Tanno and Higuchi 1999). Moreover, most Peruvian migrants were incorporated into a specific sector of the Japanese labor market to engage in specific kinds of work. This type of work-specific migration hindered the possibility of building community institutions.

Another reason had to do with the nature of their work and dispositions developed as a result of their vulnerable class position in Japan. Trying to put in as much time as possible to work, migrants rarely had time and energy to devote to community activities. Many also saw little need for a community. Eduardo Oshiro, who failed in leading associations, commented: "In Peru, Nikkei Peruvians live comfortable lives, but here (in Japan) they are just laborers. Nikkei here are different from Nikkei in Peru. They are stressed and selfish. They don't bother to help one another. Nikkei here only think of work and work, so they have no mentality for mutual help." Lack of solidarity stems, once again, from their vulnerability (and their vulnerable class position) in Japan.

Ethnic and class cleavages

Internal cleavages also hindered unity among Peruvian migrants in Japan. Particularly noticeable was a cleavage along lines of descent, namely between Peruvians of Japanese descent and non-Japanese-Peruvians. The difference originated in Peru where Japanese immigrants and their descendants have maintained a tight-knit community with a distinct identity (Takenaka 2003b). The cohesive Japanese community in Lima was defined both in terms of ethnicity and class; core participants were mostly middle-class Japanese-Peruvians,[5] while poorer Japanese descendants, who tended to be racially mixed, often felt excluded because of racial differences or fees required in participating in community activities. Antonio Sasaki, a quarter Japanese who came to Japan to work, said: "The *colonia* (the Japanese community in Lima) didn't let me in, because I don't have slanted eyes. I had to go with a Nikkei friend (to participate in their activities). Nikkei always stared at you and examined you, just as Japanese treat foreigners (in Japan). It is a closed community."

Once in Japan, these differences have further increased due to two class-related factors. One had to do with a difference in class origins in Peru; compared to the predominantly middle-class origins of Japanese-Peruvians (particularly of racially "unmixed" backgrounds), other Peruvians tended to come from more modest economic backgrounds. This was particularly so, as more non-Japanese Peruvians in greater economic need (rather than middle-class professionals) migrated to Japan by falsifying documents. According to my survey results, 55 percent of Japanese-Peruvians previously held white-collar occupations in Peru, whereas only 25 percent of non-Japanese Peruvians did. Perceptions of class differences were also widespread among Peruvians, fueled undoubtedly by publicized crimes committed by some Peruvians (of non-Japanese descent). Most recently, Manuel Torres Yake, who entered Japan on fraudulent documents as Juan Carlos Pizarro Yagi, was reported to have murdered a 7-year-old Japanese girl in Hiroshima in December 2005. "Peruvians (of non-Japanese descent) in Japan are mostly from lower classes and commit crimes," said Oscar Murata, himself a Japanese descendant, "I cannot accept such low-level Peruvians as criminals, though I have no trouble accepting high-level Peruvians." The fact that many non-Japanese Peruvians entered Japan illegally or on fraudulent documents further reinforced the perception of class differences. Rafo Saito said, "Peruvians are canny. They are even more so here in Japan. Look how they came to Japan (illegally) even without shame. And when it comes to crime, they are so crafty, excellent robbers. Japanese are not used to that, because they trust everyone too much. So, Peruvians take advantage of that." Isabel Kanai also murmured: "Peruvians in Japan are so bad. I wonder how so many *cholos* and even *negritos* (mestizo and black Peruvians) managed to sneak into Japan."

Class heightened the cleavage also because all Peruvians were placed in the same class position in Japan *despite* their class differences back in Peru. Antonio Yamada, a second-generation Japanese-Peruvian, explained: "Of course, we were shocked that the Japanese treat us as *gaijin* (foreigner), but, after all, that's what we are. But what really bothers us is ... the Japanese don't distinguish between *Nikkei* and Peruvians." "It's shocking," reiterated Keiko Shimabukuro, "because in Peru, we looked down on (poorer) Peruvians and discriminated against them. But here in Japan, we are treated the same." While (middle-class) Japanese-Peruvians were disturbed, poorer Peruvians were "amazed," as Lucho López, a former street vendor from Lima, put it: "It's amazing that I do the same work here as Nikkei. In Peru, Nikkei live like kings, you know?" Coming from modest economic backgrounds, Lucho, staying illegally in Japan, was delighted that he worked alongside Nikkei. Being lumped together with "lower-class" Peruvians, Japanese descendants, then, consciously tried to distinguish themselves from them by using ethnic and legal differences.

This was most clearly manifested in the labels they used for other Peruvians: "Peruvian" or "native Peruvian," in addition to "bambas," "truchas," "chichas," "ilegals," or "false Nikkei," all in reference to their illegal status, in distinct from "descendants" or "Nikkei. " To further clarify the boundaries, the terms "real Peruvian," "pure Peruvian," "authentic Peruvian," and "Peruvian-Peruvian" were also used, as opposed to "real Nikkei," "pure Nikkei," and "Nikkei-Nikkei" (Takenaka 2003a). In an article headlined, "False *Nikkei*, A Problem For Our Community," Lima's Nikkei community newspaper, *Peru Shimpo* (February 4, 1990), expressed its concern over how (non-Japanese) Peruvians, including "terrorists and criminals," might ruin "our prestigious *Nikkei* community achieved through years of our hard work and honesty" (Takenaka 2003a). In this way, "non-Nikkei" were often blamed for having hurt the image of the entire Peruvian population in Japan.

Then, distinct values were attached to these labels. According to Takashi Iha, a Japanese descendant, "bambas" were more dishonest, loud, and party-loving who drink a lot and always end up fighting, as opposed to Nikkei who were more reserved, quiet, and respectful. Many, like Yoshi Higa, who grew up with close ties to Lima's Japanese community, attributed the difference to their distinct upbringing: "Our customs are naturally different. We ate Japanese food at home. And our values are different – there was more emphasis on honesty, responsibility, and hard work."

Consequently, these two groups moved around different social circles. According to Adolfo Sasaki, a quarter Japanese-Peruvian, most of those who hung out at Latino discos and bars in Roppongi (Tokyo's night life district) to "look for Japanese girls" were "pure Peruvians"; Nikkei, he said, just stay at home watching TV. Also, Peruvian restaurants were disproportionately filled by non-Japanese Peruvians, as were public events, such as parties, religious services, and a Peruvian procession (held in Kanagawa in 1997). Sometimes, Japanese-Peruvians deliberately excluded other Peruvians from their social activities. Hiro Matsumoto, a Japanese-Peruvian, told me a number of times not to bring "Peruvians" or "not real (or 100 percent) Nikkei" to his salsa dance classes, because, he said, they always confused classes with parties (he let only Nikkei and Japanese in). In the end, Japanese-Peruvians often expressed more comfort with fellow "Nikkei" due to "more trust." Compared to "Peruvians who come to

Japan by abusing documents," Nikkei were more trustworthy, they said, because "we know that Nikkei have certain educational levels. We were brought up with certain (read, middle-class) values" (Jaime Iha).

Then, these differences were reinforced by legal privileges associated with ethnicity. Since Japan's immigration policy accorded privileges only to Japanese descendants, this set an ethnic hierarchy, raising the status of Nikkei over that of other Peruvians. Ethnically-privileged Japanese-Peruvians, then, used ethnicity as a strategy to make known the internal differences fueled by class, which were largely unnoticed by the larger Japanese public. In this process, prior class differences have taken on ethnic embodiment in Japan, while prior ethnic divisions increased through class strategies. Altogether, this has resulted in reinforcing divisions, instead of forging unity, among Peruvian migrants in Japan, thereby hindering yet another means to move out of manual factory jobs.

Ethnicity as a class resource: who has made it and how?

While most Peruvian migrants remained a marginal work force, a few have moved out of unstable, unskilled dispensable jobs. Over the course of their stay in Japan, some were able to earn higher income, acquire more security by purchasing homes or obtaining social benefits, or else, pursue a career they wanted. Many made it by way of venturing into independent business. In most cases, they succeeded by exploiting "ethnic" resources – e.g. teaching Spanish, soccer and Latin dances, and cooking Peruvian dishes. Daniel Días, a former professional soccer player in Peru, became economically successful (with a self-reported monthly income of $12,000) by establishing a soccer school for Japanese children. He purchased a 5-room apartment in Tokyo's fashionable district where he lives with his Japanese wife and two Japanese-born children. Rafael Rodriguez launched a career as a musician, his long-term dream, playing traditional Peruvian and Latin music in a band for Latin American and Japanese audiences. Pedro Sánchez succeeded in running an upscale Peruvian restaurant, in the name of "authentic Peruvian cuisine," catering mostly to affluent urban Japanese consumers. Utilizing various "ethnic" resources, they were able to penetrate into the mainstream Japanese market in one way or another.

Curiously, most of these Peruvians were of non-Japanese descent who were allegedly less familiar with, and more distant from, Japanese culture than Japanese descendants, and accordingly, were not granted privileged legal status like Japanese-Peruvians. Labor statistics of foreigners (Ministry of Health, Labor, and Welfare 2004) show a similar trend; while 90 percent of all South American employees in the manufacturing sector were Japanese descendants (i.e. *Nikkeijin*), *Nikkeijin* constituted only 68 percent, 74 percent, and 23 percent in restaurant and food related businesses, retail, and education, respectively. Thus, 77 percent of those South Americans engaged in education (as teachers and researchers, etc.), for instance, were of non-Japanese descent.

Contrary to common expectations, non-Japanese-Peruvians, in general, were better integrated into Japanese society than Peruvians of Japanese descent

(Takenaka 2003a). According to marriage statistics registered at the Peruvian embassy in Tokyo, as of 1997, non-Japanese Peruvians married Japanese partners in greater proportion (75 percent; or 100 out of 133 marriages involving Peruvians without Japanese surnames) than Japanese-Peruvians (31 percent, or 119 out of 382 marriages involving Peruvians with a Japanese surname).[6] Likewise, among 40 Japanese-Peruvians and 20 non-Japanese Peruvians I interviewed during 1996–97, a greater percentage of non-Japanese-Peruvians had Japanese spouses or partners (though non-Japanese Peruvians tended to be single or separated from their spouses in Peru due to their illegal status in Japan; and their illegal status might have encouraged them to marry a Japanese to legalize their status). Out of 40 Peruvian household heads more recently surveyed, five Peruvians married to Japanese natives were either non-Japanese-Peruvian or those of mixed backgrounds who had just one Japanese grandparent. Japanese-Peruvians of unmixed racial background (i.e. racially "pure" Japanese descendants) were proportionately least likely to marry Japanese natives.

Peruvians of non-Japanese descent also tended to acquire a better command of the Japanese language over time. In the survey I conducted, non-Japanese-Peruvians scored the highest on a self-reported scale of Japanese language ability, while that of unmixed Japanese descendants was the lowest. According to a Japanese language teacher employed by JICA, non-Japanese descendants often had an extra incentive to learn the language because "Japanese is a completely foreign language to them"; Japanese descendants, on the other hand, see it as the language of their parents or grandparents and "do not try to learn as hard." Some Japanese descendants were also discouraged from learning the language, because they felt ashamed not to be able to speak and comprehend the language proficiently (despite their descent), and also found it more convenient not to speak it, because Japanese natives often regarded them as culturally deficient. When Hiro Matsumoto asked Japanese passers-by for directions, they simply pointed out to signs, he said, assuming that he could read Japanese. "The Japanese treat you as an idiot, if you have a Japanese face but don't speak or read Japanese," he despaired. To avoid this type of confusion (and insult), Japanese-Peruvians often preferred to use their Peruvian first names in Japan, even if they went by their Japanese names in Peru.

Moreover, non-Japanese Peruvians, overall, were less isolated from the mainstream Japanese society. In my survey, Peruvians of non-Japanese descent reported to use the Japanese language more frequently at home, work, and in their neighborhood and interact more frequently with Japanese natives. Indeed, non-Japanese Peruvians without legal papers tended to establish more contact with Japanese natives through aid agencies and religious and volunteer organizations, compared to Japanese-Peruvians who tended to interact amongst themselves through their own social activities. Non-Japanese Peruvians were more likely to rely on these aid organizations, partly because of their greater need for assistance due to their often illegal, and generally more vulnerable, status. They were also the ones who frequented Latino discos and bars more often – key sites of interaction with Japanese, especially with Japanese women. (Most of those non-Japanese

Peruvians married to Japanese natives reported to have met their future spouses at Latino discos and parties, or else, through volunteer and community activities.)

Furthermore, non-Japanese Peruvians, who generally came from more modest economic backgrounds, were more likely to be satisfied with the life (and money) in Japan than Japanese descendants who were "shocked" about their downward mobility and treatment by the Japanese as *gaijin* (foreigner) despite their descent and prior identity as Japanese. Subsequently, non-Japanese-Peruvians were less likely than Japanese descendants to go back to Peru frequently or re-migrate (or aspire to re-migrate) to another country, although obviously their illegal status limited their international movements. Paradoxically, non-Japanese Peruvians were, in a way, more "settled" in Japan than Japanese descendants who were expected to assimilate more smoothly because of their shared descent (Yamamoto 1999; Igarashi 2000).

In sum, while Japanese-Peruvians were more concerned about restoring their status by focusing on their prior class backgrounds in Peru, other Peruvians were more forward-looking. It is generally harder for middle-class migrants to "move up" the economic ladder than those who start from lower class positions. Faced with barriers to move up the socio-economic ladder, ethnically Japanese, middle-class Peruvians found it easier to remain "temporary" workers with a sojourning mentality and derive their satisfaction purely in monetary and material terms instead of occupational status. Other Peruvians, in the meantime, tended to be more content and have a clear set of long-terms goals. Also, non-Japanese Peruvians were able to exploit "ethnic" resources better than Japanese-Peruvians for two reasons.

First, being perceived to be more different from the native Japanese population, non-Japanese-Peruvians were in a better position to utilize their ethnic resources vis-à-vis the Japanese. In the eyes of the average Japanese, it would probably appear more credible if a Cuzqueño, a native of Cuzco, prepared "authentic" Peruvian food than a Japanese-looking Peruvian. Thus, compared to Japanese-Peruvians, who often suffered from a dilemma of feeling, and being treated as, neither completely Japanese nor completely foreign, Peruvians of non-Japanese descent tended to exploit their "ethnic" resources better and more fully.

Second, their ethnic resources were class-specific resources. The kinds of cultural resources Peruvian migrants used – e.g. playing soccer, dancing, playing Latino music, and being a Peruvian chef – were often associated with lower classes in Peru; they were certainly not the type of careers typically aspired by members of the middle class, such as doctors, engineers, and lawyers. (This is akin to Japanese-Brazilians in Japan who were mostly from middle-class backgrounds in Brazil and were unfamiliar with "working-class" cultural practices, such as dancing samba [see Tsuda 2003; Roth 2002].) While Japanese-Peruvians of middle-class origins were disillusioned with abrupt downward mobility and their inability to "make it" through their skills and education (that is how middle-class people typically expect to achieve upward mobility), poorer Peruvian migrants availed themselves more of ethnic resources.

In their comparative study to the U.S., Tsuda *et al.* (2003) report that levels of human capital (i.e. education and skills) matter little in determining foreign migrants' wages in Japan. That is, regardless of their education, skills, and experience, foreign migrants are relegated to marginal class positions. In a society where human capital matters little, middle-class Japanese-Peruvians were deprived of both class *and* ethnic resources. Meanwhile, poorer Peruvians, generally more content with their class situation in Japan, had an extra incentive to use available resources. Armed with fewer class (alternative) resources, they also had little hesitation to use "lower-class" ethnic resources to "make it" in Japan.

Conclusion

Although Peruvian migration to Japan was officially triggered by ethnic ties, class played a significant role in shaping the experiences of Peruvian migrants. Nikkei and non-Nikkei Peruvians, regardless of their descent and economic backgrounds, were placed in the same class position within the Japanese class structure as manual casual laborers. In an attempt to regain status, Japanese descendants (particularly middle-class, racially unmixed Japanese-Peruvians) consciously tried to distinguish themselves from "lower-class" Peruvians on the basis of their class differences back in Peru. They did so by asserting their identity as "Nikkei" that is neither completely Japanese nor completely Peruvian. Meanwhile, non-Japanese Peruvians steadily made efforts to adjust their legal status or simply learn to survive in a society where they completely felt foreign and vulnerable. While they were largely viewed as ethnically and culturally different in Japan, it was this difference that they often utilized as a resource and a strategy to move out of their vulnerable position as manual, unstable, and often illegal, laborers.

What does this tell us about the role of ethnicity in Japan's class structure? Much research on ethnic minorities has reported disadvantages associated with ethnic minority status in Japan; ethnic minorities are perpetually confined to the bottom of the socio-economic hierarchy due to their ethnic or cultural difference, implying rigid boundaries between Japanese and non-Japanese. My study, however, has shown that ethnic "difference," or what is perceived to be different, plays double roles for minorities' social mobility. It is not simply a source of discrimination and a barrier to upward mobility; ethnic difference can also serve as a strategy to penetrate, and succeed in, the mainstream Japanese society. This is indeed reflected in Japan's immigration policy that gives privileges to foreigners with "skills not possessed by Japanese nationals" (Ministry of Justice 2002). A disproportionate number of "skilled" foreign migrants, therefore, have been admitted under categories, such as "international educators" (e.g. foreign language teachers), "special skilled workers" (e.g. foreign cooks), and "cultural entertainers and ambassadors." (Many end up working as bar hostesses and dancers.)

The ability, as well as the need, to use ethnic resources, however, depends on one's class backgrounds. Thus, foreign migrants of different class backgrounds use different mobility strategies. Middle-class migrants often try to move up by using globally transferable human capital (e.g. IT knowledge, management skills), whereas for less-skilled migrants, ethnic resources may suit them better. Ethnic resources may be particularly useful for those migrants who do not have access to large ethnic communities and ethnic entrepreneurship opportunities.

Generational succession may also be a crucial mechanism for foreign migrants' upward mobility. It remains to be seen whether their children, raised and educated in Japan, will be able to experience upward mobility through education, credentials, and skills like Japanese natives. Thus far, studies on these children have painted a grim picture, noting high school drop-out rates (15–30 percent of school-aged foreign children are reported not to be in school, depending on municipalities) and very low rates of college attendance. According to the 2000 Japanese census, out of 1,755 Peruvians of ages 15–19, only 731, or 42 percent, were in school on a full-time basis; among Peruvians of ages 20–24, the equivalent rate was only 3 percent. Perhaps, then, their children, or even their children, would be able to compete in the mainstream market on the basis of individual merit and credentials. Until that day comes, utilizing ethnic and cultural resources may remain a crucial way for Peruvian migrants to move beyond manual contract labor, unless cohesive and sizable ethnic communities become established to provide them with entrepreneur opportunities.

Notes

1   The figure includes the number of long-term Korean residents who have been in Japan for generations yet have remained "foreign" in legal terms. Excluding those long-term residents, the percentage of more recent foreign migrants is about 1 percent of Japan's total population (Ministry of Justice 2005).

2   This has to do with their greater economic incentives, as poor Japanese descendants in Peru tended to be racially mixed (based on my fieldwork in Peru). The greater proportion of non-Japanese descendants among Peruvians relative to other South Americans is attributable, in part, to the lax manner in which old population records were kept in Peru's rural areas. These records were reported to be bought and sold more frequently in Peru than in other South American countries. In order to gain entry to Japan as Japanese descendants, prospective migrants must present a number of documents demonstrating their ties to their Japanese ancestors. According to official estimates in 2004, there were 7,300 undocumented Peruvians as opposed to 4,700 undocumented Brazilians.

3   Social mobility refers here to occupational changes, and particularly to changes from manual work to other types of work. For the majority of Peruvians who initially take up manual factory jobs, moving out of such jobs is a vital step toward upward mobility. Even though most Peruvians initially migrated to Japan for the strict purpose of earning and saving money, many, especially those of middle-class origins, regard their jobs degrading, and wish to "succeed" in Japan. "Success," to them, means "abandoning the factory" (Peruvian migrants), either by establishing independent businesses or moving on to jobs where they can exercise what they were trained.

4   The findings reported in this chapter are based on the study I conducted on Peruvian migrants in Japan during 1996–1998 and 2003–2004. During the first period, I conducted extensive field work on Peruvian migrants' daily and community activities, including participant-observation in a factory. I also interviewed over 80 Peruvian migrants (1996–97, 2003–4) and conducted a survey among 40 Peruvian households

in the Tokyo metropolitan area (in 2003–4). The survey yielded life histories of 128 individuals (household members), and the data were collected on a non-random basis in collaboration with the Latin American Migration Project and Álvaro del Castillo. Personal names used in this chapter are all pseudonyms.

5 A majority of Japanese descendants in Peru are members of the middle to upper-middle classes, measured by occupation, education, and places of residence (i.e. neighborhoods) (e.g. Morimoto 1991) in a largely poor country.

6 It is unclear, however, whether those Peruvians who entered Japan on forged documents used their real or forged Japanese surname.

References

Castles, S. and Miller, M.J. (1998) *The Age of Migration*, 2nd edn, New York: Guilford.

Higuchi, N. and Tanno, K. (2003) "What's driving Brazil-Japan migration? The making and remaking of the Brazilian niche in Japan," *International Journal of Japanese Sociology*, 12: 33–47.

Hōmushō Nyūkoku Kanrikyoku [Ministry of Justice, Immigration Bureau]. (1990) "Nikkeijin no U-turn genshō wo ou [Tracing the U-Turn migration phenomena of Nikkei]," *Kokusai Jinryū* [Immigration Newsmagazine], (7): 11–16.

—— (1992) *Dai 1 ji Shutsunyūkoku Kanri Kihon Keikaku* [Basic Plan for Immigration Control, 1st edition], Hōmushō Nyūkoku Kanrikyoku [Ministry of Justice, Immigration Bureau].

—— (2002) Version *Shutsunyūkoku Kihon Keikaku* [Basic Plan for Immigration Control], Hōmushō Nyūkoku Kanrikyoku.

Igarashi, Y. (2000) "Gaijin kategorī wo meguru 4-rui gata: shokuba ni okeru jinshukan kankei no jirei kenkyū kara [Four categories of "gaijin": A study on race relations in the work place]," *Shakaigaku Hyōron* [Sociological Review], 51(1): 54–70.

Ishi, A. (1997) "Daisotsu gishi ga 3K rōdōsha ni natta toki: dekasegi nikkei burajiru jin no shigoto to identity [When university graduates become 3-K laborers: Nikkei Brazilian migrant laborers' work and identity]," in H. Kawai and K. Uchibashi (eds) *Shigoto no Sōzō* [Creating Work], Tokyo: Iwanami Shoten.

JICA (Japan International Cooperation Agency) (1992) *Nikkeijin Hompō Shūrō Jittai Chōsa Hōkokusho* [Report on Nikkei Laborers in Japan], Tokyo: Japan International Cooperation Agency.

Kajita, T. (1998) "Dekasegi 10-nen go no nikkei burazirujin [Nikkei Brazilians 10 years after their economic migration]," *Kokusai Kankeigaku Kenkyū*, [The Study of International Relations], 25: 1–22, Tokyo: Tsudajuku Daigaku.

Kim, M. (2003) "Ethnic stratification and inter-generational differences in Japan: a comparative study of Korean and Japanese status attainment," *International Journal of Japanese Sociology*, 12: 6–16.

Kim, M. and Inazuki, T. (2000) "Zainichi kankokujin no shakai idō [Social mobility of Koreans in Japan]," in K. Takasaka (ed.) *Nihon no Kaisō Shisutemu 6: kaisō shakai kara atarashii shimin shakai e* [Social Stratification in Japan 6: from stratified society to new civil society], Tokyo: Tokyo Daigaku Shuppankai.

Komai, H. (1997) *Teijū gaikokujin* [Foreign Residents in Japan], Tokyo: Akashi Shoten.

Kōsei Rōdōshō [Ministry of Health, Labor and Welfare (MHLW)]. (2004a) *Gaikokujin Koyō Jyōkyō Hōkoku* [Report on Employment Conditions of Foreign Workers], Tokyo: Kōsei Rōdōshō.

—— (2004b) *Jinkō Genshō Jidai ni okeru Shutsunyūkoku Kanri Gyōsei no Tōmen no Kadai* [Policy issues on Immigration in an Age of Population Ageing], Hōmushō Nyūkoku Kanrikyōku.

Koyo Kaihatsu Sentā [Employment Advance Research Center (EARC)]. (1991) *Gaikokujin Rōdōsha Mondai Shiryōshū* [Information Packet on Foreign Workers' Issues], Tokyo: Koyō Kaihatsu Center.

Ministry of Justice. (2004) *Statistics on the Foreigners Registered in Japan*. Tokyo, Japan: Ministry of Justice.

Ministry of Justice. (2005) *Statistics on the Foreigners Registered in Japan*. Tokyo, Japan: Ministry of Justice.

Morimoto, A. (1991) *Población de Origen Japonés en el Peru: Perfil Actual* [People of Japanese Origin in Peru: a current profile], Lima: Comisión Conmemorativa del 90 Aniversario de la Inmigración Japonesa del Peru: Lima, Peru.

NIKKEIS. (1994) *Orientación para Trabajar en el Japón: Guía para Nikkeis* [Orientation for Workers in Japan: Guide Book for Nikkeis], Tokyo: Nikkeis, Sangyō Koyō Antei Sentā [Employment Service Center for Foreigners].

Okano, K. (1997) "Third-generation Koreans' entry into the workforce in Japan," *Anthropology and Education Quarterly*, 28(4): 524–49.

Portes, A. and Rumbaut, R. (1996) *Immigrant America: a portrait*, Berkeley, CA: University of California Press.

Roth, J.H. (2002) *Brokered Homeland: Japanese Brazilian migrants in Japan*, Ithaca, NY: Cornell University Press.

Takenaka, A. (2003a) "Paradoxes of ethnicity-based immigration: Peruvian and Japanese-Peruvian migrants in Japan," in R. Goodman, C. Peach, A. Takenaka and P. White (eds) *Global Japan: the experience of Japan's new immigrants and overseas communities*, London: Routledge Curzon.

—— (2003b) "The mechanisms of ethnic retention: later-generation Japanese immigrants in Lima, Peru," *Journal of Ethnic and Migration Studies*. 29(3): 467–83.

Tanno, K. and Higuchi, N. (1999) "Nikkeijin no hōsetsu yōshiki to shakai mondai [The incorporation of Nikkei and social problems]," in T. Kajita (ed.), *Toransunashonaru na kankyōka ni okeru atarashii ijū purosesu* [New migration process in the age of transnationalism], Kagaku Gijutsu Shinkō Chōseihi Kenkyū Seika Hōkokusho [Japan Science and Technology Agency: Science and Technology Promotion Adjustment Expense Research Outcome Report], 19–40.

Tsuda, T. (2003) *Strangers in the Ethnic Homeland: Japanese Brazilian return migration in transnational perspective*, New York: Columbia University Press.

Tsuda, T., Valdez, Z. and Cornelius, W.A. (2003) "Human versus social capital: immigrant wages and labor market incorporation in Japan and the United States," in J. Reitz (ed.), *Host Societies and the Reception of Immigrants*, La Jolla, CA: Center for Comparative Immigration Studies, University of California, San Diego.

Yamamoto, K. (1999) "Teijūka suru gaikokujin towa dareka [Who are the foreigners settling in Japan?]," *Shakaigau Ronkō* [Sociological Studies], 20: 21–43.

Index

9 780415 667197